1996

Abuse, Neglect, and Exploitation of Older Persons

Strategies for Assessment and Intervention

Abuse, Neglect, and Exploitation of Older Persons

Strategies for Assessment and Intervention

Edited by

Lorin A. Baumhover
and
S. Colleen Beall
University of Alabama

HEALTH
PROFESSIONS
PRESS

Baltimore • London • Toronto • Sydney

Health Professions Press, Inc.
Post Office Box 10624
Baltimore, Maryland 21285-0624

Copyright © 1996 by Health Professions Press, Inc.
All rights reserved.

Typeset by Pro-Image Corporation, York, Pennsylvania.
Manufactured in the United States by The Maple Press Company,
York, Pennsylvania.

Library of Congress Cataloging-in-Publication Data
Abuse, neglect, and exploitation of older persons : strategies for assessment
and intervention / edited by Lorin A. Baumhover, S. Colleen Beall.
     p.   cm.
   Includes bibliographical references and index.
   ISBN 1-878812-29-7
   1. Abused aged—Services for—United States. 2. Aged—Abuse
of—United States—Prevention. 3. Social work with the aged—United
States. 4. Community health services—United States. I. Baumhover,
Lorin A. II. Beall, S. Colleen.
HV1461.A26   1996
362.6–dc20   95-42646
                                                          CIP

British Library Cataloguing in Publication Data are available from the
British Library.

Contents

About the Editors

Lorin A. Baumhover, Ph.D., is Professor of Behavioral and Community Medicine and Director of the Center for the Study of Aging in the College of Community Health Sciences at the University of Alabama. An active researcher, Dr. Baumhover has been principal investigator for approximately 15 externally funded research grants and more than 20 externally funded training and technical assistance programs. He has published extensively in the areas of elder abuse, Alzheimer's disease, and gerontology education.

S. Colleen Beall, M.S.W., Dr.P.H., is Assistant Professor in the Department of Family Medicine at the University of Alabama. She began to work in the area of elder abuse in 1986 as a research associate at the Center for the Study of Aging, and she continues to work collaboratively with the Center on a number of research and training projects. Additionally, she coordinates educational programs in gerontology at the University of Alabama.

Contributors

Edward F. Ansello, Ph.D.
Director, Virginia Center on
  Aging
Medical College of Virginia
Virginia Commonwealth
  University
Richmond, Virginia 23298-0229

Lorin A. Baumhover, Ph.D.
Director, Center for the
  Study of Aging
Professor, Behavioral and
  Community Medicine
University of Alabama
Tuscaloosa, Alabama 35487-0326

S. Colleen Beall, Dr.P.H.
Assistant Professor
Department of Family Medicine
University of Alabama
Tuscaloosa, Alabama 35487-0326

Bridget Booth, M.S.N.
Program Coordinator, Geriatric
  In-Home Support Program
Western Psychiatric Institute
  and Clinic
Pittsburgh, Pennsylvania 15201

**Audrei A. Bruno, M.S.N., R.N.,
  C.N.A.**
Professor of Nursing
Community College of
  Allegheny County
Pittsburgh, Pennsylvania 15212

Terry T. Fulmer, R.N., Ph.D.
Professor of Nursing
Division of Nursing
New York University
New York, New York 10012-1165

Elaine S. Gould, M.S.W.
Director, Geriatric Education
  Center
New York University
New York, New York 10012-1165

Susan W. Haikalis, L.C.S.W.
Director, Client Services
San Francisco AIDS Foundation
San Francisco, California 94102

Melanie Hwalek, Ph.D.
President, SPEC Associates
Detroit, Michigan 48226

Beth Hudson Keller, M.A.
Director of Education and
  Training
Coalition of Advocates for the
  Rights of the Infirm Elderly
Philadelphia, Pennsylvania 19107

Jordan I. Kosberg, Ph.D.
School of Social Work
Florida International University
North Miami Beach, Florida
  33181

Robert Marin, M.D.
Associate Professor of Psychiatry
University of Pittsburgh School
  of Medicine
Western Psychiatric Institute and
  Clinic
Pittsburgh, Pennsylvania 15213

Daphne Nahmiash, M.S.W.
Adjunct Professor
School of Social Work
McGill University
Montreal, Quebec, Canada
  H3A 2A7

Lisa Nerenberg, M.S.W., M.P.H.
Director, San Francisco
  Consortium for Elder Abuse
  Prevention
Mt. Zion Institute on Aging
San Francisco, California 94118

James G. O'Brien, M.D.
Associate Dean for Community
  Programs
College of Human Medicine
Michigan State University
East Lansing, Michigan 48824

Sue M. Parkins, M.D.
Medical Director, Adult
  Protective Team
St. Vincent Medical Center
Toledo, Ohio 43608

Kathleen M. Quinn, B.A.
Chief, Bureau of Elder Rights
Illinois Department on Aging
Springfield, Illinois 62701

Holly Ramsey-Klawsnik, Ph.D.
Klawsnik & Klawsnik
  Psychotherapy Associates
Canton, Massachusetts 02021

**Dorrie E. Rosenblatt, M.D.,
  Ph.D.**
Division of Geriatric Medicine
University of Michigan Medical
  School
Ann Arbor, Michigan 48109-0405

**Mary C. Sengstock, Ph.D.,
  C.C.S.**
Professor of Sociology
Wayne State University
Detroit, Michigan 48202

Carolyn Stahl Goodrich, B.A.
Consultant, SPEC Associates
Houston, Texas 77030

Sally C. Steiner, M.S.W., C.S.W.
Mental Health & Elder Abuse
  Specialist
Michigan Office of Services to
  the Aging
Lansing, Michigan 48909

Rosalie S. Wolf, Ph.D.
Executive Director, Institute
  on Aging
Medical Center of Central
  Massachusetts
Worcester, Massachusetts 01605

Foreword

It has been more than 20 years since Baker's (1975) comments on "granny battering" appeared in a British medical journal. During this period of time, elder abuse has become a matter for concern, not only in the United States but throughout the world. Although we may not be entirely satisfied with the rate of progress in developing prevention and treatment programs, the field has come a long way from the days when reports were met with skepticism and disbelief.

With the passage of time, the concept of elder abuse has undergone various transformations. Originally, the abuse and neglect of older persons was viewed in the context of protective services; next, it was framed as an issue of aging. Next, it was viewed as an issue of family violence, and, later, crime. These multiple interpretations have made it possible for individuals and organizations in the field to reach out to new constituencies, to increase awareness, and to develop joint programs. More importantly, the various interpretations have helped to legitimate the elder abuse movement to a degree that was not possible when it was regarded exclusively as a public welfare or social service issue.

In declaring family violence/crime a public health issue, the federal government is promoting a new paradigm that calls for closer collaboration between the health care establishment and the family violence movements. It is well known that the medical profession did not participate in shaping the response to elder abuse (in contrast to its efforts on behalf of abused children), although a few physicians did take an early interest. The American Medical Association's family violence project, initiated in the fall of 1992, signifies a more proactive policy for the organization. Instituting this policy has resulted in the publication of diagnostic and treatment guidelines for both spouse and elder abuse; in calling for a national conference on family violence, which included representation from the child, spouse, and elder abuse movements; and in the creation of the Coalition of Physicians Against Family Violence.

Unlike physicians, the nursing profession has played a significant role in the history of elder abuse. As staff members of home health agencies and hospital emergency rooms, nurses have often been the first to identify an incident of elder mistreatment. They have been instrumental in developing assessment protocols, implementing treatment and prevention programs, conducting training sessions, and promoting public awareness. They can also take credit for producing some of the notable research in the field.

The importance of health care professionals of all types in the prevention and treatment of elder abuse cannot be overestimated. Of the 241,000 domestic elder abuse reports received by the states in 1994 (National Center on Elder Abuse, 1995), the largest proportion (21.6%) came from physicians and other health care personnel, family members and other relatives accounted for 14.9%, and agencies serving older people accounted for 9.4%, with the remainder from various sources.

It is crucial that training in the signs and symptoms of elder mistreatment and the assessment process be available to physicians, nurses, therapists, and other care providers in health care settings. Information about state elder abuse laws, the system for referring a suspected case (whether it occurs in a community or long-term care setting), elder services and financial resources, ethical issues, and case management should also be part of the curriculum.

As members of multidisciplinary teams or community-wide coalitions, health care professionals have the opportunity to educate other professional groups about aging and the diseases of aging. They can also encourage and participate in the development of primary prevention activities, such as informing older people about risk factors and where to turn for help; bringing about a closer relationship among the mental health system, elder services, and substance abuse programs in order to serve elders and family members with alcohol and emotional problems; establishing support groups for persons at risk for abuse and abusing; reaching out to minority communities with culturally specific programs; and training caregivers of family members with Alzheimer's disease in behavior management techniques.

The opportunities for caregivers in health care settings to make a contribution both to the treatment and prevention of elder abuse and neglect are many. The editors of this volume have wisely chosen to focus on one very basic topic: the art and science of diagnosing and managing elder abuse cases. To produce a practical guide, they called upon an outstanding group of clinicians and researchers. The authors responded to the challenge. The result is an excellent book that promises to be an invaluable resource in the medical care setting as well as the classroom.

Rosalie S. Wolf
National Committee for the Prevention of Elder Abuse

REFERENCES

Baker, A.A. (1975, August 5). Granny battering. *Modern Geriatrics, 5*(8), 20–24.
National Center on Elder Abuse. (1995). *Understanding the nature and extent of elder abuse in domestic settings* [Fact sheet]. Washington, DC: Author.

Preface

This book was designed as a practical guide for practitioners in health care settings who need a current and accurate reference for detecting and managing abuse and neglect cases. It is intended to go beyond the 1992 American Medical Association guidelines and other hospital-based protocols. Specific chapters in this work are intended to amplify position papers provided by professional organizations and to integrate theory and practice in a single handbook. It is our belief that this volume fills an important need in the field and that the authors represent some of the most knowledgeable persons available in their respective areas of expertise in abuse and neglect.

The volume is a culmination of over a decade of research, education, and training in elder mistreatment. We were involved in a large project in the mid-1980s to implement a series of counseling sessions for potential abusers in five mental health centers. Abusive or potentially abusive caregivers were trained during eight sessions in anger management, coping strategies, relaxation techniques, understanding normal aging, and ways to deflect their anger and frustration at the caregiving situation. We have conducted several large surveys concerning knowledge of and responsiveness to elder abuse among physicians in primary care, physicians and technicians in emergency departments, and nurses in public health and private home health agencies. In addition to two national conferences on elder abuse in 1991 and 1994, we have conducted several large training projects on elder abuse for public health nurses and frontline Adult Protective Services staff.

We are pleased to acknowledge the encouragement and patience of Barbara Karni from Health Professions Press. We are appreciative of the support we have received from the staff at the Center for the Study of Aging at the University of Alabama, and from the College of Community Health Sciences. We also are appreciative of our circle of social support, our immediate family members—Lorraine, Joe, Stephanie, and Kristen Baumhover; Jean Beall; and Diane Elder—and our close friends, who continue to help us in their own ways. Finally, we must recognize the people who have gone before us, both as gerontologists who have attempted to describe and categorize elder mistreatment and as victims of mistreatment, whose case studies and experiences are directly and indirectly described in this book.

Abuse, Neglect, and Exploitation of Older Persons

Strategies for Assessment and Intervention

Introduction

Lorin A. Baumhover and S. Colleen Beall

The medical community is becoming increasingly aware that general health and overall well-being are influenced by many factors outside of the health care delivery setting. Pediatricians are realizing the overall impact of malnutrition, drugs, and interpersonal violence on their patient population. Emergency room physicians and nurses have been victimized by the violence that has followed their patients in from the streets (increasingly, visitors and family members must pass through a metal detector to enter emergency rooms). The white coats of home health nurses, which once afforded them safety in violence-prone neighborhoods, now provide notice that drugs and needles may be at hand. Health care providers are becoming aware that their patients bring a variety of related problems into the examining room. Numerous environmental, ecological, and community variables affect how health care is delivered in the United States. These variables also affect elder abuse.

Although physicians were in the forefront in the detection, diagnosis, and treatment of child abuse cases, this does not appear to be true of elder mistreatment. This is particularly ironic when the indicators for the detection of abuse and neglect are perhaps most readily visible to physicians and nurses, and particularly home health care providers. Considerable support is found in the literature for the fact

1

that the individuals most likely to report and act on cases of elder abuse are health care professionals involved in primary care. Clark-Daniels, Daniels, and Baumhover (1989) found that the individuals most likely to report cases of elder mistreatment are home health nurses, more so than other family members, the victims themselves, clergy, social workers, or other health care providers. It is also becoming apparent that insufficient attention is being paid to domestic violence and elder abuse issues in medical education, in clinical rotations, and in real-life work settings.

The United States is undergoing a convergence of aging and individual mistreatment. Although an awareness exists that the American population is aging, it has only been in the last 2 years that researchers have found that aging family members are victimized at a much higher rate than earlier anticipated (Tatara, 1994). The population group most likely to be victimized, people over age 75, is growing more rapidly than any other subset of the elderly population. Individuals who are the most frail and have the greatest number of chronic conditions, and people who are widowed or otherwise alone, are more likely to be targeted for abuse and neglect.

Elder abuse is frequently seen only as physical abuse. If no lacerations, burn marks, punctures, or bruises can be found on the body, it is too often assumed that no abuse or neglect has occurred. Neglect, the type of mistreatment most frequently found among the older population, often leaves no outward signs nor reveals any particular symptoms. Psychological abuse also leaves no external wounds. This book attempts to sensitize health care practitioners to the full range and types of abuse and neglect, including physical abuse, neglect (passive or active), psychological abuse, financial exploitation, and violation of civil rights.

This book also emphasizes that elder mistreatment is more covert than spouse or child abuse. Elderly victims frequently deny the occurrence of abuse, neglect, or both out of fear, guilt, shame, or passivity, and elder abusers attempt to justify and rationalize their actions. Elder mistreatment is more easily hidden from public view in both the home and the long-term care setting. Older people are more isolated than other age groups, have fewer social engagements and role obligations, and are more likely to be either physically or mentally impaired.

This book is the culmination of over a decade of research, education, and training in elder mistreatment. It offers a comprehensive set of guidelines that can be utilized by health care personnel in assessing whether elder abuse and neglect has occurred. The chapters include some theoretical and conceptual elements, but are largely geared toward the practical application of the art and science of diagnosing and managing elder abuse cases. The book is intended to serve as a practical guide for practitioners, and as a stimulus for developing new protocols in health care settings in which these instruments do not exist and for possible new research and training. The text focuses on both acute and long-term care issues.

The volume is organized into four parts. Part I, "Understanding the Problem," opens with a chapter by Edward Ansello, who reviews the primary causes of elder abuse and some possible explanations as to why elder mistreatment continues to occur.

Chapter 2, by Jordan Kosberg and Daphne Nahmiash, presents a detailed outline of characteristics that may be associated with elder abuse. These characteristics are related not only to the victims and perpetrators of abuse, but also to the social and cultural context in which abuse incidents occur. The authors are careful to point out the limitations of current data related to individual characteristics.

In Chapter 3 James O'Brien focuses on the identification of abuse within the context of a clinical interview and physical examination. O'Brien points out that opportunities to screen for abuse are within the purview of primary care physicians. He calls upon physicians to become aware of the type of information useful in assessing abuse and of the necessity for careful documentation whenever abuse is suspected.

The focus in Part II, "Assessment," is a detailed description of the case-finding process. Holly Ramsey-Klawsnik opens this section by examining the roles of health care providers in the assessment of possible elder physical and sexual abuse. Symptoms and dynamics of physical and sexual abuse are presented, as are specific guidelines for assessment in such cases. Requirements and professional limits of responsibility also are addressed.

In Chapter 5 Terry Fulmer and Elaine Gould discuss the assessment of neglect within a framework that recognizes the contribution of aging processes, disease, and neglect to the older person's condition; distinguishes self-neglect from caregiver neglect; and acknowledges the role of intent and competence in determining whether neglect is active or passive. Fulmer and Gould present an assessment instrument, the Elder Abuse Assessment Form, to assist practitioners in assessing and documenting neglected older people.

Mary C. Sengstock and Sally Steiner extend the assessment framework to include psychological mistreatment and exploitation in Chapter 6. The signs and symptoms with which victims of such mistreatment present are not generally physical and, therefore, are easy to overlook in a clinical setting where the focus is on physical illness and injury. Service providers are challenged to notice psychological affect, subtle behaviors, and interpersonal interactions in order to identify nonphysical mistreatment and to institute measures to safeguard the welfare of victims.

The final chapter in Part II is coauthored by Melanie Hwalek, Carolyn Stahl Goodrich, and Kathleen Quinn. In it, the authors act as facilitators, explaining the "black box" of Adult Protective Services (APS) to health care providers. They call attention to the different meanings of risk assessment within APS and health care settings and to the role of a standardized APS risk assessment to guide investigations, interventions, and evaluations. Roles for health care professionals within the investigation and intervention process are defined.

The emphasis in Part III, "Intervention," is on clinical activities with victims of elder mistreatment. The continued importance of the documentation that was inaugurated during the initial assessment is the focus of Dorrie Rosenblatt's chapter. Although it serves many functions, such as supporting legal interventions or funding requests, the primary reason for careful documentation is that it provides the basis for good patient care. Documentation is the first step in developing a care plan that is specific to the patient's or client's needs and resources, obtaining services to carry out the plan, and facilitating communications among service providers.

A promising model for intervention within hospitals is the multidisciplinary team. In Chapter 9 Sue Parkins describes the events that led to the formation of a multidisciplinary team in one setting (St. Vincent's Medical Center, Toledo, Ohio), describes the composition of the team, and provides examples of how multidisciplinary involvement facilitates a coordinated approach to developing effective intervention strategies.

A key component of intervention for many victims and their caregivers is psychological therapy, addressed in Chapter 10 by Bridget Booth, Audrei Bruno, and Robert Marin. To be effective, psychological treatment must be guided by the clinician's knowledge of the causes and consequences of mistreatment as they coexist in a particular case. Suggestions are offered for primary, secondary, and tertiary interventions.

Part IV, "Some Solutions to the Problem," addresses victim followup, abuse in institutions, and the outlook for elder abuse. The final step of clinical care for the victim of mistreatment often is discharge planning. In Chapter 11 Lisa Nerenberg and Susan Haikalis discuss some of the pressures and obstacles that may hinder effective discharge planning. By serving as the interface between in-hospital and in-home services, discharge planners can contribute to overcoming and removing these barriers. This is accomplished by engaging in planning and advocacy efforts in the community and by educating care providers that aggressive, proactive approaches to abuse can be cost effective.

Chapter 12, by Beth Hudson Keller, examines the typical kinds of mistreatment, often subtle and largely unnoticed, that may occur in a long-term care setting. She outlines a training program designed to sensitize care providers to their own possibly abusive behaviors and to replace such behaviors with actions that are more adaptive for care providers and contribute to a better quality of life for older adults. Although the focus of Hudson Keller's chapter is on nursing facility care, similar approaches are advocated for care providers in the home health and boarding home industries.

The editors conclude the volume with a chapter that summarizes and reexamines common barriers that are likely to continue to frustrate health care providers as they attempt to identify and manage a growing number of elder abuse victims. Drawing from recommendations by contributors to the volume, as well as their own experience in the field, the editors offer prescriptions for overcoming these barriers.

REFERENCES

Clark-Daniels, C.L., Daniels, R.S., & Baumhover, L.A. (1989). Physicians and nurses' responses to abuse of the elderly: A comparative study of two surveys in Alabama. *Journal of Elder Abuse & Neglect, 1*(4), 57–72.

Tatara, T. (1994). *Elder abuse: An information guide for professionals and concerned citizens* (4th ed.). Washington, DC: National Center on Elder Abuse.

I

Understanding
the Problem

1

Causes and Theories

Edward F. Ansello

THE "WHY?" OF ELDER ABUSE

In addressing elder abuse, "why?" is as important a question as "what?" or "how much?" The search for answers to the "why?" of elder abuse began only after a period of time during which both the existence and the extent of elder abuse were vigorously debated. Reports of elder abuse were initially denied. Because of this denial and, by circuitous logic, because little "related literature" existed on which to base an investigation, it was difficult to obtain financial support for research on the battering of elderly people as recently as the mid- to late 1970s. The first studies, conducted in Michigan, Maryland, and Massachusetts, seemed to ignite a wildfire. Despite a paucity of data (U.S. House of Representatives, Select Committee on Aging, 1981), suddenly 1 million people per year were declared to be elder abuse victims. The "what?" of elder abuse broadened as definitions began to include nonphysical as well as passive forms of abuse and neglect. Speculations as to how much elder abuse existed kept pace with the broadening of the scope of the "what?," with prevalence estimates growing to 4%, 6%, or more of the older population.

Debates about definitions and prevalence of elder mistreatment have stimulated many descriptive studies but produced few truly theoretical investigations that explain why elder abuse and neglect occur.

Perhaps now that time has moderated earlier exaggerations of prevalence, as confirmation of alleged cases often proves difficult (Shiferaw, Mittlemark, Wofford, Anderson, Walls, & Rohrer, 1994; Tatara, 1993), there can be systematic testing of theories as to the reasons for elder abuse and neglect. Finding a definitive cause for abuse and neglect will elude theorists, for reasons to be discussed.

"WHY?" PREDISPOSES ACTION

Theory formulation and theory testing are not idle exercises. Why something happens is of vital, if not immediate, interest to the health care practitioner. The immediate concern upon encountering an abused or neglected elderly person is most likely treatment; but the vital interest is remedial intervention in order to prevent future occurrences. To guide interventions, the practitioner employs a theory, a reasoned set of propositions supported by evidence, to explain certain phenomena. The theory is developed either deductively or inductively. In the *deductive* process one reasons from the general to the particular. The general principle is applied to particular instances; in other words, theory drives practice. In the *inductive* process one reasons from the particular to the general. Specifics are assembled to form an explanatory general principle; in other words, practice forms theory. The inductive process describes theory building in elder abuse and neglect, as data are pieced together inductively in an attempt to understand the causes.

Formulating a theory about the causes of elder mistreatment has been difficult. Theorists have had to contend with a lack of comparable data sets or studies from which to induce a theory (i.e., to conclude that support exists for an explanatory general principle). Studies have employed different definitions of elder abuse, making induction difficult. Theorists have also had to contend with a lack of normative data on behavior toward elderly people. Where is the threshold on the continuum from appropriate to inappropriate behavior beyond which behavior is "abusive"? It is also unclear what the normative expectations for response are when parents are "not themselves," difficult to relate to, or burdensome in their needs or demands. An extreme situation of physical abuse is self-evidently wrong, but what if yelling obscenities at each other has been a way of life for years? The threshold also shifts when theorists face the issue of intention versus lack of understanding prior to the execution of a behavior. These and other issues make theory building in the area of elder abuse and neglect the caboose of the train rather than its engine.

INADEQUATE CARE AND REMEDIATION

While theory builders and theory testers encounter these obstacles and continue their attempts to develop explanations for elder abuse and neglect, health care practitioners continue to encounter and treat patients whom they suspect have been abused, neglected, or self-neglected. Notwithstanding the fundamental importance of theories in guiding behavior, health care practitioners must treat patients, even as the process of explanatory theory building continues.

Fulmer and O'Malley (1987) propose that practitioners move ahead. Legislation in almost every state requires members of the helping professions to report suspected cases of elder abuse and neglect. (Ironically, penalties in several states against these professionals for failing to report are stiffer than the penalties against the abuser or neglector.) This pressure to report notwithstanding, health care practitioners must diagnose amidst competing definitions of what it is they are to look for (i.e., definitions of elder abuse and neglect), and must treat amidst competing explanations of probable cause (i.e., theories of elder abuse and neglect). Fulmer and O'Malley conclude that practitioners need to move beyond the issues of elder abuse and neglect to the broader issue of inadequate care, and to move beyond blaming and ensuring punishment to remediating the identified inadequate care. These remedial interventions will still be guided by the practitioner's understanding of the etiology of the situation, and thus, the loop of theory–research–practice will continue. However contradictory the theories for elder abuse and neglect may appear at times, knowing them will inevitably enrich the reasoned treatments that health care professionals must provide. Fulmer and O'Malley's proposal to look for inadequate care as a red flag for abuse or neglect is appropriate. They observe that in a health care setting it is often easier to detect inadequate care of elderly people than it is to draw some fine line between abuse and neglect.

The experiences of old age confound practitioners' abilities to diagnose elder abuse or neglect, even when it is self-directed. Little consensus exists as to what later life should be, or in fact is, and what constitutes "normal aging." In contrast to child development, there are few if any norms for growth and development in later life. Gerontology and geriatrics are late twentieth century concepts. Practitioners in gerontology and geriatrics continue to debate the terms "productive," "successful," "normal," and "meaningful" as they apply to the later years. Complicating the matter further is the evidence that in many ways people seem to become more heterogeneous as they age (Ansello, 1991). Unfortunately, these subtleties are lost on the public. All too common is the belief that deterioration is normal in aging; therefore, it is pointless to investigate it when it is encountered. Indeed, the normative expectation is often, at best, stagnation, and, at worst, decline and impairment with advancing age. Thus, not only is the occurrence of neglectful or abusive behavior made more difficult to identify amidst these expectations, but also the mind-set for treatment may be compromised by the related common assumption that frail elderly people are marginal members of society and unlikely to respond to treatment.

Fulmer and O'Malley's directive to look for inadequate care and to treat remedially is sensible. As an orientation "inadequate care" can accommodate emerging developments in theory testing. Some researchers now speculate that elder abuse may be a reflection of the characteristics of the abuser (e.g., dependency on the older person, substance abuse, poor social history) rather than of the abused. These are not well-meaning caregivers. Other researchers speculate that the well-meaning overwhelmed caregiver in chronic caregiving is typical in elder neglect.

THE SEARCH FOR CAUSES

Theories regarding the causes of elder abuse can and do draw on investigations of other forms of domestic violence, such as child and spouse abuse, but the differences among the various forms of domestic violence are probably as great as the similarities. For example, in child abuse, the victim is legally a minor, and the abusive adult has legal, physical, and resource control over the victim. In spouse abuse, two adults are in a consensual relationship. In elder abuse, there may or may not be the dependency that characterizes child abuse or the consensual relationship that characterizes spouse abuse, and often the victim at one time had control over the abuser. Nonetheless, lessons can be learned from research into domestic violence.

First, there does not appear to be any single theoretical explanation for any one form of domestic violence (e.g., child abuse), let alone for the whole phenomenon of domestic violence. Acknowledging the lack of a unicausal theory of elder abuse, Steinmetz (1988) proposes using several theories as "interactive perspectives" to understand the dynamics of elder abuse better. There may be theories that practitioners find suitable to explain abuse that do not pertain to neglect, or theories that are appropriate for neglect but not for self-neglect (Rathbone-McCuan & Fabian, 1992). The theories, in any event, cannot fully determine causes or causation. Human behavior has long frustrated researchers attempting to define cause and effect. The best researchers can do is to search for strong associations that predict a human event.

Second, the study of elder abuse will likely continue employing an inductive approach to theory formulation in an attempt to fit discrete findings into a pattern of explanation or a theory. Testing a theory for elder abuse deductively in practice by starting from a general principle and applying it to particular settings while gathering empirical evidence is not feasible. If certain adverse conditions were theorized to cause elder abuse, one could not assign elderly people at random to experimental groups in which these conditions were applied in order to test the theory deductively.

Third, some agreement exists on correlates of or risk factors for elder abuse and neglect; these correlates include conditions present in the would-be abuser, in the would-be victim, and in the context of abuser–victim interactions. Some researchers are matching these risk factors to theories inductively in order to explain the presumed causes of abuse and neglect, as mentioned later in the chapter.

Finally, the health care practitioner will likely formulate theories or assumptions of cause regardless of the obstacles involved because it is part of the professional's training. The practitioner will find it is better to understand current theories of elder abuse and neglect, however untested, than to rely on supposition or stereotype in formulating an explanatory theory, or to respond only to the symptom and not to the cause.

ASSUMPTIONS BEHIND THE PREVAILING THEORIES

The prevailing theories of the "why?" of elder abuse are based on the following assumptions:

1. *Elder abuse and neglect, including self-abuse and self-neglect, are neither normal nor to be condoned.* Although this statement may seem incontestable, it does reflect a tension between what may be and what should be cultural values. In a work on family violence, Gelles (1983, p. 157) notes, "Publicly, at least, we think of the family as a loving, tranquil, peaceful social institution to which one flees *from* stress and danger. Privately, the family is perhaps society's most violent institution." With regard to self-abuse and neglect, there have always been recluses and hermits, but they have always existed on the fringes of society. The consensus is that elder abuse and neglect are non-normative and inconsistent with a developed society.

2. *Neglect is the most common form of elder mistreatment.* Active maltreatment of another accounts for the minority of confirmed cases of elder abuse. Much more prevalent are cases of self-neglect and neglect by another. Summarizing data obtained from 30 states in 1991 (during the fiscal year), Tatara (1993) reports that over half of all the substantiated cases of abuse involve self-neglect and that almost half of all the substantiated cases of abuse that exclude self-neglect are cases of neglect by others. In an analysis of visits by elderly people to emergency rooms, Fulmer, McMahon, Baer-Hines, and Forget (1992) found neglect to be the most common form of maltreatment. A 1994 statewide study in Louisiana by the Governor's Office of Elderly Affairs (*Aging News Alert*, 1995) found self-neglect and neglect to be the most common forms of

elder maltreatment. A key to understanding neglect by others may be the study by Wolfson, Handfield-Jones, Glass, McClaran, and Keyserlingk (1993) of adult children's perceptions of their responsibility to care for their elderly parents. The adult children ranked what they "could" do for their parents financially, emotionally, and physically consistently lower than what they "should" do. Specifically, the parents' characteristics, especially aggressive behavior and incontinence, influenced the adult children's responses. The discrepancy between "should" and "could" means inaction. In turn, this inaction is associated with neglect.

3. *Multiple causes or conditions may be present that must be addressed.* Unicausal theories of abuse and neglect have proven to be inadequate across the spectrum of domestic violence. The dynamics of interpersonal interactions and of person–environment interactions are more complex than can be accounted for by any single theory. For example, in studying the quality of care provided by nursing assistants in an intermediate level nursing home, Foner (1994) questioned whether they are "saints or monsters." Foner's data indicate that they are both. The complexities of interactions in the nursing facility cause some nursing assistants to play both roles during the same shift, and to present with a mixture of compassion and exasperation.

RISK FACTORS INDUCE THEORIES

"Risk factors" rather than "causes" is the preferred terminology in elder abuse research for many reasons, including the inability of inductive theory building to demonstrate cause and effect empirically. The lists of risk factors are numerous. Most factors assume some type of caregiving setting. Over time, these risk factors have come to serve as embryonic theories through an inductive process of theory building. Johnson (1991) and Kosberg (1988) reviewed available data and organized risk factors into lists of characteristics pertaining to the elderly person, the caregiver, and the environment. When combined, Johnson's and Kosberg's risk factors for elder abuse and neglect include the following:

- *Elderly person:* Female, dependence, impairment, drinking problem, excessive loyalty, history of abuse, isolation, provocative behavior
- *Caregiver:* Substance abuse, mental or emotional illness, lack of experience in caregiving, economic dependence, stress, history of abuse, blamer, isolation, hypercritic
- *Environment:* Lack of family support, marital problems, sudden and unwanted change, ageism

Drawing upon a small sample of 61 abused elderly people in Boston, Pillemer and Finkelhor (1989) give different weight to these risk factors. They place the emphasis squarely on the characteristics of the caregivers, and maintain that abuse is not the result of the dependency of care recipients on caregivers but of the socioemotional problems of the caregivers. Rather than being overburdened in caring, these caregivers are less than suitable. Carrying this theory to an institutional context, Pillemer and Moore (1989) interviewed approximately 600 staff members in 31 intermediate care nursing facilities, and concluded that abusive staff members are more likely than nonabusive staff to possess negative attitudes about elderly people, to have emotional problems, and to view their work environment as stressful.

A review of the literature (e.g., Fulmer & O'Malley, 1987) identifies several risk factors that appear regularly in analyses of elder abuse and neglect. Although sheer repetition does not confer credibility, it does carry weight in defining the debate and in shaping theory building. The most commonly accepted risk factors for elder abuse and neglect, including self-abuse and self-neglect, are also factors that are the most closely linked to the few relatively well-developed theories of presumed causation. The most commonly accepted risk factors are as follows:

1. A history of substance abuse or mental pathology in either the older person or the caregiver
2. A previous history of elder abuse in the caregiving context
3. Financial dependence of the caregiver upon the older person
4. Chronic illness or impairment affecting the older person who lacks informal support
5. Chronic illness or impairment affecting the older person, which exceeds the capacity of the caregiver (e.g., family member, paid assistant) to help

The prevailing theories for elder abuse and neglect, including self-abuse and self-neglect, relate to the most commonly cited risk factors. These theories ascribe elder abuse and neglect to the following:

1. Psychopathology of the abuser
2. Transgenerational violence
3. Exchange theory, which includes social exchange and symbolic interaction
4. Vulnerability/impairment of the elderly person
5. Excessive situational demands

The following sections briefly review each of these theories. The theories are not mutually exclusive, and elements of more than one theory may be relevant to a given case of elder abuse or neglect, including self-neglect.

Psychopathology of the Abuser

Gelles (1983) calls a focus upon the psychopathology of the abuser "the intraindividual level of analysis." This theory attributes causation to pathological characteristics of the caregiver or of the self-abusing elderly person. Assessments of child and spouse abuse cases in the 1960s and 1970s actively adopted this theory, assigning blame to psychologically disturbed offenders. Fulmer and O'Malley (1987) note that this theory posits that character disorders precipitate abusive behavior. These disorders include psychotic conditions, substance abuse, and inadequate capacity to care (the latter may result from the consequences of substance abuse or a mental impairment). Gelles' (1983) review of 10 years of interviews with offenders in cases of domestic violence led him to conclude that the proportion of abusers with psychological disorders is no greater than the proportion of the public with these disorders.

Nevertheless, psychopathological behavior may operate within the abusive situation. Hart and Brassard (1993) maintain that rejection may be present in all maltreatment, and may take any of five forms: spurning (verbal battering), withholding emotional response, terrorizing, isolating, and exploiting and corrupting. (In elder abuse cases the latter may include encouraging the infantilization of the older person.) Pillemer and Finkelhor (1989) find that characteristics of the caregiver rather than of the care recipient are more strongly correlated with situations of abuse. They report that abusive caregivers are severely troubled people, with histories of unstable, antisocial behavior.

Quinn and Tomita (1986, p. 77) note that in domestic violence "alcohol appears to be involved in more than half of the cases, but it is still unclear whether alcohol is the stimulus, the effect, or the frequent companion to domestic violence."

The psychopathology theory is appealing, but it probably explains only a small number of cases and has the effect of distancing health care providers from people in need of intervention. Because of his or her sociopathological personality or drug-damaged brain the psychopathological elder abuser may be the most difficult abuser with whom to work. He or she cannot be relied upon to comprehend or to follow through with remedial steps, even after making charming or remorseful promises. Removal from the abusive situation and psychotherapy or psychiatric treatment may be the only effective interventions for the abuser and the self-abusing elderly person. The self-abuser's profile tends to include an incapacity for activities of daily living (ADLs) and a likelihood of substance abuse.

Transgenerational Violence

The theory of transgenerational violence maintains that elder abuse is a manifestation of learned violent behavior, and that the violence is cyclical. The theory has some support in the literature. For example, Gelles (1983) found a correlation between exposure to and experience with violence as a child and violent behavior as an adult. Walker

(1984) found that previous experience with violence in the home or acts of violence committed against their pets were among the best predictors of violence in men who battered their wives. Walker also found that men who battered their wives were more than three times as likely (81% versus 24%) as nonviolent men to have seen or experienced spouse or child abuse in their homes of origin. In turn, battered women were more likely than women who were not abused to discipline their children physically. The cycle of violence is completed when the abused child, now an adult in control, is able to "pay back" an infirm parent.

Violence occurs in degrees, and some violence is a learned behavior, passed down through the generations and considered "normal" (e.g., "spare the rod and spoil the child"). Violence can be threatened as well as carried out, with similar effects. In their brief review of psychological maltreatment, Hart and Brassard (1993, p. 6) refer to a study of child-abusing mothers that found that "their backgrounds harbored rejection and *threats* of abandonment and violence instead of backgrounds of *actual* abandonment or violence." Violence in abusive situations also can be bidirectional, reflecting the living history of its origin in that family. Steinmetz's (1981) study of the interactions of 60 caregivers and their older dependents identifies "double-directional violence"—efforts by caregivers and older people under their care to control each other by screaming, yelling, and slapping. Studying the relationship between dementia and elder abuse in 1,000 caregiving settings, Coyne, Reichman, and Berbig (1993) reported that 33% of the time the care recipient directed abuse toward the caregiver during the course of caregiving. The theory of transgenerational violence is also supported by the growing literature on post-traumatic stress and violent behaviors in some Vietnam War veterans.

The transgenerational theory suggests that once learned, violence can be unlearned or at least more appropriate behaviors can be substituted, especially within a supportive, nonthreatening environment. However, to be effective, behavioral interventions often require participation by both partners in an abusive dyad. Moreover, initial assessments by health care practitioners in cases of suspected elder abuse should always include questions about family violence in the person's history.

Exchange Theory

Social Exchange Broadly interpreted, exchange theory includes both social exchange theory and symbolic interaction theory. Social exchange theory assumes that social interactions involve the exchange of rewards and punishments between people, and that people seek to maximize rewards and minimize punishments in these exchanges. Rewards are obtained from the exchange of sentiments, resources, and services. Punishment is obtained from exchanging negative sentiments, withholding resources, or delivering punishing behaviors. Social interactions operate under the law of *distributive justice*, which dictates that rewards should be proportional to the costs incurred in obtaining them (Phillips, 1986). This theory posits that human behavior is guided by the principle of exchange: We provide resources to others because we receive them in return. Gelles (1983, p. 157) explained the principle of exchange in this way: "An individual who supplies reward services to another obliges him to fulfill an obligation, and thus the second individual must furnish benefits to the first."

Walker and Allen (1991) used exchange theory to study the qualitative fit in relationships between caregiving daughters and their mothers. Noting the degree of reported costs, rewards, and conflicts in the relationships, these researchers found some sociodemographic correlates. For example, in relationships with the most positive exchanges, the daughters spent fewer years in caregiving and have fewer children. In studying the behaviors of nursing assistants, Foner (1994) observed that assistants tend to have favorite patients to whom they provide the greatest amount of and the highest quality of attention. Foner discovered that, in turn, these favored residents ask about the nursing assistants' families and personal lives.

According to social exchange theory, social exchange goes awry in abusive situations. When distributive justice fails, resentment, anger, and violence can result. Phillips (1986) notes that the theory of social exchange can be used to explain child, spouse, and elder abuse. In each type of abuse the aggressor and the victim have few alternatives to the abusive domestic situation; where would the child, the wife, or the elderly person go? The victim is dependent on the aggressor, and is not, in the opinion of the aggressor, rewarding the aggressor's behaviors sufficiently. The aggressor has the monopoly on rewards, with no deterrent to being unjust toward the victim. Indeed, some abusers rationalize punishment on the grounds that the personal rewards they derive from the exchange are not commensurate with the costs they incur in maintaining the relationship. The abuse occurs and will continue as long as the abuser can capitalize upon it.

A quirk in this theory developed when Hwalek, Sengstock, and Lawrence (1984) and Pillemer (1986) found that some abusers were actually more dependent upon the elderly person than vice versa, especially with regard to finances and housing. Pillemer argues that abuse arises out of the abuser's resentment over his or her powerlessness. Lacking the resources for a normal exchange, the abuser employs the resources of control and violence.

Because it is focused on the idiosyncratic interactions of the people in the abusive scenario, social exchange theory is not able to predict elder abuse. However, social exchange theory does suggest avenues of intervention, including a range of options from values clarification and economic supports for the abuser to the insertion of a third party into the abusive scenario. If the abuse occurs only as long as the abuser can get away with it without sanctions or punishment, a third person, in the form of a house visitor or home health aide, may disrupt this pattern. Human services agencies in the community, such as Area Agencies on Aging or Departments of Social Services, can provide intervention resources.

Symbolic Interaction Symbolic interaction theory argues that social interaction is a process that is continuous, evolves through phases, and requires constant renegotiation of the meaning of the interaction. Steinmetz (1988, pp. 13–14) uses this theory in her study of 104 caregivers and their 119 elderly family members and explains:

> Attempting to understand not only the behaviors engaged in by the caregiver and elder, but also the symbolic interpretation of these behaviors by the actors, makes this approach useful. Earlier work on family violence suggested that the subjective perception of the situation was as important, and perhaps more so, than the actual objective characteristics measured.

The research on caregiver burden has operationalized this perspective, as the focus has shifted over the years from attempting to quantify and determine the objective level of care that becomes burdensome to attempting to qualify the caregivers' perceptions or sense of burden.

The phases that symbolic interactions pass through are cognitive, expressive, and evaluative. Phillips (1986) explains that in the cognitive process phase each individual assigns meaning to the encounter based on his or her personal background, beliefs, and current roles. This definition of the situation predisposes expectations and planned behaviors, based on self-image and the image one has of the other person. During this process the individual assumes roles for him- or herself and ascribes motives and characteristics to the other person. As the interaction continues, each person redefines the situation as feedback is received and processed. Studying family caregivers' views of nursing facility staff, Duncan and Morgan (1994) reveal that these family members assign to nursing assistants characteristics that they consider to be requisite for delivery of high-quality care, and then monitor and measure the treatment of their elderly family member against this unspoken standard.

In the expressive process phase the interactors behave in ways consistent with the roles assumed and assigned. *Role synchrony* describes both persons having similar perceptions of the relationship and of the assumed and assigned role identities. Role synchrony keeps the interaction going, even when the roles are synchronized on invalid perceptions, such as the adult child being the parent and the elderly parent being the child. *Role asynchrony* refers to a mismatch in how the interaction is defined by the interactors. This asynchrony has negative consequences when one is not free to suspend the dissimilar perception, as may be the case with a dependent elderly person.

In the evaluative process phase each person assesses the situation and the roles assumed and assigned, and redefines the personal identity of the other person. Viewed from the perspective of symbolic interaction, elder abuse arises from faulty or inappropriate role enactments that are based on cognitive processes in which the interactors assume and assign roles to each other (Phillips, 1986). For instance, in a family context the image of the elderly person may change over time, and the symbolic meaning of past and present images of the elderly person lies within the evaluator (e.g., family caregiver). The evaluator may ascribe harmful motives and characteristics to the perceived change in the older person. Phillips (1986) reports that in families in which elder abuse is present, the elderly members are stigmatized and devalued, or a large, negative discrepancy exists between past and present images of the elderly person. The family assigns negative motives and characteristics to the elderly person's behavior and adopts roles that are consistent with its negative image of the older member, such as harsh warden to the unruly older person. Counseling is a logical intervention that addresses, clarifies, and rectifies dangerous "meanings" operating in the family context. Because internalized meanings may have devious, if not incredible, histories for the suspected abuser or neglector, counseling may be an extensive process of peeling back layers of rationalizations.

Vulnerability of the Elderly Person

The vulnerability theory posits that characteristics of the elderly person, specifically, incapacities and impairments, render the elderly person frail and vulnerable. This vulnerability may predispose exploitation by a second party. Researchers in child abuse have noted that certain characteristics of children placed them at greater risk for abuse by their parents. These characteristics included having disabilities; being chronically ill; being disfigured; being born prematurely; and making economic, social, or psychological demands. With the exception of the characteristic of prematurity, which can be mirrored as *postmaturity* (viewed by others as living too long) in frail elderly people, this child abuse theory may be readily transferred to elder abuse. Interestingly, Gelles (1983) uses the same body of child abuse research to explain social exchange theory. He reports that children with deformities or impairments "may be perceived as not providing sufficient gratification in return for the parents' investment of time and energy" (p. 160). The theories are not mutually exclusive, and the same observations and data may be used inductively to support different theories.

The interconnection of the vulnerability theory with the social exchange theory helps to explain a troubling feature of vulnerability theory: Why would the presence of an impairment precipitate abuse? Fulmer and O'Malley (1987) found that the older person with severe physical or mental impairment is more likely than other older people to be abused, not because he or she foments the abuse, but because the dependency causes vulnerability. This statement begs the question: If vulnerability is the proximate condition for elder abuse, what is the immediate or precipitating condition for the abuse? Anticipating still another theory, the situational demand theory of elder abuse, it may be that the person with impairments is neglected or abused because care demands exceed the caregiver's capacity to provide care, and the caregiver either walks away from the caregiving situation or strikes out at the older person.

Aside from the merits or possible predictive value of a vulnerability theory of elder abuse (i.e., elder abuse will become more prevalent as the number of elderly people with impairments increases), this theory poses some troubling prospects for health care practitioners concerned about elder abuse. In tracking annual data from the National Health Interview Survey from 1985 to 1992, Cohen and Van Nostrand (1995) report that limitations in ADLs such as eating, bathing, and dressing remained constant, at about 12%–13% among people age 70 and over. Likewise, limitations in routine care areas, such as household chores and shopping, remained constant from 1985 to 1992, at about 17%–18%. However, the number of elderly people is growing, as is the number of old-old people (age 85 and over). The needs of these people for assistance are greater than the needs of their younger counterparts. Therefore, even if prevalence rates for limitations remain constant, the absolute numbers of elderly people with these limitations will grow. Kunkel and Applebaum (1992) project that even with the most optimistic of four models for longevity and disability (i.e., longer life and lower disability), the population of elderly people with disabilities is likely to rise 84% between 1986 and 2020, or from 5.1 to 9.4 million. Their projection does not factor in the unprecedented survival to later life of large numbers of people with lifelong developmental disabilities, a phenomenon Ansello and Eustis (1992) and other researchers have noted.

On a practical level, a theory that maintains that dependency predisposes vulnerability, which predisposes elder abuse and neglect, suggests numerous interventions for the health care provider. These interventions include lessening or moderating dependency (e.g., using assistive devices) and mobility training. Coupled with social exchange theory, the vulnerability theory suggests interventions to improve the reciprocity of the care receiver–caregiver interaction (e.g., family therapy). When coupled with excessive situational demand theory, the vulnerability theory suggests interventions to lessen the pressure of demands placed upon the caregiver and/or to increase the caregiver's competence to respond to these demands (e.g., respite assistance, skills training).

Excessive Situational Demands

The excessive situational demand theory, especially as it relates to stress and domestic violence, has had an enduring history. In 1977 Skolnik and Skolnik posited that family violence appears to be a product of psychological tensions and external stresses that affect all families. In a review of the situational theory of violence, Phillips (1986) found an "inconsistent fit between the situational model and the empirical data" (p. 201). However, Phillips noted the many methodological problems in early studies from which the situational theory was induced, including widely varying definitions of elder abuse and nonoverlapping samples of individuals studied. The logic of a situational model would also predict different precipitators for different forms of elder abuse, such as physical abuse as opposed to financial exploitation.

The descriptive literature on elder abuse and neglect repeatedly documents the stresses and strains of caregiving. Montgomery (1989) provides a good review of caregiver strain studies up to that time. In 1993 Clipp and George demonstrated the interactive nature of the caregiving situation by comparing spousal caregivers of adults with dementia and of adults with cancer. Situational demands and caregiver perceptions apparently interweave in such a way that caregivers of people with dementia were found to have significantly more negative affect, more stress symptoms, more feelings of being overwhelmed, less life satisfaction, worse self-rated health, and greater use of anti-anxiety drugs. Interestingly, quantified hours of care provided by caregivers did not correlate with these caregiver outcomes.

Biegel, Sales, and Schulz (1991) reviewed studies of caregiving of family members with cancer, heart disease, stroke, Alzheimer's disease, and chronic mental illness. They found instructive similarities in the studies. The patient illness characteristics that seem most related to stress and strain reported by family caregivers are greater illness severity, suddenness of onset, and greater changes in preexisting patient behaviors. They conclude that certain contextual variables act as mediators to transform or filter the caregiver's reaction to the family member's illness. They found the following:

1. Female caregivers generally report significantly higher levels of distress.
2. Spouses generally report experiencing more severe strain than nonspouse family caregivers in all cases except providing care after a heart attack.

3. Parental caregivers of children with chronic mental illness report more subjective burden than do caregivers of other conditions, although their objective burden is lower.
4. Older caregivers (e.g., spouses) report greater emotional distress than younger caregivers.
5. Caregivers who had good psychological adjustment skills prior to the care recipient's illness report an ability to withstand caregiving stress better than caregivers who lacked good psychological adjustment skills prior to the illness.

Thus, Biegel, Sales, and Schulz provide a picture of the situational demand theory in which dynamic interaction occurs between the characteristics of the care recipient and the caregiver that contributes to perceived stress. Steinmetz's (1988) study of family caregivers and their elderly care recipients compared stressed and nonstressed caregivers in 12 stress-producing categories in order to learn whether abuse did or did not result. Steinmetz concludes,

> It appears that instrumental tasks, household, financial, transportation, getting the elder to eat (adequately) and special diets are, in general, less likely to produce abusive caregiving than are expressive tasks, such as dealing with a mobile but senile elder, their [sic] demands, or providing social/emotional support. (p. 177)

Steinmetz observes that the perception by caregivers that caregiving is stressful and burdensome increases the likelihood that they will use "negative forms of control maintenance techniques," including abuse.

The excessive situational demand theory recognizes that abusive situations comprise the characteristics of caregiver and care recipient, the caregiver's perception of the caregiving context, and the process of social exchange. The element of perception (or "meaning" in symbolic interaction theory) is essential to understanding elder abuse. The perception of stress or burden may not coincide with an objective accounting of demands placed on the caregiver. Stull, Kosloski, and Kercher (1994) maintain that caregiver burden is not simply the obverse of generic well-being; generic well-being and the caregiver's sense of burden can coexist. The authors argue that caregiver burden is both an outcome of antecedent conditions in the elderly person (e.g., needing help with ADLs, instrumental ADLs, and a greater level of assistance; dementing illness) and a predictor of other specific outcomes (e.g., chore/homemaker services and adult day services, nursing facility placement). Stull, Kosloski, and Kercher (1994) demonstrate another aspect of the interactive nature of the caregiving situation in which the characteristics of the care recipient affect the caregiver's perceptions, which, in turn, affect actual and intended behaviors.

THE ENVIRONMENTAL PRESS MODEL PROTOCOL

The excessive situational demand theory is perhaps the most complex and inclusive of the explanatory theories of elder abuse and neglect. It can incorporate aspects of the other four theories. Thus, it is prudent to explore a practical protocol for analysis and intervention, the environmental press model (Figure 1.1). Although not a theory of elder abuse and neglect, the environmental press model possesses robust practical implications for diagnosing likely reasons for inadequate care of an elderly person and for recommending courses of remediation. The environmental press model has been used to train physicians, nurses, pharmacists, and nursing home administrators.

The environmental press model relates especially well to the situational demand theory for inadequate care, but its utility also extends to the vulnerability theory and the exchange theories. The dynamic or interactive premise of the environmental press model includes both parties in an abusive or neglecting situation, and applies to both domestic and institutional settings. (See Ansello, King, and Taler [1986] for a complete examination of the specific workings and application of the environmental press model.)

The model grew out of the premise that people seek to adapt to, or become minimally aware of, their environment so that qualities in the environment (see below) are neither so strong nor so weak that people must attend to them rather than to other tasks that express competence. Adaptation, then, is the appropriate balance or fit between the environment's degree of "press," or impingement, on an individual and the individual's level of competencies (Lawton, 1980; Lawton & Nahemow, 1973). The many dimensions of the environmental press model have been studied extensively in institutional settings (the model was actually developed in institutional settings), with ready applications to family and work life. The dimensions of press or qualities in the environment can be reduced to three practical concerns: How much stimulation, change, and responsibility does the environment allow the individual? Under circumstances of balance or adaptation to the environmental press, an individual can fully use the four primary types of competence: biological, sensorimotor, cognitive, and emotional. Low competence would fit with weak press; higher competence would require stronger press. If competence and press are not in balance, maladaptation occurs; the strength or weakness of the environmental demand essentially captures the individual's attention and dictates responses. The outcome of either adaptation or maladaptation is expressed in two ways, behavior and affect.

A key insight from environmental press research is that the press of the environment (e.g., stimulation) must continuously renew itself; that is, it must vary or change. Without renewal, an appropriate level

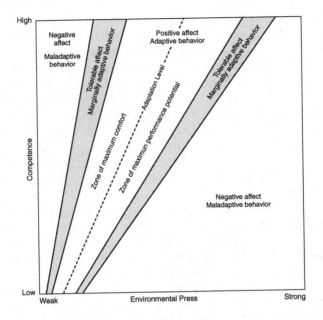

Figure 1.1. The environmental press model. (From Eisdorfer, C., & Lawton, M.P. [Eds.]. [1973]. *Psychology of adult development and aging*, p. 318. Washington, DC: American Psychological Association; reprinted by permission.)

of press progressively becomes weaker. Without renewal, what is initially stimulating becomes less so. For example, as environmental press weakens, an elderly person may consciously or unconsciously become less competent in order to remain in balance with or adapted to the weakened environment. For instance, sometimes the elderly person has nowhere else to go.

Inadequate care relates to the two maladaptation scenarios: competence exceeds press, and press exceeds competence. When competence exceeds press, an individual tends to exhibit *passive maladaptation*. The environment does not offer sufficient stimulation, change, or responsibility. A person may experience symptoms such as boredom, mental withdrawal, and physical or mental escape, and may sabotage a relationship with another person in order to create change. Passive maladaptation typifies the lives of many elderly people, especially if their environments contain things (e.g., furnishings, daily routines) and people that seldom or never change. Ironically, the chronic caregiver becomes less stimulating and becomes a feature in the older person's diminishing press the longer the caregiver continues the routine of caregiving. Thus, the care recipient's seemingly exaggerated response to the occasional telephone call from a distant son can be seen not as a figurative slap at the ever-present caregiving daughter, but as a momentary peak in the elderly person's environmental press.

In older people diminishing competence is associated with self-neglect, as they become less capable physically or emotionally of coping with increasing environmental demands. Rowles (1978) notes that in facing this potential maladaptation, older people may choose to compensate, to constrict their geographical lifespace (i.e., to narrow their realm of action to the home); to intensify their investment in certain places, especially emotionally, as when a particular route for walking is favored because of obstacles elsewhere; and to expand their geographic experiences through fantasy, as when they imagine their children's daily lives.

An excess of press over competence is a key feature of the excessive situational demand theory of elder abuse and neglect or inadequate care. This excess frequently corresponds to the caregiver's reality of providing chronic care to an elderly person whose biological, sensorimotor, cognitive, and emotional competencies are declining. The caregiver's own competencies may be overwhelmed by the care recipient's progressive deterioration; by the need to provide more complex care; and by multiplying, simultaneous demands, such as coping with the older person's incontinence and medication regimen, with the caregiver's own physical exhaustion and sense of burden, and with the rest of the family's requirements for meals, transportation, and scheduling. The lack of assistance from other relatives in providing care may significantly increase the caregiver's sense of burden and precipitate family conflict (Strawbridge & Wallhagen, 1991). Compounding the excessive press may be the care recipient's seemingly "provocative" or "demeaning" behaviors. For example, the older person may display a lack of appreciation for continuing care when momentary peaks in the elderly person's environmental press occur, such as a telephone call from a distant relative.

Interventions that flow from the environmental press model should follow reasoned appraisal by the health care provider of the overall situation in which the older person and the alleged abuser are found. Historically, removal of the abuser has been the initial, almost knee-jerk reaction. By understanding the person–environment fit of the environmental press model the practitioner may realize that no other resource exists for the elderly person's care than this caregiver, or that dynamics are at play other than the abusive behavior that must be addressed, such as stimulus deprivation or diminished competence (Biegel, Sales, & Schulz, 1991; Clipp & George, 1993). Interventions should incorporate situational demand, vulnerability, and exchange theory considerations.

Intervening on behalf of the elderly person who is receiving inadequate care seeks both to increase any or all of the four areas of competency and to increase the elderly person's environmental press. In intervening on behalf of the caregiver, one recognizes that stress tends to be intrinsic to chronic caregiving. The environmental press may already be on overload. Therefore, intervention is intended to reduce the caregiver's environmental press and/or to increase any or all of the four areas of competency because caregiving may progressively deplete a caregiver's physical, sensorimotor, cognitive, and emotional resources as it simultaneously presents demands in each of the four areas of competency.

CONCLUSION

This chapter provides background for the assessments and interventions that health care practitioners institute upon encountering suspected elder abuse and neglect or inadequate care. No unicausal theory explains the etiology of all elder abuse, neglect, or inadequate care, nor can one theory prescribe the best course of action in response to suspicion or identification of abuse and neglect. Conceptually, the theories are more complementary than mutually exclusive. Practitioners may use them eclectically to develop a reasoned course of action. The environmental press model provides an operational framework within which to apply the theories of abuse and neglect.

REFERENCES

Aging News Alert. (1995, February 22). p. 12.

Ansello, E.F. (1991). Aging issues for the year 2000. *Caring, 10*(2), 4–12.

Ansello, E.F., & Eustis, N.N. (Eds.). (1992). Aging and disabilities: Seeking common ground [Special issue]. *Generations: Journal of the American Society on Aging, 16*(1).

Ansello, E.F., King, N.R., & Taler, G. (1986). The environmental press model: A theoretical framework for intervention in elder abuse. In K.A. Pillemer & R.S. Wolf (Eds.), *Elder abuse: Conflict in the family* (pp. 314–330). Dover, MA: Auburn House.

Biegel, D.E., Sales, E., & Schulz, R. (1991). *Family caregiving in chronic illness: Alzheimer's disease, cancer, heart disease, mental illness, and stroke.* Newbury Park, CA: Sage Publications.

Clipp, E.C., & George, L.K. (1993). Dementia and cancer: A comparison of spouse caregivers. *Gerontologist, 33*(4), 534–541.

Cohen, R.A., & Van Nostrand, J.F. (1995). *Trends in the health of older Americans: United States, 1994.* (Series 3: Analytic and epidemiological studies; No. 30). Hyattsville, MD: National Center for Health Statistics.

Coyne, A.C., Reichman, W.E., & Berbig, L.J. (1993). The relationship between dementia and elder abuse. *American Journal of Psychiatry, 150*(4), 643–646.

Duncan, M.T., & Morgan, D.L. (1994). Sharing the caring: Family caregivers' views of their relationships with nursing home staff. *Gerontologist, 34*(2), 235–244.

Foner, N. (1994). Nursing home aides: Saints or monsters? *Gerontologist, 34*(2), 245–250.

Fulmer, T.T., McMahon, D.J., Baer-Hines, M., & Forget, B. (1992). Abuse, neglect, abandonment, violence, and exploitation: An analysis of all elderly patients seen in one emergency department during a six-month period. *Journal of Emergency Nursing, 18*(6), 505–510.

Fulmer, T.T., & O'Malley, T.A. (1987). *Inadequate care of the elderly: A health care perspective on abuse and neglect.* New York: Springer Publishing.

Gelles, R.J. (1983). An exchange/social control theory. In D. Finkelhor, R.J. Gelles, G.T. Hotaling, & M.A. Straus (Eds.), *The dark side of families: Current family violence research* (pp. 151–165). Beverly Hills, CA: Sage Publications.

Hart, S.N., & Brassard, M.R. (1993). Psychological maltreatment. *Violence Update, 3*(7), 1ff.

Hwalek, M.A., Sengstock, M.C., & Lawrence, R. (1984, November). *Assessing the probability of abuse of the elderly.* Paper presented at the 37th Annual Scientific Meeting of the Gerontological Society of America, San Antonio, TX.

Johnson, T.F. (1991). *Elder mistreatment: Deciding who is at risk.* Westport, CT: Greenwood Press.

Kosberg, J.I. (1988). Preventing elder abuse: Identification of high risk factors prior to placement decisions. *Gerontologist, 28*(1), 43–50.

Kunkel, S.R., & Applebaum, R.A. (1992). Estimating the prevalence of long-term disability for an aging society. *Journal of Gerontology: Social Sciences, 47*(5), S253–S260.

Lawton, M.P. (1980). *Environment and aging.* Monterey, CA: Brooks/Cole.

Lawton, M.P., & Nahemow, L. (1973). Ecology and the aging process. In C. Eisdorfer & M.P. Lawton (Eds.), *Psychology of adult development and aging* (pp. 619–674). Washington, DC: American Psychological Association.

Montgomery, R.J.V. (1989). Investigating caregiver burden. In K.S. Markides & C.L. Cooper (Eds.), *Aging, stress and health* (pp. 201–208). New York: John Wiley & Sons.

Phillips, L.R. (1986). Theoretical explanations of elder abuse: Competing hypotheses and unresolved issues. In K.A. Pillemer & R.S. Wolf (Eds.), *Elder abuse: Conflict in the family* (pp. 197–217). Dover, MA: Auburn House.

Pillemer, K.A. (1986). Risk factors in elder abuse: Results from a case-control study. In K.A. Pillemer & R.S. Wolf (Eds.), *Elder abuse: Conflict in the family* (pp. 239–263). Dover, MA: Auburn House.

Pillemer, K.A., & Finkelhor, D. (1989). Causes of elder abuse: Caregiver stress versus problem relatives. *American Journal of Orthopsychiatry, 59*(2), 179–187.

Pillemer, K., & Moore, D.W. (1989). Abuse of patients in nursing homes: Findings from a survey of staff. *Gerontologist, 29*(3), 314–320.

Quinn, M.J., & Tomita, S.K. (1986). *Elder abuse and neglect: Causes, diagnosis, and intervention strategies.* New York: Springer Publishing.

Rathbone-McCuan, E., & Fabian, D.R. (Eds.). (1992). *Self-neglecting elders: A clinical dilemma.* Westport, CT: Auburn House.

Rowles, G.D. (1978). *Prisoners of space? Exploring the geographical experience of older people.* Boulder, CO: Westview Press.

Shiferaw, B., Mittlemark, M.B., Wofford, J.L., Anderson, R.T., Walls, P., & Rohrer, B. (1994). The investigation and outcome of reported cases of elder abuse: The Forsyth County aging study. *Gerontologist, 34*(1), 123–125.

Skolnick, A., & Skolnick, J.H. (Eds.). (1977). *The family in transition* (2nd ed.). Boston: Little, Brown.

Steinmetz, S.K. (1981, January–February). Elder abuse. *Aging,* pp. 6–10.

Steinmetz, S.K. (1988). *Duty bound: Elder abuse and family care.* Newbury Park, CA: Sage Publications.

Strawbridge, W.J., & Wallhagen, M.I. (1991). Impact of family conflict on adult child caregivers. *Gerontologist, 31*(6), 770–777.

Stull, D.E., Kosloski, K., & Kercher, K. (1994). Caregiver burden and generic well-being: Opposite sides of the same coin? *Gerontologist, 34*(1), 88–94.

Tatara, T. (1993). *Summaries of the statistical data on elder abuse in domestic settings for FY90 and FY91: A final report.* Washington, DC: National Aging Resource Center on Elder Abuse.

U.S. House of Representatives, Select Committee on Aging. (1981). *Elder abuse: An examination of a hidden problem* (Committee Publication No. 97-277). Washington, DC: U.S. Government Printing Office.

Walker, A.J., & Allen, K.R. (1991). Relationships between caregiving daughters and their elderly mothers. *Gerontologist, 31*(3), 389–396.

Walker, L.E. (1984). *The battered woman syndrome.* New York: Springer Publishing.

Wolfson, C., Handfield-Jones, R., Glass, K.C., McClaran, J., & Keyserlingk, E. (1993). Adult children's perceptions of their responsibility to provide care for dependent elderly parents. *Gerontologist, 33*(3), 315–323.

2

Characteristics of Victims and Perpetrators and Milieus of Abuse and Neglect

Jordan I. Kosberg and Daphne Nahmiash

Health care providers often function in settings (e.g., clinics, emergency rooms, private dwellings, long-term care facilities) in which the abuse and neglect of elderly people can be identified. Care providers must be able to recognize the specific characteristics of actual or potential abuse victims and their abusers. This chapter presents an overview of the characteristics of elder abusers and their victims, which have been identified from research study findings and practical experience.

Elder abuse is defined as adverse acts of omission or commission against an elderly person, and includes the following:

- Physical mistreatment, such as striking and burning
- Verbal, emotional, or psychological abuse, in which the older person is subjected to repeated insults, humiliation, and threats
- Material or financial abuse, such as misuse of the victim's property or finances
- Passive and active neglect, including withholding items or care that is necessary for daily living

- Violation of civil rights, in which an older person is forced to do something against his or her wishes

These forms of abuse can result from either the intentional or unintentional actions or inactions of the perpetrators of abuse.

Self-neglect, which occurs when an older person endangers him- or herself or fails to provide adequate self-care (e.g., excessive drinking, malnutrition, failure to seek needed medical care), is often included as a form of abuse. This form differs from the others because no second party is the abuser. However, family and friends may be aware of the neglectful behavior and may fail to intervene.

The incidence of elder abuse is highest within private dwellings in the community. Often, abusers are members of the elderly person's family, but abusers may also be home health care providers, friends, or neighbors. Elder abuse in community-based settings also may include the mistreatment by or unprofessional behavior of physicians, psychologists, adult day services workers, and other formal (professional and paraprofessional) caregivers. Such community-based abuse is largely an invisible social problem and is difficult to detect (Kosberg, 1988).

Elder abuse in institutional settings is also an invisible social problem (Kosberg, 1994). Abusive acts may be perpetrated within long-term care facilities by paid staff members who are responsible for giving care to residents. No consistent definitions exist of "inappropriate care" of residents in long-term care settings (O'Malley, 1987). Pillemer and Moore (1989) defined inappropriate care as physical abuse within institutions, which includes the use of restraints, hitting, and slapping. Psychological abuse (Pillemer & Finkelhor, 1989) and acts of omission (Beaulieu & Belanger, 1995) within long-term care facilities also are included as examples of inappropriate care.

Because of the roles they play and their status within health care institutions, nursing personnel and other paid caregivers are believed to possess the greatest potential for mistreating residents (Beaulieu & Belanger, 1995). Paradoxically, care providers are the most likely to identify incidents of abusive behavior. Personality conflicts and conflicting expectations between staff and residents have been identified as among the possible explanations for abuse inflicted by staff members.

Abuse in long-term care facilities also results from material or monetary theft by staff or mismanagement by administrators or owners of long-term care facilities (e.g., charging for services or items unrelated to resident care, collecting monies from Medicare or Medicaid for deceased or discharged residents, charging for therapy or medication that was not provided) (Hornick, MacDonald, & Robertson, 1990). Embezzling a resident's funds is another example of this form of abuse (Vladek, 1980).

All of these forms of elder abuse are perpetrated in part because abusers perceive that older people are more vulnerable than younger people. Many explanations exist for the vulnerability of older people to the abusive behavior of others (Kosberg, 1990). The most basic explanation pertains to prevailing societal attitudes toward elderly people. Because elderly people are widely perceived as being impaired and dependent, often little or no social value is ascribed to older people, particularly in North America (Breckman & Adelman, 1988). Sexism is another explanation for negative societal attitudes, particularly toward older women (Driedger & Chappell, 1987).

Older people, especially older women, tend to live alone (Rubenstein, Kilbride, & Magy, 1992), often in areas with high crime rates. These factors increase the probability that they will be physically isolated and the likelihood that they will be victimized. One of the effects of isolation, loneliness, may lead older people to develop friendships with unscrupulous strangers. Material or financial abuse of older people may result from the abuser's perception that older people are unable to safeguard personal property (Quinn & Tomita, 1986). Publicized incidents of such abuse may result in fear of becoming a victim, which, according to Brillon (1987), is common among elderly people. Paradoxically, although fear may deter older people from becoming victims, it also has the negative consequences of isolating older people within their dwellings and adversely affecting the quality of their lives.

Elderly people are also likely to have chronic physical disabilities or impairments that diminish their strength, hearing, sight, touch, and mobility, making them less able than younger people to defend themselves or to escape from threatening situations. Brillon (1987) found that the consequences of psychological abuse are more serious for older people than for younger people and that elderly people are more likely to be victimized repeatedly by the same offender or offenders (Goldsmith & Tomas, 1974). The regular receipt of government, retirement, or investment benefits or checks causes older people to be vulnerable to exploitation or theft by relatives, neighbors, and strangers.

These older people also tend to be dependent on the people upon whom one is traditionally dependent, family members, neighbors, friends, or formal caregivers, for their daily care. Even when health care professionals and paraprofessionals are aware of abuse resulting from family care of an elderly person, they are often reluctant to intervene.

Although health care professionals often view family care of an elderly person as a panacea, some relatives may be inappropriately suited (e.g., disagreeable temperament, mental or physical impairment, lack of motivation) to be caregivers and cannot be counted on to meet the needs of an older person (Kosberg, 1988).

Some formal long-term caregivers may be inappropriately suited to work in long-term care facilities as well. To ensure their suitability to caregiving, long-term care staff need to be screened, just as family members should be screened. Caregiving surveillance by outsiders (e.g., professionals, advocacy groups) should be provided because elderly patients may be the most "invisible, voiceless, and dependent population in society" (Kosberg, 1994).

Events in the lives of elderly people or their caregivers can trigger abuse. These events may include changes in living arrangements, the death of a spouse, and conflicts that lead to lost trust between two family members (Kozak, Elmslie, & Verdon, 1995).

A review of the literature reveals many different ways in which to view the dynamics of elder abuse. Evidence in the literature suggests that health care and social service providers should consider not only the individual characteristics of elderly victims and their abusers, but also the broader context within which the abuse occurs. Table 2.1 provides a conceptual framework through which to view characteristics and milieu. Admittedly, the four areas—characteristics of abused and abusive people and characteristics of the social and cultural milieus within which the abuse takes place—overlap. The following sections expand on the information contained in Table 2.1.

CHARACTERISTICS OF VICTIMS

Gender

Studies from the 1970s and 1980s revealed that women were more likely than men to be the victims of elder abuse (Lau & Kosberg, 1979; Douglass, Hickey, & Noel, 1980; Wolf, Strugnell, & Godkin, 1982; O'Malley, 1987; Pillemer & Finkelhor, 1988). Among the explanations are the larger proportion of older women to older men, the lack of physical strength to resist abuse, and the sexual molestation of women. However, Tatara (1993) suggested that the majority of elder abuse victims in the United States are men. Tatara cited reasons such as that men are often older and more impaired than their spouses, men are "paid back" for the abuse of their children or spouses, and men are more likely to engage in excessive inappropriate behaviors (e.g., drinking, gambling) that lower their defenses and affect their ability to make appropriate judgments about the care they receive.

It is important to acknowledge that victims of elder abuse can be either women or men. Many cases of abuse may remain unreported if professionals exclude elderly men from screening protocols for elder abuse.

Marital Status

Many studies have noted that the victims of elder abuse are disproportionately widows (Kosberg, 1988; Pillemer & Finkelhor, 1988). This

Table 2.1. Conceptual framework for the characteristics of elder abuse victims and perpetrators and the milieus of abuse

Elderly victims	Elder abusers
Gender	Substance abuse
Marital status	Mental/emotional illness
Health	Lack of caregiving experience
Chronological age	Reluctance
Substance abuse	History of abuse
Living arrangements	Stress and burden
Psychological factors	Dependency
Problem behavior	Dementia
Dependence	Personality traits
Isolation	Lack of social support
Social context	**Cultural norms**
Financial problems	Ageism
Family violence	Sexism
Lack of social support	Attitudes toward violence
Family disharmony	Reactions to abuse
Living arrangements	Attitudes toward people with disabilities
	Family caregiving imperatives

is not surprising because most elderly people are women, many of whom are widowed. However, Giordano and Giordano (1983) and Pillemer and Suitor (1992) also identified spouses as elder abuse victims. Marriage does not nullify the fact that both negative and positive feelings can and often do coexist within the same relationship (Troll & Smith, 1976). Negative feelings can result in abusive treatment of the spouse.

Health

Numerous studies indicate that most, but not all, victims of elder abuse are in poor physical or mental health. In rural areas being mentally ill has been identified as a potential risk factor for abuse (Weiler & Buckwalter, 1992). Elder mistreatment has been associated with the extent and severity of the physical or mental impairment (Block & Sinnott, 1979; Wolf, Strugnell, & Godkin, 1982). Elderly people in poor health require a great deal of care and thus can place greater demands on their formal or informal (e.g., family) caregivers. It is commonly believed that caregivers who are under excessive stress are most likely to engage in abusive behavior against the source of the perceived or real problems, the elderly person (Kosberg & Cairl, 1986).

Healthy older people also may be mistreated. Godkin, Wolf, and Pillemer (1989) and Pillemer and Suitor (1992) showed that impairment is not necessarily a characteristic specific to abuse victims. Older people who are not victims of abuse may be as physically and mentally impaired as older people who are victimized.

Chronological Age

Kosberg (1980) and O'Malley (1987) suggested that the older the person, the greater the risk of mistreatment. Chronological age is associated with poor health conditions. However, Hudson (1994) found that abuse also occurs among young-old people (60–69 years of age). Abuse in this age group may not occur only in one direction—perpetrator to victim—but may be reciprocal (Hudson, 1994). Although health care professionals and paraprofessionals must not exclude the possibility that people 60–69 years old are abused or mistreated, research shows that this group of elderly persons is less likely than their older counterparts to become victims of abuse (Tatara, 1993).

Substance Abuse

An older substance abuser is susceptible to the abusive behavior of others because the individual is less inclined to care properly for him- or herself (Kosberg, 1988), and because substance abusers often practice lifestyles that may exacerbate their problems. For example, an alcoholic lifestyle may place an older person in situations in which there is an increased likelihood of abuse by others, or in situations in which satisfying the addiction is more important than obtaining good nutrition (Pillemer, 1986; Kosberg, 1988).

Living Arrangements

The setting within which an elderly person lives may determine whether he or she is at risk for abuse. Floyd (1983) and Pillemer (1986) found that the majority of the abuse victims they surveyed live with a relative. Thus, cohabitation is associated with certain types of abusive situations (such as spouse abuse, sexual abuse, or neglect).

Other studies show that many elderly abuse victims live alone (Harshbarger, 1993), particularly in urban areas, in which they may be isolated, easily identifiable, and lonely. These older people can become targets of financial scams, larceny, and embezzlement by family, formal caregivers, and strangers. It is suspected that self-neglectful behavior occurs and may continue without intervention when no other people reside with the older person (Kosberg, 1988).

Psychological Factors

A person who is depressed or resigned to a particular situation may become an abuse victim, according to Phillips (1983). Similarly, stoicism that is based on a philosophy of tolerance of the behavior of others has been found to be a characteristic of some victims of elder abuse (Kosberg, 1988). Depression, stoicism, or resignation may be symptomatic of abuse; such characteristics also may be antecedents or consequences of abuse.

Other individuals with high-risk personality traits are people who internalize blame, engage in self-blame, or display excessive loyalty to family members (Kosberg, 1988). It is likely that such persons will neither seek help nor report their problems (Quinn & Tomita, 1986).

Presence of Problem Behavior

The exhibition of problem behavior was noted in some victims of abuse (Paveza et al., 1992). The behavior of people with advanced Alzheimer's disease serves as an example of problem behavior. When an older person demonstrates aggressiveness toward a caregiver or a caregiver's family, the result may be abuse of the impaired, acting-out person with Alzheimer's disease.

Estimates suggest that 57%–67% of people with dementia manifest aggressive behavior (Ryden, 1988; Hamel et al., 1990). Caregivers have described some elderly people as overly demanding, unsympathetic, and ungrateful for the care received. People with dementia are considered by some care providers to be provocateurs, and their behavior and attitudes can exacerbate the problems faced by their caregivers (Douglass, Hickey, & Noel, 1980; Kosberg & Cairl, 1986). Indeed, some caregivers justify their abusive behavior by claiming that it is the result of their anger at the older person's behavior, even though they may realize that the behavior was unintentional (Garcia & Kosberg, 1993).

Dependence

Debate has arisen as to whether the dependence of the care recipient on the care provider increases the likelihood of the care recipient becoming a victim of abuse (Quinn & Tomita, 1986) or whether the abuser is more likely to be dependent on the victim of abuse (Pillemer, 1985; Fulmer, 1990). Researchers who support the contention that the functional dependence of elderly people upon their caregivers heightens their vulnerability suggest that mistreatment is often the result of the stress generated by the caregiving situation. Godkin, Wolf, and Pillemer (1989) and Pillemer and Suitor (1992) found that abusive incidents occur when the care receiver and the caregiver become increasingly interdependent, as a result of the loss of family support, increased social isolation, or the increased financial dependency of the abuser on the victim. The economic dependence of a caregiver on an older person may lead first to hostility and then to abuse (Gelles, 1974; Maddox, 1975). "Blaming the victim" is common among elder abusers who are codependent on their victim.

Victims of abuse and neglect often feel powerless (Blunt, 1993) and may be unwilling to disclose their problems to others. Abused elderly people usually have low self-esteem, display a need to "save face," and avoid betraying the abusive acts of family members. Such characteristics may emerge as a consequence of long-term abuse rather than as etiologic factors.

Isolation

Social isolation and the lack of social support from relatives of the abused older person have been suggested as reasons that victims of elder abuse are seldom detected. Enforced isolation can enable victimization to continue without outside detection and intervention (Pillemer, 1984). Although social isolation of abuser and abused often occurs in rural areas, it can also occur within large cities.

CHARACTERISTICS OF ABUSERS

Researchers have found that the typical elder abuser is a son or daughter caregiver, under 60 years of age, who is living with or in close proximity to the elderly victim (Quinn & Tomita, 1986; Wolf, Strugnell, & Godkin, 1982). Abusers in institutions are usually women (Gnaedinger, 1989) who work predominantly in low-paying, high-stress jobs. Both types share ten common characteristics, which are summarized in the following sections.

Substance Abuse

The elder abuse literature contains many references on the abusive consequences of having a substance abuser act as a care provider (Floyd, 1983; Pillemer & Wolf, 1989). Indeed, one can conclude that the substance abuse of a caregiver is the single best predictor for elder abuse. Not only is the abuser unable to make appropriate care decisions, but the economic need to support the addiction probably will take precedence over the needs of the elderly person. Misappropriation of the older person's financial assets by the substance abuser is likely to occur.

Mental/Emotional Illness

Ongoing mental illness or emotional problems have been identified as characteristic of some elder abusers (Kosberg, 1988). Like substance abusers, caregivers with emotional problems are often unable to curb behavior that interferes with their ability to meet the needs of vulnerable elderly persons.

As a result of improved medical care, groups that had been dependent upon their parents for care (e.g., adult children with emotional or intellectual limitations) are now living into old age. Thus, the possibility exists that, as parents age and become increasingly dependent, those who had been dependent become the caregivers of their elderly parents. Such a possibility begs the question of the effectiveness of the caregiving provided by adult children who may be physically or emotionally unable to provide the care needed by their parents.

Lack of Caregiving Experience

One of the characteristics of many abusers is their lack of caregiving experience or training. It cannot be assumed that a person who has never undertaken the task of caring for another can perform the job appropriately (Kosberg, 1988). Family members who have had to meet only their own needs may be unable to shift their attention to the needs of another. Little gratification may be gained from the role of caregiver, whether the caregiver is a family member or a member of the staff in a long-term care facility. Although motivation is necessary, caregiving also necessitates the ability to know how to provide care.

Reluctance

Cairl, Keller, and Kosberg (1984) noted that some family members are reluctant to assume the caregiving role. The personal value systems of some health care professionals and their belief that the family care option is quick and relatively inexpensive as compared to institutional care may cause some professionals to seek to influence a reluctant family member to take on the caregiving role.

Health care professionals must consider the possible reasons for this reluctance and the likely adverse consequences for the older person. The reluctance may be the outgrowth of a poor relationship between the elderly person and the family member or the result of problems within the family (e.g., unemployment, dependent children, an over-crowded household). Either reason may preclude a family member from feeling that he or she is able to provide adequate care.

History of Abuse

Elder abuse is more common in families with established patterns, or histories, of violent behavior (Gelles, 1974; Sengstock & Hwalek, 1985). Violent behavior may be a consequence of a learned response or it may result from conscious or unconscious motivations for retribution. For example, elder abuse may represent a "turning of the tables" of a longstanding pattern of spouse abuse. A resentful, retaliatory wife may abuse her once-abusive husband, who is now infirm and vulnerable. Adult children may abuse an elderly father who abused them, or they may wish to "get even" for the treatment experienced by their mother at the hands of their father (Canadian Panel on Violence Against Women, 1994; Floyd, 1983).

Stress and Burden

As the size of families declines and the number of older persons requiring care increases, some families find themselves under increasing pressure to provide an appropriate level of care to older relatives. Caring for an aging parent can place stress on adult children, particularly women in an intergenerational household (Brody, 1985). Issues of stress and burden that are commonly cited are lack of personal time, lack of privacy, and a decrease in financial resources.

Hudson (1986) noted that stressed and overburdened caregivers may be more likely to abuse their relatives than are caregivers who are able to handle their stress. Abuse may result from accumulated stresses or from a single stressful event (Block & Sinnott, 1979; Galbraith & Davison, 1985; Hickey & Douglass, 1981). Studies conducted by Steinmetz and Amsden (1983) and Zarit, Reever, and Bach-Peterson (1990) found that actual (*objective*) stress may be a less important predictor of abuse than the caregiver's perception (*subjective*) of the stress.

Like family members, formal caregivers may react to work-related stress by becoming abusive toward the elderly people to whom they provide care. Unfortunately, formal education and training of staff does not guarantee suitability for work in institutional care (Smyer, Brannon, & Cohen, 1992). In institutional settings, staff members who receive low wages, whose working conditions are poor, who are employed in "dead-end jobs," and who work under overly demanding supervisors and indifferent administrators are the people who are considered most likely to abuse residents (Davis, 1991). These staff members sometimes describe the residents under their care as overly demanding and ungrateful for the care they receive. The nature of caregiving work with institutionalized elderly populations, which comprise elderly people with numerous impairments, including Alzheimer's disease, may cause low morale, high rates of staff "burnout" and turnover, and inadequate care of residents, including abuse.

Dependency

Older people who are dependent on their caregivers may seem to be the most vulnerable to abuse, although some studies (e.g., Pillemer, 1985) suggest that the opposite is true. Pillemer found that more frequently caregivers are dependent upon older people for financial, emotional, or social support. Caregivers may be angry, embarrassed, or frustrated about their dependency, and these feelings may contribute to the abuse of older people. Dependency also may take the form of interdependence, in that the elderly person may be dependent for activities of daily living on a caregiver who, in turn, is dependent on the elderly person for financial assistance or housing.

Dementia

The abuse of older people with dementing illnesses, such as Alzheimer's disease, was observed by Steinmetz (1988) and Hamel et al. (1990). Abusive caregivers also may be demented, confused, or elderly with a cognitive impairment (Giordano & Giordano, 1983).

Cognitive impairment was linked to the violent and aggressive behavior of caregivers and care recipients by Ryden (1988) and Hamel et al. (1990). Interactive abuse between caregiver and care recipient was noted by Steinmetz (1983).

Personality Traits

Several personality traits have been associated with abusive behavior. These traits include people who exhibit hypercritical and impatient behavior, people who display unsympathetic attitudes toward the needs of others (Reis & Nahmiash, in press; Sengstock & Hwalek, 1985), people who blame the elderly person for caregiving problems, people who harbor unrealistic caregiving expectations, and people who lack an understanding of the care recipient's condition (Quinn & Tomita, 1986). Anger, frustration, disillusionment, and abusive behaviors often arise from these personality characteristics. Other traits that have been associated with abusive behavior are depression (Paveza et al., 1992) and loss of self-control (Bendik, 1992; Reis & Nahmiash, in press). The loss of self-control, in particular, results from the caregiver's relative lack of independence and loss of his or her sense of freedom (Pillemer, 1986; Gottlieb, 1991).

Lack of Social Support

The lack of family, friends, and associates—people who can intervene and perhaps end the abuse—has been linked with abusive behavior. Social isolation was found to be a characteristic of families in which child, spouse, and elder abuse occurs (Pillemer, 1984). Threatening behavior displayed by an abuser toward other people may inhibit social contacts by driving people away who could intervene in the abusive situation. This encourages the abusive behavior to continue. This estrangement may mean that the abusive situation is never identified, and thus the abusing caregiver never obtains professional assistance. Gottlieb (1991) found that caregivers of frail, chronically ill elderly persons lacked the psychological support of others, support that may reduce or alleviate abusive behavior. However, there may be family members who are willing to help the caregiver, but who have not been asked to assist.

In the institutional environment abuse occurs most often at night and on weekends, periods when few staff members or people from the community are in the facility.

SOCIAL CONTEXT WITHIN WHICH ABUSE OCCURS

Certain elements within the social context of the caregiving scenario may suggest why elder abuse occurs.

Financial Difficulties

Many caregivers do not possess the financial resources to care for an elderly parent or resident. These economic pressures may foster resentment in a person in a caregiving situation. Adult children may be forced to terminate employment in order to provide adequate care to an aged parent, and conscious or unconscious resentment may grow out of this situation (Lau & Kosberg, 1979). The resentment may run so deep that abuse may result. Societal pressures to be productive and acquire material possessions may cause a person to become greedy, and greed may induce a caregiver to abuse an older person financially. This can occur both in the community and in long-term care facilities.

Family Violence

Pillemer and Wolf (1993) defined elder abuse as a "family affair." This "affair" may be hidden from outsiders because family members often are reluctant to reveal their problems to others, and abused elderly people may be fearful of creating or exacerbating conflicts within the family (Steinmetz, 1988). Patterns of intrafamily violence may be so ingrained that the dynamic is viewed as normal by family members (Myers & Shelton, 1987; Griffin, 1994).

Problems between parents and children do not decrease with the passage of time and may even intensify as a parent becomes increasingly dependent on an adult child (Blenkner, 1965). The legacy of violence can be transmitted intergenerationally through modeling. Parents who were raised to place importance on disciplining children might be hesitant to report slapping or hitting that they receive from their adult children (Pillemer & Finkelhor, 1989).

Lack of Social Support

Social support, whether from family, friends, or representatives of community agencies or organizations, has been demonstrated to reduce social isolation, caregiving burden, and the vulnerability of older people (Zarit, Reever, & Bach-Peterson, 1990). However, some families lack the community resources and the finances to access support (Kosberg, 1990).

Pillemer (1984) noted that abused elderly people tend to have fewer social contacts than nonabused elders. Social isolation also was found by Pillemer and Finkelhor (1988) to be associated with neglected older people insofar as they have no established support system to which they can turn for help. Vulnerable, elderly members of families that are isolated from the support of other people by distance or by design are probably at greater risk than elders who have social support, and abusive behavior may go undetected.

Family Disharmony

Intrafamily conflicts, such as marital disputes, appear to increase the potential for elder abuse (Douglass, Hickey, & Noel, 1980). These conflicts may create stressful or potentially explosive situations that result in abusive behavior against elderly, dependent relatives. Parent–child conflicts were studied by Cicirelli (1981); Steinmetz and Amsden (1983) focused on mother–daughter rivalry regarding the appropriate way to manage households, husbands, and children. The daughters' feelings of frustration and resentment placed additional strain on the caregiving role.

When a family member or a professional is the only person available to provide care, or when no other people can provide respite to the caregiver, the caregiver may feel an overwhelming sense of burden (Gold & Gwyther, 1989). This burden can be alleviated by enlisting others to share the caregiving responsibility, but if family members cannot agree on the sharing of responsibility, this disharmony may result in increased stress on the principal caregiver (Fiore, Becker, & Coppel, 1983).

Living Arrangements

Much has been written about the benefits and limitations of elderly parents sharing households with adult children and their families (Quinn & Tomita, 1986; Steinmetz, 1988). Stoller (1985) noted that a willingness to assist elderly people should not be equated with a desire for a long-term commitment to provide care. Research by Anetzberger (1987) disclosed that elderly relatives often share this belief. Even when elderly relatives become ill, they are often reluctant to move in with their relatives. Studies (e.g., Pillemer, 1985) found violence to be associated with abuser–victim cohabitation or residency in close proximity. Overcrowded living spaces and lack of privacy were associated by Kosberg (1988) with intrafamily conflict, which many times resulted in feelings of anger toward the older relative.

CULTURAL NORMS

Cultural attitudes and values such as those enumerated in the following sections may influence individuals to engage in, or may deter them from engaging in, the mistreatment of elderly people.

Ageism

Older adults are frequently depicted in society as frail and dependent individuals (Kosberg, 1990). These depictions can contribute to the way in which society perceives and treats older people. If one group is viewed to be less worthy than other groups, the mistreatment of the "less worthy" group may be seen as relatively inoffensive. A negative view of elderly people may thus result in a climate that is favorable to elder abuse.

Sexism

Canadian researchers have pointed out that older Canadian women are the primary victims of violence (Canadian Panel on Violence Against Women, 1994), and that the unequal status of women in general and older women in particular must be addressed. Women, especially recent immigrants, are particularly vulnerable to abuse because cultural norms and societal expectations prevent them from seeking help (Canadian Panel on Violence Against Women, 1994; Dow Pittaway et al., 1995). Doubtless this is also true within the United States and elsewhere in the world.

Cultural Attitudes Toward Violence

Cultural norms and values influence attitudes toward intrafamily violence. Many variations in attitudes and values exist within and among ethnic groups. Nahmiash (1994) reported that some ethnic groups rely extensively on the cultural value of "family," and thus are reluctant to report incidents of intrafamily violence, such as elder abuse. When working with people from various ethnic backgrounds, professionals must be sensitive to cultural values that support or enable the use of violence against dependent members of a family (e.g., children, women, elderly persons). Certain groups of people (defined by ethnicity and by urban or rural residence) are more likely to engage in aggressive intrafamily behavior, whereas other groups are not as likely to engage in this behavior. For example, Griffin (1994) found that rural African-American families are unlikely to physically abuse their elderly relatives.

Denial of the existence of abuse by the family makes the identification of incidents of abuse particularly difficult. Victims are often reluctant to report abuse, and their culture may mandate that abuse is a private family affair to be concealed from outsiders because of poverty, resistance to formal assistance, and the religion of the family (Dow Pittaway et al., 1995).

Reactions to Abuse

Health care workers may not always understand individual reactions to abusive situations because they may be unaware of the personal beliefs of victims and abusers. Personal beliefs may emanate from religious convictions, family histories, or cultural backgrounds. The perceptions by elderly people of a situation as abusive or not abusive may influence whether the older people seek help (Moon & Williams, 1993). This pertains not only to an elder abuse victim but also to the abuser or others aware of the abuse.

Attitudes Toward People with Disabilities

Cultural values may impose a moral or legal imperative against the mistreatment of people who are perceived to be disabled (or otherwise "different"). Heisler (1991) found that in some cultures people with disabilities are deemed less worthy, and that abusive behavior against such individuals is not seen as wrong. Thus, in certain cultures elderly people with disabilities may be at risk for abuse. Heisler (1991) emphasized that in order to ensure the safety of these older people, abusive behavior in the community or in institutional settings should be labeled a criminal act.

Imperatives for Family Caregiving

Family caregiving can be undervalued by society (Pepin, 1992). If no alternatives exist to family caregiving, the family may be caught in a difficult situation for which no solution is adequate. Thus, the cultural expectations of family caregiving, coupled with a lack of professional assistance and care alternatives, can place the older care recipient in a potentially dangerous situation.

Some differences are evident in various cultural beliefs or perceptions of caregiving responsibilities. Whose responsibility it is to be the caregiver—the eldest son, an unmarried daughter, the entire family, or the "community" (ethnic, religious, or secular)—is influenced by such beliefs. Culturally produced imperatives do not take into account whether a family or a particular member of a family can effectively provide care. This unquestioning family imperative may result in added burden on a caregiver, conflict between members of a family, ineffective care, and perhaps acts of abuse against an elderly relative.

CONCLUSION

This chapter identified and described the characteristics of abused elderly people and their abusers. These characteristics were categorized into four different areas. Through awareness of the characteristics, health care workers and others can become more aware of the dynamics involved in elder abuse and can begin to consider methods of prevention and intervention. The first step, of course, is to be aware of the possible existence of elder abuse; the second step is to become knowledgeable about the causes and consequences of this invisible and often taboo social problem.

Health care and social service workers (e.g., physicians, nurses, social workers) are more able than the casual observer to identify elderly people who are or may be victimized by the abusive behavior of others because they work in private dwellings, clinics, and long-term care facilities. These caregivers are able to investigate the reasons behind unexplained traumas, neglected medical problems, pressure sores, malnutrition, and other possible behavioral and physical manifestations of abuse and neglect, in private dwellings or in long-term care facilities (Kosberg, 1986). In addition to being able to assess the characteristics of victims and abusers, social workers and health care workers should understand the contributions made by the social and cultural dynamics that influence attitudes and behavior to mistreatment and abuse.

REFERENCES

Anetzberger, G.J. (1987). *The etiology of elder abuse by adult offspring.* Springfield, IL: Charles C Thomas.

Beaulieu, M., & Belanger, L. (1995). Interventions in long-term care institutions with respect to elder mistreatment. In M. MacLean (Ed.), *Abuse and neglect of older Canadians: Strategies for change* (pp. 27–37). Toronto: Thompson Educational Publishing.

Bendik, M.F. (1992). Reaching the breaking point: Dangers of mistreatment in elder caregiving situations. *Journal of Elder Abuse and Neglect,* 4(3), 39–59.

Blenkner, M. (1965). Social work and family relationships in later life with some thoughts on filial maturity. In E. Shanas & G. Streib (Eds.), *Social structure and family generational relations* (pp. 46–59). Englewood Cliffs, NJ: Prentice Hall.

Block, M.R., & Sinnott, J.D. (Eds.). (1979). *The battered elderly syndrome.* College Park, MD: University of Maryland Center on Aging.

Blunt, A.P. (1993). Financial exploitation of the incapacitated: Investigation and remedies. *Journal of Elder Abuse and Neglect, 5*(1), 19–32.

Breckman, R.S., & Adelman, R.D. (1988). *Strategies for helping victims of elder mistreatment.* Beverly Hills, CA: Sage Publications.

Brillon, Y. (1987). *Victimization and fear of crime among the elderly.* Toronto: Butterworths.

Brody, E. (1985). Parent care as normative family stress. *Gerontologist, 25,* 19–29.

Cairl, R.E., Keller, D.M., & Kosberg, J.I. (1984, November). *Factors associated with the propensity to take on a caregiver role.* Paper presented at the annual meeting of the Gerontological Society of America, San Antonio, TX.

Canadian Panel on Violence Against Women. (1994). Older women report. In *Changing the landscape: Ending violence—achieving equality* (pp. 10–15). Ottawa: Canadian Ministry of Supply and Services.

Cicirelli, V.G. (1981). *Helping elderly parents: The role of adult children.* Boston: Auburn House.

Davis, M.A. (1991). On nursing home quality: A review and analysis. *Medical Care Review, 48*(2), 129–166.

Douglass, R.L., Hickey, T., & Noel, C. (1980). *A study of maltreatment of elderly and other vulnerable adults.* Ann Arbor, MI: University of Michigan Institute of Gerontology.

Dow Pittaway, E., Gallagher, E., Stones, M., Nahmiash, D., Kosberg, J., Strain, L., & Bond, J. (1995). *Report on services for abused older Canadians.* Victoria, British Columbia: University of Victoria Center on Aging.

Driedger, L., & Chappell, N. (1987). *Aging and ethnicity: Toward an interface.* Toronto: Butterworths.

Fiore, J., Becker, J., & Coppel, D.B. (1983). Social network interactions: A buffer or a stress? *American Journal of Community Psychology, 11,* 423–439.

Floyd, J. (1983). Collecting data on abuse of the elderly. *Journal of Gerontological Nursing, 10*(12), 11–15.

Fulmer, T.T. (1990). The debate over dependency as a relevant predisposing factor in elder abuse and neglect. *Journal of Elder Abuse and Neglect, 2*(1/2), 51–57.

Galbraith, M.W., & Davison, D.E. (1985). Stress and elderly abuse. *Focus on Learning, 1*(9), 86–92.

Garcia, J.L., & Kosberg, J.I. (1993). Understanding anger: Implications for formal and informal caregivers. *Journal of Elder Abuse and Neglect, 4*(4), 87–99.

Gelles, R. (1974). Child abuse as psychopathology: A sociological critique and reformulation. In S. Steinmetz & M. Straus (Eds.), *Violence in the family* (pp. 190–204). New York: Dodd, Mead.

Giordano, N.H., & Giordano, J.A. (1983, November). *Family and individual characteristics of five types of elder abuse: Profiles and predictors.* Paper presented at the annual meeting of the Gerontological Society of America, San Francisco.

Gnaedinger, N. (1989). *Elder abuse: A discussion paper for family violence prevention division.* Ottawa: Health Canada.

Godkin, M.A., Wolf, R.S., & Pillemer, K.A. (1989). A case-comparison analysis of elder abuse and neglect. *International Journal of Aging and Human Development, 23*(3), 207–225.

Gold, D.T., & Gwyther, L.P. (1989). The prevention of elder abuse: An educational model. *Family Relations, 38*(4), 9–14.

Goldsmith, J.T., & Tomas, N.E. (1974). Crimes against the elderly: A continuing national crisis. *Aging, 236,* 10–13.

Gottlieb, B.H. (1991). Social support and family care of the elderly. *Canadian Journal on Aging, 10*(4), 359–375.

Griffin, L.W. (1994). Elder maltreatment among rural African-Americans. *Journal of Elder Abuse and Neglect, 6*(1), 1–29.

Hamel, M., Gold, P.D., Andres, D., Reis, M., Dastoor, D., Grauer, H., & Bergman, H. (1990). Predictors and consequences of aggressive behavior by community-based dementia patients. *Gerontologist, 3,* 206–211.

Harshbarger, S. (1993). From protection to prevention: A proactive approach. *Journal of Elder Abuse and Neglect, 5*(1), 41–54.

Heisler, C.J. (1991). The role of the criminal justification in elder abuse cases. *Journal of Elder Abuse and Neglect, 3*(1), 5–35.

Hickey, T., & Douglass, R.L. (1981). Mistreatment of the elderly in the domestic setting: An exploratory study. *American Journal of Public Health, 71,* 500–507.

Hornick, J.F., MacDonald, L., & Robertson, G.B. (1990). *Elder abuse in Canada: Prevalence, legal and service issues.* Paper presented at the XXII Banff International Conference on Behavioral Sciences, Banff, Alberta, Canada.

Hudson, M.F. (1986). Elder mistreatment: Current research. In K.A. Pillemer & R.S. Wolf (Eds.), *Elder abuse: Conflict in the family* (pp. 125–166). Dover, MA: Auburn House.

Hudson, M.F. (1994). Elder abuse: Its meaning to middle-aged and older adults (Part II: Pilot results). *Journal of Elder Abuse and Neglect, 6*(1), 55–83.

Kosberg, J.I. (1980, November). *Family maltreatment: Explanations and interventions.* Paper presented at the annual meeting of the Gerontological Society of America, San Diego, CA.

Kosberg, J.I. (1986). Understanding elder abuse: An overview for primary care physicians. In R.J. Ham (Ed.), *Geriatric medicine annual* (pp. 114–127). New York: Medical Economic Books.

Kosberg, J.I. (1988). Preventing elder abuse: Identification of high risk factors prior to placement decisions. *Gerontologist, 28,* 43–49.

Kosberg, J.I. (1990). Assistance to crime and abuse victim. In A. Monk (Ed.), *Handbook of gerontological services* (2nd ed., pp. 450–473). New York: Columbia University Press.

Kosberg, J.I. (1994). *The state of institutional care for the elderly in the U.S. and Canada.* Paper presented at the Conference on Institutional Care and Support Systems for the Elderly—The Development of the Korean Model, Seoul, South Korea.

Kosberg, J.I., & Cairl, R.E. (1986). The Cost of Care Index: A case management tool for screening informal care providers. *Gerontologist, 26,* 273–278.

Kozak, J., Elmslie, T., & Verdon, J. (1995). Epidemiology of the abuse and neglect of seniors in Canada: A review of the national and international research literature. In M. MacLean (Ed.), *Abuse and neglect of older Canadians: Strategies for change* (pp. 129–141). Toronto: Thompson Educational Publishing.

Lau, E.E., & Kosberg, J.I. (1979, September–October). Abuse of the elderly by informal care providers. *Aging,* 10–15.

Maddox, G. (1975). Families as context and resource in chronic illness. In S. Sherwood (Ed.), *Issues in long term care.* New York: Halstead Press.

Moon, A., & Williams, O. (1993). Perceptions of elder abuse and help-seeking patterns among African-American, Caucasian-American and Korean-American elderly women. *Gerontologist, 33,* 387–393.

Myers, J.E., & Shelton, B. (1987). Abuse and older persons: Issues and implications for counsellors. *Journal of Counselling and Development, 65*(7), 376–380.

Nahmiash, D. (1994). *A comparison of social welfare services in the community in Japan with Quebec.* Paper presented to the Heiwa Nakajima Foundation, Tokyo.

O'Malley, T.A. (1987). Abuse and neglect of the elderly: The wrong issue? *Pride Institute Journal of Long-Term Health Care, 5,* 25–28.

Paveza, G.J., Cohen, D., Eisdorfer, C., Freels, S., Semla, T., Ashford, W.J., Gorelick, P., Hirschman, R., Luchins, D., & Levy, P. (1992). Severe family violence and Alzheimer's disease: Prevalence and risk factors. *Gerontologist, 32,* 493–497.

Pepin, J.I. (1992). Family caring and caring in nursing. *Gerontologist, 24,* 127–131.

Phillips, L.R. (1983). Abuse and neglect of the frail elderly at home: An exploration of theoretical relationships. *Journal of Advanced Nursing, 8,* 379–392.

Pillemer, K.A. (1984). Social isolation and elder abuse. *Response, 8*(4), 2–4.

Pillemer, K.A. (1985). The dangers of dependency: New findings on domestic violence of the elderly. *Social Problems, 33,* 146–158.

Pillemer, K.A. (1986). Risk factors in elder abuse: Results from a case-control study. In K.A. Pillemer & R.S. Wolf (Eds.), *Elder abuse: Conflict in the family* (pp. 239–263). Dover, MA: Auburn House.

Pillemer, K.A., & Finkelhor, D. (1988). The prevalence of elder abuse: A random sample survey. *Gerontologist, 28,* 51–57.

Pillemer, K.A., & Finkelhor, D. (1989). Causes of elder abuse: Caregiver stress versus problem relatives. *American Journal of Orthopsychiatry, 59,* 179–187.

Pillemer, K.A., & Moore, D.W. (1989). Abuse of patients in nursing homes: Findings from a survey of staff. *Gerontologist, 29,* 314–320.

Pillemer, K.A., & Suitor, J. (1992). Violence and violent feelings: What causes them among family caregivers? *Journal of Gerontology (Social Sciences), 47,* 165–172.

Pillemer, K.A., & Wolf, R.S. (1989). *Helping elderly victims: The reality of elder abuse.* New York: Columbia University Press.

Pillemer, K.A., & Wolf, R.S. (1993). Domestic violence against the elderly: Who depends on whom? What difference does it make? In R. Gelles & D. Loesike (Eds.), *Controversies in family violence* (pp. 237–250). Newbury Park, CA: Sage Publications.

Quinn, M.J., & Tomita, S.U. (1986). *Elder abuse and neglect: Causes, diagnosis and intervention strategies.* New York: Springer Publishing.

Reis, M., & Nahmiash, D. (in press). When seniors are abused: An intervention, guidebook and research. *Gerontologist.*

Rubenstein, R.L., Kilbride, J.C., & Magy, S. (1992). *Elders living alone: Family and the perception of choice.* New York: Aldine de Gruyter.

Ryden, M. (1988). Aggressive behavior in persons with dementia living in the community. *Alzheimer Disease and Associated Disorders: International Journal, 2*(4), 342–355.

Sengstock, M.C., & Hwalek, M. (1985). *Comprehensive index of elder abuse.* Detroit, MI: Wayne State University.

Smyer, M., Brannon, T., & Cohen, M. (1992). Improving nursing home care through training and job design. *Gerontologist, 2,* 327–333.

Steinmetz, S.K. (1983). Dependency, stress and violence between middle-aged caregivers and their elderly parents. In J.I. Kosberg (Ed.), *Abuse and maltreatment of the elderly: Causes and interventions* (pp. 134–149). Littleton, MA: John Wright-PGS.

Steinmetz, S.K. (1988). *Duty bound: Elder abuse and family care.* Newbury Park, CA: Sage Publications.

Steinmetz, S.K., & Amsden, D.J. (1983). Dependent elders, family and abuse. In T.H. Brubaker (Ed.), *Family relationships in later life* (pp. 178–192). Beverly Hills, CA: Sage Publications.

Stoller, E.P. (1985, June). Elder–caregiver relationships in shared households. *Research on Aging, 2,* 175–176.

Tatara, T. (1993). Understanding the nature and scope of domestic elder abuse with the use of state aggregate data: Summaries of the key findings of a national survey of state APS and aging agencies. *Journal of Elder Abuse and Neglect, 5*(4), 35–59.

Troll, L., & Smith, J. (1976). Attachment through the life span: Some questions about dyadic bonds among adults. *Human Development, 19,* 156–190.

Vladeck, B.C. (1980). *Unloving care: The nusing home tragedy.* New York: Basic Books.

Weiler, K., & Buckwalter, K.C. (1992). Abuse among rural mentally ill. *Journal of Psychosocial Nursing and Mental Health Services, 30*(9), 32–36.

Wolf, R.S., Strugnell, E.P., & Godkin, M.A. (1982). *Preliminary findings from the model projects on elderly abuse.* Worcester, MA: University of Massachusetts Center on Aging.

Zarit, S.H., Reever, K.E., & Bach-Peterson, J. (1990). Relatives of impaired elderly: Correlates of feelings of burden. *Gerontologist, 20,* 649–655.

3

Screening: A Primary Care Clinician's Perspective

James G. O'Brien

Elder abuse victims often turn to health care settings for assistance (Hickey & Douglass, 1981). It is unfortunate that many health care practitioners are ill-equipped to respond when confronted with elder abuse or neglect. Although health care providers are becoming aware of the phenomenon of elder abuse, many believe their communities or medical practices are exempt from such abuse. Thus, health care professionals have a low index of suspicion that some of their older patients may have been abused. Unless the effects of abuse are obvious, abuse or neglect may be overlooked. Indicators of abuse or neglect may be confused with the sequelae of normal aging (O'Brien, 1994). Elderly people bruise more easily, fall more frequently, and fracture bones more readily than younger people. The potential for recognition of abuse may be lessened when signs of abuse are attributed to the changes of normal aging. The sensory losses and communication difficulties experienced by many older adults also may prevent physicians from recognizing elder abuse or neglect.

The setting in which a victim presents may affect detection of abuse. A home health care nurse (home is the most common site of elder mistreatment outside of institutions) may identify a neglected, isolated victim, whereas the same individual may arouse little suspicion when encountered in a physician's office because he or she has been made socially presentable. A separate home visit may reveal a restrained victim whose overburdened, but well-intentioned caregiver is out running errands. Restraining an elderly person in a nursing facility or hospital setting may not be identified as abuse, but may be labeled "in the best interest" of the elderly person.

The type of abuse encountered may offer different opportunities for various professional disciplines. Physical abuse and neglect are more likely to be identified by physicians and nurses and material abuse is more likely to be identified by social workers, lawyers, and bankers.

BARRIERS TO DETECTION AND ACTION

The barriers to detection and to taking action for primary health care clinicians are numerous and include the low index of suspicion mentioned at the beginning of the chapter (Blakely & Dolon, 1991). A time-pressured encounter may force clinicians to narrow their focus to medical concerns such as hypertension, diabetes, or a pain syndrome, and may not allow time for a victim to express fears or concerns that are not strictly medical.

Most victims are reluctant to admit that abuse or neglect has occurred for a variety of reasons, including implicating or stigmatizing a family member who may also be a caregiver. A fear of reprisal or a concern that intervention may result in a less desirable option, such as nursing facility placement, may serve as a powerful deterrent to reporting. A lack of trust in the clinician, particularly with regard to confidentiality, may prevent the victim from revealing the presence of abuse (Long, 1981).

Clinicians may harbor ageist attitudes and not react as readily to elder abuse as they might to child abuse, perhaps believing that the older individual provoked or deserved the abuse (Fulmer, 1989). Clinicians may also believe that family privacy is paramount, or that abuse is not strictly a medical problem and is more appropriately handled by social workers and the courts. Physicians may feel that reporting abuse will undermine the doctor–patient relationship, and they may attempt other strategies. Reimbursement by Medicare and Medicaid typically does not cover the total cost of a protracted office encounter, and cannot be justified based on medical interviewing or complexity.

Detection in an emergency room setting includes many of the previously mentioned barriers, but also includes other deterrents, such as a lack of knowledge of the victim and family and the competing demands of other medical emergencies. Another bias of some clinicians that may affect detection of abuse is their cynicism that nothing can be done to ameliorate the situation, particularly if the practitioner has had a negative experience that resulted in a victim's refusal of help, threatening behavior by the abuser, or a lack of response from the protective services agency. Finally, physicians prefer "medical certainty" before taking action. Given that no test exists that can verify the presence of abuse, physicians may be reluctant to identify a syndrome as the result of abuse (O'Brien and Piper, 1991).

SCREENING FOR ABUSE

Physicians should approach elder abuse the way they approach diseases that compromise the quality of life and independence. Physicians, particularly, are willing to screen for treatable diseases, such as hypertension, that can cause significant morbidity and mortality. Hypertension is a disease that is amenable to treatment and also one in which earlier treatment results in an improved outcome. Similarly, certain types of abuse escalate over time, and it is probable that earlier identification and intervention will yield an improved outcome. However, identifying an overwhelmed caregiver and providing support and respite before abuse or neglect can occur is likely only when a particular line of questioning is initiated.

Elder abuse occurs with sufficient prevalence in the community to warrant screening (Pillemer & Finkelhor, 1988). It occurs more frequently than suicide among older adults, and causes significant morbidity and occasional mortality. Complex or expensive technology is not required for screening. Typically, interventions offered, such as respite care, counseling, and legal assistance, do not constitute unusual treatments, are available in most communities, and are not necessarily expensive. Finally, in most states failure to detect a reportable problem may result in a penalty or possible litigation for failure to address the problem. It is well within the purview of most physicians and nurses to screen for abuse and neglect (Haviland & O'Brien, 1989).

Screening in a primary care clinician's office should be targeted at obtaining an accurate depiction of the elderly person in the context of his or her home environment. Vital information should include data on personal health, functional abilities, mental capacity, social and economic resources, and information about the living situation (Ferguson & Beck, 1983). Much of this information can be gathered in cumulative fashion in primary care settings in order to create a profile or database on each elderly patient. Specific questions that serve to elicit this information are included in Table 3.1. These questions may help to identify an individual at a high risk of being abused or may detect a previously unrecognized victim.

A patient database is developed using a variety of sources, in particular the anecdotal reports of office staff who interact with patients and their families more frequently than do clinicians. For example, office staff may notice verbal exchanges in the waiting room between

Table 3.1. Abuse/neglect screening questions for primary care physicians

1. Are you sad or lonely?
2. Do you know anyone who is reliable and can help you in a crisis?
3. Are your finances adequate?
4. Do you support someone?
5. Do you need any assistance with taking care of yourself?
6. Do you take your own medicines and balance your own checkbook?
7. Describe a typical day.
8. Do you have enough privacy in your home?
9. Are you uncomfortable with anyone in your family?
10. Who makes decisions about your life, such as how or where you will live?
11. Does anyone in your family drink too much or have problems with drugs or medicine?
12. Have you had any injuries, hospitalizations, or emergency room visits recently? Describe them.

patient and family that may indicate abuse. Visiting nurses are in an ideal position to appreciate and note living situations and family dynamics. They also may be in a position to obtain information from such useful sources as other family members, neighbors, or fellow church members. However, much of the data may not be pooled and shared because individuals are not always sure about where or to whom they should voice their concerns.

INTERVIEWING VICTIMS OF ABUSE OR NEGLECT

When abuse or neglect is suspected, questioning by clinicians needs to progress from generalities to specifics. Special interviewing techniques should be followed (Table 3.2), and the questions should be direct, as follows (Hwalek & Sengstock, 1986):

	Yes	No	
1.	❑	❑	Has anyone tried to hurt or harm you?
2.	❑	❑	Have you been forced to do things you did not want to do? Give an example.
3.	❑	❑	Have you been threatened with being placed in a nursing facility?
4.	❑	❑	Has anyone stolen from you or taken your possessions without permission?
5.	❑	❑	Has anyone sworn at you or threatened you?
6.	❑	❑	Has anyone confined you at home against your will?

7. ❑ ❑ Has anyone refused to provide you with food or with your medications?
8. ❑ ❑ Has anyone beaten or assaulted you?
9. ❑ ❑ Have you ever signed any documents that you did not understand?
10. ❑ ❑ Are you afraid of anyone in your home?

Any questions answered in the affirmative should be explored in order to determine how, when, and how often mistreatment occurs; who perpetrates it; and how the patient feels about and copes with it.

The clinician conducting an interview with a suspected victim should have a clear sense of the type of information that is required. Unfortunately, most clinicians lack a formal protocol to guide them in questioning. Many excellent protocols are available to assist with this process, including the American Medical Association's diagnostic and treatment guidelines (American Medical Association, 1992), the Hwalek-Sengstock protocol (1986), the Health, Attitudes, Living Arrangements, and Finances (H.A.L.F.) protocol (Ferguson & Beck, 1983), the Tomita protocol (1982), and the Mount Sinai Victim Services Agency instrument (1988). Even lacking an official guide, the clinician must document (see also Chapter 8). The following sections outline the information that must be included in documentation.

Safety
Ensuring the safety of the victim is paramount. If the victim is in immediate danger, prompt action must be taken, either via admission to the hospital, referral and transport to a victims' shelter, or use of a

Table 3.2. Guidelines for interviewing victims

- Ensure privacy.
- Separate victims from caregivers.
- Ensure confidentiality.
- Allow adequate time for response.
- Progress from general (screening) to specific (direct) questions.
- Keep questions simple and appropriate for educational level.
- Respect cultural, ethnic differences.
- Do not blame victims.
- Do not blame or confront perpetrators.
- Do not show frustration.
- Acknowledge that this process may require multiple interviews.
- Determine whether cognitive impairment is present.
- Use other people, such as office or emergency room nurses, to conduct the interview if this is less threatening to victims.

court protective order to ensure safety. The consequences of not being cognizant of the risks to the victim can be devastating, as in the following illustrative case:

> Mrs. Kossel, a 78-year-old white female, was admitted to the hospital with dehydration, uncontrolled hypertension, and poor hygiene. Her condition was gradually stabilized over several days. Her only visitor during her hospitalization was her son, who seemed quite attentive. He appeared somewhat dishevelled, however, and occasionally was observed by staff eating from his mother's tray. Prior to discharge, Mrs. Kossel remarked to one of the nursing assistants that she thought she was going to die. Her discharge was delayed. She was reevaluated, but no life-threatening illnesses were noted. Also, she was identified as not being suicidal or clinically depressed. Her son was questioned regarding her fears and was unable to provide any insight. Mrs. Kossel was discharged home to the care of her son. Two days later, a home health care nurse discovered Mrs. Kossel in bed with a plastic bag over her head that was tied at the neck with a shoelace. Her son was charged with homicide.

This case demonstrates the need to assign the highest priority to ensuring the safety of the victim. A home investigation that included questioning the neighbors and a more appropriate questioning of the son and victim may have identified the presence of abuse and may have led to a different outcome.

Health and Functional Status

A second priority in screening is determining the victim's health and functional status. Clinicians may use the following questions as a guide:

- What medical problems exist?
- Is a condition present that may have resulted from abuse?
- Has a medical problem worsened as a result of withheld treatment?
- Is a condition present that may reflect an overuse of a medication?
- Is a medical problem, such as insulin-dependent diabetes, present that requires close monitoring and supervision?

A determination of functional abilities should be made using one of the assessment tests of activities of daily living (ADLs), which include the abilities to feed, dress, and bathe. The ability to perform instrumental activities of daily living (IADLs), the more complex skills, such as transportation, shopping, and telephoning, that are required for independent living, should also be assessed. (For further information on these assessment tests, see Chapter 8.) It is preferable for the practitioner to observe these skills rather than to accept a report of competence. Attention to discrepancies between victim and caregiver reports should be noted. Asking the victim to transfer, ambulate, follow commands, and write a sentence is an invaluable, simple method of evaluation, and may help determine the victim's vulnerability and inability to protect against physical abuse or neglect. Further determination of a victim's functional status can be made by asking the following questions: If the elderly person is dependent, who provides the assistance? Is all the care supplied exclusively by a single individual, who may be overwhelmed and abusive, or can the burden be shared with others?

Cognitive Status

Cognitive status is perhaps the most difficult assessment to make and requires great sensitivity and tact on the part of the clinician. Subjecting an elderly individual to a poorly introduced test of mental status is often embarrassing and demeaning. Mental status tests such as the Mini-Mental State Exam (MMSE) (see also Chapter 8) (Folstein, Folstein, & McHugh, 1975) and the Short Portable Mental Status Questionnaire (SPMSQ) (Pfeiffer, 1975) have proven reliability in outpatient settings and will suffice in many instances. In situations in which a person experiences early cognitive losses yet insight persists, other strategies may be necessary. The strategies of *repeating* a Social Security number, *writing* a sentence, *recalling* phone numbers of friends and relatives, or *relating* recent news items can all be validated for accuracy. A low score on an MMSE does not necessarily imply a lack of capacity to report abuse or to make a decision to remain in an abusive situation. An elderly individual may retain the ability to understand his or her situation and to make an informed decision regarding placement. Mental capacity is typically challenged when a decision made by the victim does not agree with the opinion of the clinician.

The clinician also has a responsibility to determine if the victim is cognitively impaired and the level of that impairment. If the victim is cognitively impaired, the clinician must determine whether the impairment is chronic and irreversible or reversible and related to the medications, depression, or the stress of being in a strange environment. Using information from others may be helpful in determining prior competence. Repeating the examination in a more comfortable setting may yield a different outcome. Screening for the presence of depression is equally important. Using the Geriatric Depression Screen (Yesavage, Brink, & Rose, 1983) (see Chapter 8) may be helpful in this instance, as depression can affect cognitive abilities and may result from abuse. If the clinician determines that the victim has dementia, the victim is no longer considered to be a reliable source. Data should be collected and corroborated from friends, neighbors, or family members. In these situations a more paternalistic approach, such as that used in child abuse situations, is appropriate. Separating the paranoia associated with dementing illnesses from legitimate suspicions regarding a family member may challenge the most astute clinician.

Emotional Status

The presence of anxiety, fear, depression, or anger in the victim should be noted. Anxiety and fear may prevent the victim from revealing the severity of the mistreatment or from identifying the perpetrator of abuse. Denial is a common response to questions regarding abuse. Clinicians should not allow denial to deter them from further questioning. Offering reassurance and identifying resources that offer respite and protection may greatly lessen fear and lead to more open discussion. In some instances, it is only with time and multiple visits that enough trust can be built between clinician and victim to allow open discussion. Involving a trusted family member as an advocate may be particularly helpful when denial occurs.

Social and Financial Resources

The location of the victim's residence, the safety of the neighborhood, the degree of isolation, and the assistance (if any) provided by neighbors are all important data that help a clinician to create a composite that allows for a more informed judgment. Additional data may include sources of income, which may be multiple or minimal, and information about who has access to money or checks. The type of insurance carried by the older person can be easily accessed from hospital records or a physician's office. In some instances of financial abuse the caregiver may be dependent upon the victim for shelter and finances. The caregiver may have financial obligations to other family members or payments for medication that rapidly deplete a reasonable income. These data are vital to the process of identifying and providing victim support services.

Access to the Victim's Residence

Prior to discharging the victim to his or her home, the clinician should ascertain whether gaining access to the victim's home will be difficult. Enlisting the services of a home health agency should be initiated prior to discharge. Because many states mandate the reporting of elder mistreatment, state or local Adult Protective Services (APS) becomes aware of the presence of mistreatment as a byproduct of the report. Access to the victim's home also can be ensured by involving another family member who is willing to help.

Frequency, Severity, and Intent of Mistreatment

Although clinicians are not expected to "play detective," determining the frequency, severity, and intent of mistreatment influences the conclusions drawn about safety and the need for urgent intervention. It is vitally important that clinicians not alienate the victims or the perpetrators in their zeal to identify whether mistreatment was intentional or unintentional. This is a time for compassion and understanding. Victims must not be blamed and perpetrators must not be confronted or accused; the responsibility for such action rests with other individuals and institutions. Victims often continue to remain in the home with their abusers. Clinicians (physicians or nurses) may be the only lifeline to victims. Therefore, sustaining relationships with victims and caregivers is essential for continuing support and monitoring of abusive situations.

Victim Assessment

In a busy physician's office or emergency room setting, obtaining a medical history and conducting a physical examination occur nearly simultaneously. The history elicited from the victim typically guides the physical examination. However, an uninformative history supplied by a patient who is dressed may become informative when clothing is removed for the physical examination. Evidence of trauma not revealed in the verbal history is often revealed in this way. Suspicious bruises observed while examining the body may prompt additional questioning. It is essential that questions that relate to sexual abuse, rape, or molestation be asked in order to obtain a complete assessment (Benton & Marshall, 1991).

Ideally, the clinician should be knowledgeable regarding how various indicators of physical abuse and neglect may present. Even in situations in which only material or psychological abuse is thought to be present, a comprehensive physical examination should be conducted, given the frequency with which multiple types of abuse occur to the same individual.

The physical examination should also be functionally oriented. Requesting that a patient perform a range of motion may reveal previously unrecognized injuries, particularly in a patient who is unable to report an injury because of cognitive impairment. Special attention should also be paid to the following physical factors:

- The patient's general appearance should be noted, particularly the presence of obvious weight loss; poor hygiene; odor of urine; and deformity, swelling, or discoloration.
- The hair and scalp should be examined for alopecia (hair loss) from pulling, swelling from being beaten, or the presence of lice from neglecting the hair.
- The skin should be inspected for swelling, bruising, atrophy, abrasions, lacerations, and ulcerations. The pattern of bruising and color needs to be observed, and the consistency of the pattern with the reported injury needs to be noted (see Figures 3.1 and 3.2) (Fulmer, 1992; Lachs & Fulmer, 1993).
- Vital signs should be noted, including weight, temperature, pulse rate, and blood pressure. These signs may indicate starvation with

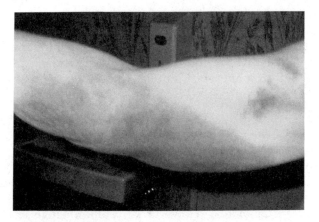

Figure 3.1. Traumatic hematoma from a direct blow.

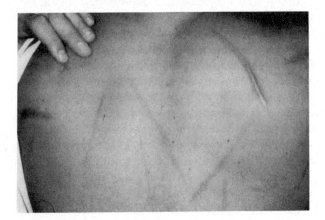

Figure 3.2. Multiple scars on an older person's back as a result of being whipped with a cord.

massive weight loss, for example. In emergency room settings, recording temperature may yield not only indications of infection, but also hypothermia from neglect, especially in colder climates.

• Functional abilities should be checked. This examination may indicate occult injuries (injuries not detectable by clinical methods alone) and fractures. A simple "get up and go" test, whereby the elderly patient is asked to rise unassisted from a chair, stand, reach above head level, walk, turn, and pick up an item from the floor, may be informative in ascertaining the ability to function independently. The "get up and go" test can be supplemented by putting the patient through a range of motion of all major joints. The following vignette illustrates the outcome of a "get up and go" test:

Mrs. Allen, 85, was brought to a geriatric assessment program at the request of her niece, who held power of attorney and lived in another state. Mrs. Allen had a live-in caregiver, who was hired when Mrs. Allen showed early signs of dementia. Mrs. Allen's niece had become concerned about what she felt was a significant deterioration in her aunt's condition. Her aunt seemed much less communicative on the telephone and more confused. The caregiver's report indicated that Mrs. Allen spent most of her time in bed and used a wheelchair.

Upon examination, which included a "get up and go" test, it was revealed that Mrs. Allen had sustained a hip fracture, which was concealed by the caregiver. The fracture was thought to be at least 3 months old. During this 3-month period, Mrs. Allen had visited her cardiologist, who conducted his examination of her while she was in her wheelchair so as not to inconvenience her. The caregiver was present during the cardiologist's examination.

The caregiver was subsequently prosecuted for inducing the hip fracture by pushing Mrs. Allen down a flight of stairs.

- Inquire about the presence of assistive devices, such as a walker or a hearing aid, but also determine their functional status.
- An oral examination must be conducted. This examination may reveal trauma, dental decay, absent or broken dentures, and evidence of malnutrition.
- All bony areas must be carefully palpated (examined by touch) to reveal deformity, swelling, or tenderness.
- "Silent" areas, including axillae (armpits), abdomen, and perineum (area around the genitals) must be inspected (Mildenberger & Wessman, 1986). An often-neglected area is the foot, especially the sole, which may reveal bruising from beating. The presence of gross neglect also may be indicated by untrimmed nails and the presence of corns and calluses.
- The pelvic exam requires great sensitivity and should be negotiated with the victim when rape is suspected by the clinician. At a minimum, a perineal inspection should be carried out. In order to conduct a comprehensive perineal examination, clinicians should use the rape kits that are available in emergency departments. Some victims may never have undergone a pelvic exam and may be frightened. Having a female physician or nurse practitioner conduct the examination may be less frightening to the victim. Some clinicians advocate the left lateral position in conducting the examination. This position involves placing the victim on her side and performing the examination without the use of stirrups. This examination is technically more difficult, but places less strain on the victim.

All findings must be carefully documented and, when appropriate, photographs should be taken after obtaining a written release from the victim or responsible party. Supportive or confirmatory testing such as blood tests (including medication levels), special x-rays, and scans may be necessary to verify, for example, dehydration, malnutrition, and inappropriate use of medications.

INTERVIEWING PERPETRATORS

Interviewing the caregiver suspected of abuse can be a daunting process. The clinician must remain unemotional and avoid confrontation or accusation, no matter how heinous the abuse. The clinician should bear in mind that an individual accompanying the older adult may not be the perpetrator, and may in fact be an advocate. The clinician should seek the individual's perspective on the abusive situation. Questions regarding the amount of support and assistance the caregiver provides should be asked (Council on Scientific Affairs, 1987). Describing a typical day may be informative, particularly if the caregiving burden is large and the caregiver is employed outside the home. Corroboration of statements by the victim should be sought. Other sources of support for caregiving, such as other family members and agencies, should be determined. During this process, the clinician should note the caregiver's appearance, responses, and behavior (Ross, Ross, & Ross, 1985). The clinician should resist taking copious notes and making little eye contact during the interview as this may be intimidating to the caregiver and may lessen rapport and communication. However, the need for rapport must be balanced with the necessity for creating documentation that is legally admissible.

The victim must be made to understand that the clinician functions in a helping role and can participate in improving the abusive situation. In states that mandate reporting, it is wise to inform the family members of the need to report the abuse or mistreatment. APS also should be identified as a support agency, not as a punitive body. Given that abuse is a complex problem requiring systemic solutions, a family systems approach is often necessary. This requires the participation of many different individuals; the primary care clinician can play a major role in offering continuity and assisting in coordinating services. The following vignette illustrates the family systems approach:

In response to questions regarding living arrangements, Mr. and Mrs. Roubelot, both in their 70s, revealed that their 40-year-old son, Donald, had moved into their small home and was now dominating their lives. He was unemployed and dependent on them for food, shelter, and money. His presence compromised their privacy, and he was assuming increasing responsibility for managing their finances, which greatly bothered Mr. Roubelot. They were unwilling to accept any outside help at the time of screening, but recognized that in the future they might need assistance in imposing limits on their son.

The passive approach taken by Mr. and Mrs. Roubelot toward their son, Donald, was shortlived. Mr. Roubelot was brought to the emergency room of the local hospital following an altercation with Donald. Mr. Roubelot had become so frustrated with his noncontributing son that he had asked him to move out. Donald refused and subsequently assaulted his father. Mr. Roubelot sustained fractures to eight ribs and his radius and ulna. He also sustained multiple abrasions, lacerations, and soft tissue injuries. He was hospitalized briefly and recovered without permanent physical sequelae. Donald pleaded with the physician not to report the beating. The physician explained his legal obligation and reported the incident to APS. Following an investigation, a restraining order was placed on Donald. The restraining order was lifted after repeated appeals by Mrs. Roubelot. Donald returned home and for the last 5 years has not engaged in any further physical abuse. Mr. Roubelot is convinced that this is related to the ongoing observational/monitoring role played by the primary care physician. Donald expressed the fear that if anything untoward were to befall his father, he would be a suspect. The family continues to be involved in counseling.

This certainly does not represent an ideal outcome, but with the degree of family dysfunction and the family's desire to live together, this was perhaps the only acceptable solution.

CONCLUSION

Primary care clinicians can contribute much to alleviating the problem of elder mistreatment (O'Brien, 1986). An increased awareness of the phenomenon of elder abuse and how it typically presents is a necessity. Opportunities to screen and detect high-risk situations and to identify abuse are well within the purview of most practitioners in primary care settings. A structured approach, using one of the many protocols available, will facilitate this process. Careful documentation, as detailed in Chapter 8, is mandated. A nonjudgmental, compassionate approach, along with careful examination, will ensure the greatest potential for success.

REFERENCES

American Medical Association. (1992). *Diagnostic and treatment guidelines on elder abuse and neglect.* Chicago: Author.

Benton, D., & Marshall, C. (1991). Elder abuse. *Clinics in Geriatric Medicine,* 7(4), 831–845.

Blakely, B., & Dolon, R. (1991). The relative contributions of occupation groups in the discovery and treatment of elder abuse and neglect. *Journal of Geriatric Social Work, 17*, 183–199.

Council on Scientific Affairs. (1987). Elder abuse and neglect. *Journal of the American Medical Association, 257*(7), 966–971.

Ferguson, D., & Beck, C. (1983). H.A.L.F.: A tool to assess elder abuse within the family. *Geriatric Nursing, 4*(5), 301–304.

Folstein, M., Folstein, S., & McHugh, P. (1975). Mini-Mental State: A practical method for grading the cognitive state of patients for the clinician. *Journal of Psychiatry Research, 12*, 289–298.

Fulmer, T. (1989). Mistreatment of elders: Assessment, diagnosis, and intervention. *Nursing Clinics of North America, 42*(3), 707–717.

Fulmer, T. (1992). Elder mistreatment assessment as a part of everyday practice. *Journal of Gerontological Nursing, 19*, 42–45.

Haviland, S., & O'Brien, J. (1989). Physical abuse and neglect of the elderly: Assessment and intervention. *Orthopedic Nursing, 8*(4), 11–19.

Hickey, T., & Douglass, R. (1981). Mistreatment of the elderly in the domestic setting: An exploratory study. *American Journal of Public Health, 71*, 500–507.

Hwalek, M., & Sengstock, M. (1986). Assessing the probability of elder abuse: Toward the development of a clinical screening instrument. *Journal of Applied Gerontology, 5*(2), 153–173.

Lachs, M., & Fulmer, T. (1993). Recognizing elder abuse and neglect. *Clinics in Geriatric Medicine, 9*(3), 665–681.

Long, C. (1981). Geriatric abuse. *Issues in Mental Health Nursing, 3*, 123–135.

Mildenberger, C., & Wessman, H. (1986). Abuse and neglect of elderly persons by family members. *Physical Therapy, 66*(4), 537–539.

Mount Sinai Victim Services Agency Elder Abuse Project. (1988). *Elder mistreatment guidelines for health care professionals: Detection, assessment and intervention.* New York: Author. .

O'Brien, J. (1986, December). Elder abuse and the primary care physician. *Medical Times, 114*(12), 60–64.

O'Brien, J. (1994). Elder abuse. In R.J. Ham & P. Sloan (Eds.), *Primary care geriatrics* (pp. 466–472). St. Louis: Mosby/YearBook.

O'Brien, J., & Piper, M. (1991). Elder abuse. In M. Pathy (Ed.), *Principles and practice of geriatric medicine* (pp. 211–220). New York: John Wiley & Sons.

Pfeiffer, E. (1975). A Short Portable Mental Status Questionnaire for the assessment of organic brain deficit in elderly patients. *Journal of the American Geriatrics Society, 23*, 433–441.

Pillemer, K., & Finkelhor, D. (1988). The prevalence of elder abuse: A random sample survey. *Gerontologist, 28*(1), 51–57.

Ross, M., Ross, P., & Ross, C.M. (1985, February). Abuse of the elderly. *Canadian Nurse*, 36–39.

Tomita, S. (1982). Detection and treatment of elderly abuse and neglect: A protocol for health care professionals. *P.T. and O.T. in Geriatrics, 2*(2), 37–51.

Yesavage, J., Brink, T., & Rose, T. (1983). Development and validation of a geriatric depression screening scale: A preliminary report. *Journal of Psychiatric Research, 17*, 37–49.

II

Assessment

4

Assessing Physical and Sexual Abuse in Health Care Settings

Holly Ramsey-Klawsnik

The National Aging Resource Center on Elder Abuse (1992) estimates that nearly 30% of elder abuse victims have been physically or sexually assaulted. Unlike some types of abuse, such as financial exploitation and psychological abuse, acts of physical and sexual abuse may leave visible medical evidence on the victim's body. Many elderly individuals are seen regularly, or at least periodically, by health care providers. Health care professionals are thus in a unique position to identify cases of elder physical and sexual abuse and to act on behalf of victims, and may be called upon to assess, or to assist in assessing, possible elder abuse. Effective assessment requires an awareness of the symptoms and clinical dynamics of elder physical and sexual abuse. In addition to providing diagnosis and treatment for illness or injury caused by abuse, health care professionals must carefully doc-

---

The illustrative cases included here are composites of several elder maltreatment cases referred to the author for clinical consultation. All identifying information has been changed to protect the confidentiality of the victims.

ument and preserve evidence of abuse. They must respond supportively and appropriately to patient or client disclosures of abuse. Providers should gently confront patients or clients regarding suspected abuse when symptoms present in the absence of disclosure. Providers must be aware of their legal obligation to file reports of suspected abuse. This chapter addresses the symptoms and clinical dynamics of elder physical and sexual abuse. Various situations in which health care providers are faced with the professional responsibility for assisting possible victims of elder physical or sexual abuse are described. Guidelines are provided for assessing physical or sexual abuse concerns in these situations.

CLINICAL DYNAMICS OF PHYSICAL AND SEXUAL ABUSE

Physical Abuse

Physical abuse is defined by the American Medical Association (1992) as acts of violence that may result in pain, injury, impairment, or disease. These acts of aggression include hitting, slapping, punching, kicking, pushing, choking, pinching, shaking, scratching, biting, burning, pulling hair, striking with objects, force-feeding or forcing a person to ingest a noxious substance, using a weapon to injure, unreasonably confining or restraining, improperly using medication, and incorrectly positioning. Pillemer and Finkelhor (1988) studied rates of physical abuse, verbal aggression, and neglect among a random sample of nonreferred elderly people and found physical violence to be the most widespread.

Indicators of physical and psychosocial abuse are provided in Table 4.1. These indicators should be considered to be particularly suggestive of physical abuse if the injury is incompatible with the explanation provided or with the medical findings. Abuse also may be suggested if the caregiver does not seek medical attention for these conditions in a timely fashion or altogether fails to seek treatment. A report by the caregiver that the elderly person is "accident prone" should be viewed with suspicion. A caregiver or elderly person who consistently avoids using the services of one primary physician or hospital may be attempting to hide evidence of physical abuse. An unusual pattern of injuries, repeated injuries, injuries at various stages of healing, and damage to areas of the body unlikely to be injured accidentally should be viewed by health care providers as suspicious for physical abuse.

Victims may display psychosocial indicators of their physical abuse. Symptoms associated with post-traumatic stress disorder may be seen, including a reexperience of the trauma through nightmares or intrusive thoughts about the abuse, numbed responsiveness through markedly diminished interest in significant activities, or intensification of

Table 4.1.   Indicators of physical and psychosocial abuse

Physical	
Bruises	Marks left by a gag
Welts	Sprains, dislocations, fractures
Lacerations	Alopecia (spotty balding) from
Scratches	pulling hair
Abrasions	Eye injuries (black eye, conjunctivitis
Puncture wounds	[redeye], detached retina)
Bleeding	Missing teeth
Human bite marks	Unexplained scars
Bilateral bruises on forearms,	Internal injuries
suggesting shaking	**Psychosocial**
Imprint injuries (i.e., marks in the	Post-traumatic stress disorder
shape of fingers, thumbs, hands,	Fear, anxiety, mistrust
belts, sticks, rulers)	Shame, humiliation
Burns (e.g., inflicted by cigarettes,	Strong ambivalent feelings toward
matches, ropes, irons, immersion	abuser
in hot water)	

Adapted from Ramsey-Klawsnik (1993b).

symptoms by exposure to events that symbolize the trauma (American Psychiatric Association, 1987).

Sexual Abuse

The vulnerability of elderly women to rape by a stranger has been recognized for some time (Cartwright & Moore, 1989; Groth, 1979; Reay & Eisels, 1983). In contrast, elder sexual abuse is a more recently identified problem (Ramsey-Klawsnik, 1991). This form of maltreatment involves the sexual assault of elderly women, and sometimes elderly men, perpetrated by family members, caregivers, and others who have ongoing access to elderly people and who are often in positions of trust and authority.

Sexual abuse is identified less often than are other forms of elder maltreatment. During 1991 sexual abuse accounted for less than 1% of the substantiated reports of elder abuse in domestic (as opposed to institutional) settings in 30 states that reported data to the National Aging Resource Center on Elder Abuse (Tatara, 1993). Tatara noted that one explanation for the low proportion is that some states list sexual abuse as a form of physical abuse in their official statistics, rather than citing it as a separate form of elder maltreatment. It is also likely that lack of awareness has caused sexual abuse to be the most underidentified form of elder mistreatment. As knowledge of elder sexual abuse has become available to health care professionals and the public, case identification has increased (Ramsey-Klawsnik, 1991).

Sexual offenders are attracted by vulnerability and availability, rather than by the physical attributes of potential victims (Groth,

1979). Offenders seek potential victims who are easy to intimidate and overpower and lack credibility in the event that they report the assault. Elderly people with the types of mental and physical impairments that render them unable to seek help during or following sexual assault are particularly vulnerable. The following case illustrates the vulnerability of elderly people with multiple impairments, including men, to sexual assault.

Eighty-seven-year-old Mr. Nissenbaum is blind, hearing impaired, and unable to speak. He resides in a nursing facility, where his wife visits regularly. As Mrs. Nissenbaum entered her husband's room one morning for a visit, she was shocked to find the nursing assistant who was assigned to bathe Mr. Nissenbaum performing oral sex on Mr. Nissenbaum.

The conditions under which sexual contact with an elderly person is abusive are as follows:
- Physically forcing older person into unwanted sexual activity
- Pressuring or manipulating (e.g., emotionally intimidating) elderly person into unwanted sexual contact
- Victim not granting informed consent to sexual contact because of lack of ability to do so
- Service provider having sex with client or patient

Sexually abusive behavior involves a range of activities, including the following (Ramsey-Klawsnik, 1991):
- Molesting the elderly person, including sexualized touching or kissing
- Oral, vaginal, or anal rape with a penis, fingers, or objects
- Forcing the elderly person to perform sexual acts on the perpetrator
- Sexual harassment
- Threatening the elderly person with rape or molestation
- Forcing the elderly victim to view pornographic material
- Exhibitionism by the abuser

An additional form of sexual abuse, harmful genital practices, was identified in the field of child abuse (Berson & Herman-Giddens, 1994; Herman-Giddens & Berson, 1989). Harmful genital practices are acts such as obsessive or painful washing of genitals, sometimes with genital or rectal penetration; frequent, unnecessary inspection of the genitals; inappropriate application of creams or medications; and the inappropriate use of enemas. In the course of providing consultation to professionals assessing abuse allegations, the author has encountered cases of harmful genital practices involving elderly victims, as in the following illustrative case:

A nurse supervising home health nursing assistants sought consultation regarding a case brought to her attention by one of the nursing assistants. The nursing assistant approached her supervisor and asked if she was obligated to provide care for an elderly patient in the way prescribed by the patient's adult daughter. The nursing assistant expressed discomfort with the manner in which the daughter wished her mother to be bathed. The daughter instructed the nursing assistant to wash the mother's genitals by covering three of her fingers with a washcloth and inserting the covered fingers into the mother's vagina. The daughter had further instructed the nursing assistant to then "scrub" the older woman internally with the washcloth to properly cleanse her mother's genitals. The nursing assistant reported that the daughter had demonstrated the technique by performing the ritual herself. The daughter subsequently stood over the nursing assistant during the bath, insisting that if she did not comply with the instructions, the bath would be incomplete. The nursing assistant reluctantly followed the daughter's orders several times before approaching her supervisor.

Unlike offenders who perpetrate other types of sexual abuse, people who engage in harmful genital practices often admit the abusive behavior and claim that the behavior is necessary for medical or hygienic reasons. Offenders are typically caregivers, often women, who may insist on continuing the abuse behavior even when instructed by health care providers to discontinue it.

The indicators of sexual abuse are listed in Table 4.2. Sexual abuse should be suspected if an elderly person displays irritation, injury, infection, bruising, bleeding, or other trauma about the genitals, breasts, mouth, or anal areas. Injury to other parts of the body also may signal sexual abuse. During sexual assault offenders may injure the face, arms, legs, neck, or buttocks by violently restraining or by physically assaulting the victim. Human bite marks can also signal the presence of sexual, as well as physical, abuse. The psychosocial indi-

Table 4.2.   Indicators of sexual abuse

Physical

Trauma (e.g., bruising, bleeding, wound, infection, scarring, redness, irritation, pain) about the genitals, breasts, rectum, mouth

Presence of sexually transmitted disease, particularly if the elderly person has not engaged in consensual sexual activity

Injury to the face, neck, chest, abdomen, thighs, buttocks

Human bite marks

Psychosocial

Post-traumatic stress disorder

Fear, anxiety, mistrust

Shame, humiliation

Strong ambivalent feelings toward abuser

Extreme discomfort or upset when bathed, toileted, or undergarments changed

Adapted from Ramsey-Klawsnik (1993a).

cators of trauma that are described in relation to physical abuse are also exhibited by many sexual abuse victims.

Victims and Offenders of Physical and Sexual Abuse

Both elderly men and women are vulnerable to abuse, although the violence perpetrated against elderly women tends to be more serious in nature and consequence than that experienced by elderly men (Pillemer and Finkelhor, 1988). The majority of elder abuse victims are women and the majority of perpetrators are men (Kosberg, 1988; Ramsey-Klawsnik, 1991; Tatara, 1993). Early research revealed that older people with physical and mental impairments are more vulnerable to abuse than are unimpaired older people (Wolf, Godkin, & Pillemer, 1984). Impaired individuals who are unable to credibly and reliably report abuse are among the most vulnerable. For example, in a study of 28 suspected victims of elder sexual abuse, 12 suffered severe psychiatric impairments, 3 had Alzheimer's disease, and 1 had experienced a stroke that left the victim aphasic (Ramsey-Klawsnik, 1991).

Elder abusers can be family members, paid or unpaid care providers, or people who have access to older adults but who are not in positions of power or authority, such as boarders and visitors. The elder abuse that occurs in domestic settings may be inflicted by spouses, adult children, other relatives, or paid caregivers. People who abuse older adults in institutional settings may be staff members, other residents, or visitors to the facilities.

Individuals who assault vulnerable elderly people can be grouped into two broad categories (Ramsey-Klawsnik, 1995). The first category consists of abusers who have no malevolent intent. They may be well-intentioned, basically capable people who normally do not abuse, but may lash out in anger or impatience when overwhelmed or stressed. The nature of the abuse tends to be episodic, rather than ongoing. Alternatively, abusers in this category can be people without abusive intent who are unable to adequately care for others because of their own physical or mental impairments or ignorance. Offenders in this category often admit their abusive action. Well-intentioned, capable family members and caregivers who have lashed out at vulnerable elderly people often feel remorseful and recognize the harmful effects of their behavior on their victims. Well-intentioned, impaired offenders may admit their harmful actions, but fail to recognize the abusive or socially undesirable nature of the actions. They may consider the abuse to be a deserved punishment or an appropriate method of teaching or coercing the elderly person into more desirable behavior. The intervention used with this category of offender, whether overwhelmed or impaired, is usually to provide services to reduce the caregiving burden and to increase the caregivers' capacity to provide high-quality care.

The second category of elder abuser consists of individuals who have malevolent intent. They may have abusive or, in some cases, sadistic personalities. These offenders purposely inflict pain and suffering and may enjoy terrifying, exploiting, and assaulting vulnerable people. The abuse inflicted tends to be multifaceted in nature and ongoing, rather than episodic. Serious and extensive physical, sexual, and psychological abuse, as well as neglect and financial exploitation, may be perpetrated. Offenders who force elderly people into unwanted sexual activity are much more likely to belong to this category, rather than the first, because being overwhelmed or ignorant does not cause people to sexually abuse. These offenders lack guilt for their abusive actions as well as empathy for their victims. They are motivated to protect themselves from the consequences of their abusive actions, and do not wish to lose access to their victims. They are unlikely to admit wrongdoing, often intimidate their victims into silence about the abuse, and pose a danger to any vulnerable individuals over whom they have power. These offenders often seek opportunities to gain power and control over vulnerable people, for example, by offering to care for an elderly, impaired relative or by seeking employment in a nursing facility. Intervention in cases involving abusive and sadistic perpetrators should be geared toward removing offenders from positions of authority, power, or caregiving over their victims and any other vulnerable elderly people. Protecting potential victims from these individuals is the rationale behind intervention methods such as central registries of identified elder offenders.

Offenders in this second category can be manipulative and convincing. Health care professionals may or may not be able to "spot" an offender. An offender who is intelligent and manipulative can often dupe professionals attempting to assess suspected abuse cases. Abusers with high socioeconomic status who present with good interpersonal skills and likable personalities can be especially difficult to identify.

Victims may display fear of and suspicion about their offenders. Fear may be expressed through flinching or overly compliant behavior, and can inhibit victim disclosure. Victims of offenders in the second category are often threatened with severe physical or psychological harm if they seek or accept help from professionals. For example, a man repeatedly physically and sexually assaulted his wife, who was physically impaired as the result of a stroke, and threatened that he would sexually assault their two young granddaughters if his wife sought assistance.

Elder abuse victims commonly experience strong feelings of shame and humiliation, particularly if the abuse has included sexual or extensive physical assault. The sense of shame can be exacerbated if the offender is a family member. Ambivalent feelings are common in victims of family abusers because they may simultaneously love and resent their offenders. Elder abuse victims may have difficulty accepting intervention, especially if they have strong affective relationships with offenders, such as spouses and adult children or grandchildren. "Traumatic bonding," in which victims experience intense psychological dependence upon their abusers, was examined by Herman (1992). This pathological attachment significantly interferes with victims' capacities to utilize intervention services. It has been observed in many women battered by husbands and partners, and is also exhibited by elderly victims abused by close relatives.

ASSESSMENT SITUATIONS

Health care providers may become aware of elder abuse in a variety of ways, which are listed in Table 4.3. Health care providers may be called upon to assess possible abuse when elderly patients disclose that they have been physically or sexually harmed. This may occur during the provision of routine patient care. Some victims reveal physical or sexual abuse in the context of trusting relationships with supportive health care providers. Health care professionals (e.g., primary care physicians, visiting nurses, home health care nursing assistants) who provide ongoing care in a private setting are particularly likely to hear these voluntary disclosures. Physical injury or infection causally related to the abuse may or may not be present at the time of disclosure.

Table 4.3.   Situations in which health care providers may assess abuse

Elderly patient discloses abuse to provider

- During routine health care patient discloses abuse—physical evidence of abuse may or may not be present
- Patient requests treatment for condition reportedly inflicted by abusive action

Physical evidence of abuse observed—no disclosure of abuse

- During routine care, injury or infection symptomatic of abuse is observed—patient does not report abuse
- Patient presents for treatment of injury or infection symptomatic of abuse—does not report abuse as the cause

Others seek assistance from health care provider

- Family members or paid caregivers suspect abuse and seek advice from elderly person's health care providers
- Health care providers are asked to provide patient's medical and social histories during abuse investigation
- Physician is asked to conduct forensically oriented medical examination for possible abuse
- Health care professional is a member of an interdisciplinary team assessing elder abuse allegations—may provide diagnostic examination and/or consultation

Mr. Weiss, a 76-year-old diabetic amputee, resides in a two-family home with his son, upon whom he depends as a caregiver. Mr. Weiss receives home health care services 3 days per week, as ordered by his physician upon recent hospital discharge. The assigned nursing assistant had been providing personal care for about 3 weeks when Mr. Weiss told her that he was very grateful that she was now helping him to bathe. He explained that in the past his son had bathed him and had consistently made the water too cold, despite Mr. Weiss' repeated requests to increase the temperature. Mr. Weiss expressed his feeling that his son did not like to help him bathe and, therefore, was not interested in providing this assistance in a compassionate way. Mr. Weiss revealed further that when he has toileting accidents and needs to be cleaned up, his son "punishes" him by washing him with very cold water.

Care providers also may encounter elderly individuals seeking treatment for a medical problem that they say was inflicted by physical or sexual abuse.

Mrs. Cerwinske, 67, a widow who lived alone in an urban area, requested treatment at the hospital emergency room for genital and rectal pain and vaginal discharge. She reported that these symptoms had been present for several months, and that she could no longer bear the pain. Upon examination, vaginal and rectal tissue was found to be torn and infected. Testing revealed the presence of a sexually transmitted disease. Mrs. Cerwinske tearfully explained to the physician that her landlord was forcing her into unwanted vaginal and rectal intercourse on a regular basis. She recounted that approximately 3 months earlier he had told her that if she did not comply with his sexual demands, he would evict her. Mrs. Cerwinske lived on a limited income, spoke English as a second language, and feared that if she did not comply, she would become homeless and unable to find alternate affordable housing.

Unlike Mrs. Cerwinske and Mr. Weiss, many victims are too embarrassed or afraid to reveal abusive experiences to their health care providers. In the course of providing routine medical or nursing care, the care provider may observe physical evidence of abuse. Symptoms may occur in the absence of any allegations or disclosures, and the patient may not request assistance for an abuse problem. Some victims request medical treatment for an injury or infection caused by physical or sexual abuse, but fail to report abuse as the origin of the problem.

Mrs. Thomas, a 72-year-old nonambulatory stroke victim, resided with her husband. A home health nurse visited Mrs. Thomas weekly to monitor her physical condition. During several visits, the nurse noticed marks of unknown origin on Mrs. Thomas' wrists and ankles. The nurse became concerned about possible abuse when she found Mrs. Thomas bleeding vaginally.

Her wrists and ankles had marks that resembled rope burns. Mrs. Thomas did not complain to the nurse and volunteered no explanation. When the nurse asked Mrs. Thomas what had caused these symptoms, Mrs. Thomas anxiously turned her face to the wall, bit her lower lip, and did not respond verbally.

Health care providers may become involved in abuse assessment when requests for assistance are made by individuals who suspect the abuse of an elderly patient. A family member or caregiver who suspects the abuse of an elderly person may seek the advice of a health care provider. During the Adult Protective Services (APS) or criminal investigation into allegations of suspected elder abuse, the suspected victim's health care providers are typically asked to provide medical and social histories and other information that may assist in determining the veracity of allegations. The individual's physician may be requested to perform a forensically oriented examination to diagnose and document injuries resulting from abuse for purposes of investigation and possible court-related intervention.

Dr. Willinger, a family physician in private practice, received a telephone call one morning from Ms. Montgomery, an investigative social worker with the state APS office. Ms. Montgomery explained that her office had received an emergency report of suspected physical abuse of Mr. Benson, one of Dr. Willinger's patients. The report had been made by the home health care agency that provided care to Mr. Benson. Earlier that morning a nursing assistant found Mr. Benson with bruises on his neck, face, forearms, and legs. The bruises had not been present at the time of the prior home visit. Dr. Willinger's assistance in assessing these allegations was requested. Specifically, he was asked to provide Mr. Benson's medical and social histories. The physician was also asked to examine Mr. Benson and to diagnose, document, and treat any injuries.

In some hospitals, clinics, and social services agencies, health care professionals function as members of interdisciplinary teams providing services and/or consultation in cases of suspected elder abuse. The physician or nurse may serve as an expert consultant to other members of the team, such as the hospital social worker or protective services worker. Direct patient care in the form of a physical examination may be provided. Alternatively, team members may provide information and consultation based upon information gathered by other team members.

GUIDELINES FOR ASSISTING SUSPECTED VICTIMS

Responding to Patient Disclosures

Clinical experience reveals that individuals who have been psychologically traumatized by the abusive acts of others benefit from discussing these experiences with supportive individuals (see, e.g., Herman, 1992). Victim disclosure also can be the crucial first step in the journey toward ending the ongoing abuse. For these reasons, it is imperative that health care providers respond appropriately to patient disclosures of physical and sexual abuse. The provider must keep three concerns in mind when responding to patient disclosures: 1) the patient's need for immediate treatment and safety; 2) the patient's long-term need for safety and psychological well-being; and 3) sociolegal considerations, such as preserving medical evidence of abuse and carefully documenting the disclosure in order to facilitate investigative efforts.

The following example illustrates some important points to remember in responding to patient disclosures. These points are also summarized in Table 4.4.

Ms. Anderson, a visiting nurse, made a routine home visit to 81-year-old Mrs. Starkoff, who received transportation services from the local council on aging. During the visit, Mrs. Starkoff confided that the van driver from the council had sexually assaulted her on several occasions, after other passengers had departed from the van.

Ms. Anderson may not have believed Mrs. Starkoff, and responded, "Are you sure? I've known that driver for years and he just doesn't seem like the type of person to do that." Statements that convey that the provider doubts the patient's credibility frequently cause abuse victims to refrain from disclosing further and seeking help. A health care provider should not display shock, alarm, or personal reactions. He or she should refrain from expressing disbelief or putting the patient on the defensive by questioning the credibility or accuracy of the statement.

A more therapeutic response would involve the expression of concern and interest, and an invitation to the patient to continue her description. Privacy for this discussion should be arranged if the disclosure is volunteered at a time when others are in close proximity. Open-ended questions should be used to avoid leading the patient or being suggestive. An appropriate response to Mrs. Starkoff's disclosure would be, "I'm sorry to hear that. Can you tell me what happened?" The care provider should listen supportively and with empathy, and should validate the patient's feelings as appropriate. For example, Mrs. Starkoff tearfully stated that she was afraid to go out because she was concerned that the driver's sexual assaults would continue and perhaps escalate. The appropriate response would be, "I certainly understand your fears."

Table 4.4. Guidelines for responding to patient disclosures of abuse

Do not display alarm, personal reactions, or disbelief

Express concern and invite the patient to provide more information

Do not conduct investigative interview unless trained to do so and in a role in which this is appropriate

Validate the patient's expressed feelings about the abuse

Explain the limits of confidentiality

Assess whether patient has any injuries, infection, or bruises

Conduct or arrange for medical examination as appropriate

Document and preserve medical evidence of abuse

Document the disclosure and observations of the patient

File all necessary reports, including report to APS

Assess patient's needs

Make referrals for required services

Use discretion and judgment in sharing disclosures with others

Providers should refrain from conducting an investigative interview unless it is within their role and they have received training in forensic abuse interviewing. It is critically important that investigative interviews be conducted using both clinically and legally sound methods. Subsequent investigative efforts can be muddied when well-meaning but untrained and inexperienced individuals attempt to conduct investigative interviews. Instead, the provider who is untrained in investigative interviewing should simply invite the patient to tell the provider more about the disclosed abuse. The health care provider thus conveys concern to the patient and collects whatever information the patient wishes to volunteer, but does not compromise investigative efforts with inappropriate questions. Investigative interviews are best conducted by APS investigators, law enforcement officers, or medical or mental health professionals with forensic training. Rather than ask specific questions about the alleged abuse, the provider should listen patiently and supportively to whatever details the patient wishes to provide. An appropriate response would be, "I'm concerned about you. We'll take steps to make sure you're safe."

The health care provider should assess whether the patient has any injuries, bruises, or medical needs that may be related to the disclosure. An immediate examination of the patient should be arranged or conducted, as appropriate. It is critical to fully document all injuries and other medical findings relative to the allegations. Guidelines for medical examination and documentation (including photodocumentation) of findings in cases of suspected elder abuse are provided by Chelucci and Coyle (undated).

Using the example of the illustrative case, Ms. Anderson should listen carefully to Mrs. Starkoff's volunteered description of sexual assault. Mrs. Starkoff reported that her assailant had driven the van to a secluded location following the discharge of the other passengers. He had made sexually charged statements to Mrs. Starkoff, fondled her breasts through her clothing, then removed his penis from his pants and rubbed it on her clothed chest. After several minutes of sexualized talk and rubbing on her, he ejaculated on her clothing. Mrs. Starkoff reported that on two previous occasions the driver had made sexually explicit comments to her when she was alone in the van with him. She reported that the most recent and most severe episode had occurred on the previous day.

The attending nurse should ask Mrs. Starkoff if she has any injuries, bruises, pain, or other medical problem that are the result of the alleged episode. Mrs. Starkoff reported that her breasts were sore from being aggressively squeezed by the driver, but that she had no bruises or injuries. The patient should be offered a medical examination, and urged to accept the examination if any pain, injury, bruising, or recent physical or sexual assault is reported. When recent oral, anal, or vaginal rape is reported, a rape kit examination should be conducted. Guidelines for conducting a rape kit examination of elderly patients are provided by Chelucci and Coyle (undated).

When recent sexual assault is reported, other forensic procedures may be appropriate, including testing of the clothing worn by the victim at the time of the assault. Because Mrs. Starkoff reported that the driver had ejaculated on her clothing, the clothing should be obtained and subjected to forensic testing. If ejaculatory fluid is found, it will become valuable evidence during procedures aimed at terminating the driver's employment and ensuring that he cannot again provide services to elderly people. Should Mrs. Starkoff decide to press criminal charges, this evidence will be extremely important during prosecution.

Health care providers should immediately document the patient's disclosure with detailed notes. Notes should be written as factually as possible; personal and professional reactions to the disclosure should not be recorded. Providers should document the alleged victim's statements, labeled as such: "Mrs. Starkoff reports that yesterday . . .," rather than phrased as a conclusion: "Mrs. Starkoff was sexually assaulted yesterday and . . . ." Notes should be detailed and include all of the patient's statements. The patient's affect and the professional observations of the patient during the disclosure should be recorded: "While discussing this, Mrs. Starkoff periodically cried and trembled."

In responding to patient disclosures of abuse, health care providers should refrain from promising confidentiality, but rather should explain the limits of confidentiality. After hearing Mrs. Starkoff's statements Ms. Anderson might explain, "I'm glad you told me about this. You deserve to be safe. I'm required by law to report this to state authorities. It's their job to keep older people safe from abusive service providers."

Health care professionals should learn and follow state legal requirements regarding the reporting of suspected elder abuse. Most states mandate that health care providers notify APS of their suspicions of elder physical or sexual abuse. Those states that do not require reporting do encourage reports and take steps to ensure the safety of elderly people when reports are made.

The patient should be involved to whatever extent possible in decision making and in taking steps toward achieving safety. Involvement in decision making helps victims regain a sense of control and minimizes feelings of victimization. For example, although Ms. Anderson is required by her state to report Mrs. Starkoff's disclosures to APS, she can provide Mrs. Starkoff with some options as to how that report will be made. Ms. Anderson may ask Mrs. Starkoff if she would like the call to be made immediately from Mrs. Starkoff's telephone. Ms. Anderson may ask Mrs. Starkoff if she would like to make the call or if she would like to speak directly to the social worker taking the call. Mrs. Starkoff may feel empowered by having the call made from her home, where she can listen to the report, even if she does not actually participate in making the report.

A patient may request that a health care provider refrain from reporting in a situation in which the provider is legally obligated to notify authorities. Although the provider must comply with legal requirements, it can be helpful to explain this to the patient in a way that conveys the provider's concern for the patient. For example, had Mrs. Starkoff told Ms. Anderson that she did not want her allegations reported, Ms. Anderson might have said, "I'm sorry, but I can't respect your wishes. I'm required by law to report allegations that an older person has been harmed by a service provider. I know that it's upsetting to have me do this against your wishes. I'm going to report this because I have to, but also because I'm concerned about you. I don't want you to be assaulted again by the driver, and I don't want you to be unable to take the van because you're afraid you'll be assaulted. Service providers who harm clients should not be allowed to continue in their jobs. I'm also concerned because the driver might have assaulted other older people. We need to have this investigated."

When health care professionals file a report of suspected elder physical or sexual abuse with APS, they must specify any immediate or emergency needs of the suspected victim. APS triages reports and is legally required in most states to respond immediately to emergency cases. In a case not identified as an emergency or priority, APS may not dispatch an investigator for several days. Reports must contain as much detail as possible, and provide all pertinent information concerning the suspected victim, alleged offender, and nature of the allegation. The health care provider should detail any medical findings concerning the alleged abuse, as well as what he or she perceives to be the elderly person's needs at the time of the report.

Caution must be exercised in deciding whether to discuss the suspicions with the alleged offender. Good judgment must also be used in deciding whether to notify the alleged offender of the APS report. In some cases it may be appropriate for health care professionals to discuss the allegations with the suspected offender and to notify this individual of the report. In other cases such discussion and notification can endanger an elderly person's safety, as well as compromise the likelihood that a victimized person will be able to cooperate with investigators. In deciding whether to confront the suspected offender, health care providers should consider factors such as the nature of the allegation and the possibility that the older person is under the care or influence of the suspected offender. Offenders, especially offenders with abusive or sadistic personalities, may threaten their victims in order to inhibit their cooperation with investigators. This is a particular risk if serious physical abuse or sexual abuse is alleged, which could result in criminal charges or loss of employment for a caregiver/offender.

Health care providers should also use caution and good judgment in deciding whether to share allegations with nonaccused family member or caregivers. In some cases these people have shared the allegations with the suspect. This action can compromise the integrity of the investigation if the suspect in turn intimidates the victim into recanting the disclosure during subsequent investigatory interviews.

An elderly victim of physical or sexual abuse may have a variety of immediate needs. For example, an elderly woman who has disclosed to her physician that her son has a substance abuse problem and assaults her when he is intoxicated may require emergency alternative housing in order to escape the violence. The health care provider should either provide or arrange for medical attention. The victim may be distraught and require emergency counseling, which may be provided by the local rape crisis center or mental health agency. Emergency referrals should be made, as appropriate, to the hospital social services department, the rape crisis center, the mental health agency, the police, or other agencies, in addition to APS. Hospital admission is sometimes warranted and can provide the crisis intervention necessary to provide immediate safety for the victim.

Responding to Indicators of Abuse in the Absence of Disclosure

In the course of providing routine care, the health care provider may observe symptoms of physical or sexual abuse in the absence of a verbal disclosure from the patient. Some patients request treatment for a specific injury or illness caused by physical or sexual abuse. The relationship between the medical problem and the abuse may not be revealed by the patient or by others who transport the patient for care. Fictitious explanations may be offered.

When symptoms of abuse present in the absence of disclosures, providers cannot assume that abuse has occurred. Factors other than victimization, such as falls and accidental injury, can result in some of the physical findings often associated with abuse. All physical findings should be fully documented and described. If the patient is able to engage in meaningful conversation, the health professional should gently inquire as to the origin of the observed indicators. The patient's statement, affect, and nonverbal response should be documented.

Questioning the patient may lead to various outcomes, including the following:

1. The patient may produce a reasonable and plausible explanation for the physical findings, other than abuse. If the physical condition is consistent with the explanation offered, the provider may conclude that no reason exists to continue to explore for abuse. This is particularly likely if the patient does not seem stressed, anxious, avoidant, or worried as he or she provides the explanation.

2. The patient may discuss abusive experiences. The health care provider should utilize the guidelines provided earlier in the chapter for responding to disclosures.

3. Questioning may fail to result in either abuse disclosures or alternative plausible explanations for the physical findings. The patient may respond in an anxious, defensive, or avoidant manner, which may further alert the provider to possible abuse. For example, in a previously cited illustrative case, a home health nurse found Mrs. Thomas with recurrent marks of unexplained origin on her wrists and ankles, and observed vaginal bleeding. When questioned regarding these symptoms, Mrs. Thomas provided no verbal response.

The following guidelines are offered for dealing with this situation, and with cases involving patients who demonstrate symptoms of abuse, but who are unable to provide reliable information because of mental or physical impairments:

• Consultation with others providing care to the patient sometimes sheds light on the question of possible abuse. For example, the nurse queried nursing assistants who cared for Mrs. Thomas on a daily basis, and learned that they had observed recurrent vaginal bleeding and marks on her wrists and ankles. One nursing assistant reported that she had observed behavior that suggested to her that Mrs. Thomas was afraid of her husband.

- Consultation with specialists may assist health care providers in assessing abuse concerns. For example, a gynecological examination of Mrs. Thomas may suggest an etiology for vaginal bleeding that is either consistent or inconsistent with abuse.
- Most states require health care professionals to report situations for which they have "reasonable cause" to suspect elder abuse. Therefore, in the illustrative case, the nurse would be required to file a report with APS. When in doubt as to the appropriateness of such a report, health care providers can telephone their state APS office and make inquiry. The patient's condition and the presenting symptoms of possible abuse can be discussed at this point without revealing the patient's identity. APS will be able to advise as to whether a report is indicated or mandatory. Providers also can consult with an attorney or with supervisory or administrative personnel as to the appropriateness of a report in any particular case.
- Providers should use caution and careful professional judgment in deciding whether to confront or question possible offenders regarding abuse concerns.
- If it is possible to do so, providers should take precautionary steps designed to ensure the elderly person's safety.

Responding to Requests by Others for Assistance

Suspicions of physical or sexual abuse of an elderly person may lead concerned individuals to seek the advice of a health care provider. Knowledge of the clinical dynamics and symptoms of abuse can enable the provider to respond in a helpful manner. After eliciting from the concerned individual the reasons for his or her suspicions, the provider may recommend a physical examination of the elderly person, gentle questioning of the elderly person regarding the suspicions of abuse, or an APS report of suspected abuse.

Health care providers can be extremely helpful to APS investigators, as well as to law enforcement officers, during investigations of suspected elder physical or sexual abuse. In fact, in many cases the investigation would be incomplete without the input of the suspected victim's physician and other health care providers. Providers wishing to acquaint themselves with the process of a thorough protective services investigation and their crucial role in such investigations are referred to Ramsey-Klawsnik (1995). Some states have passed legislation protecting physicians and other health care providers from civil or criminal responsibility for releasing confidential information to authorities investigating suspected elder abuse. In some states it is a violation of the law for health care providers to withhold requested information, even information normally considered confidential, from investigators. Providers should become familiar with the legislation on these issues in their jurisdiction. When in doubt as to the legal requirements for releasing confidential patient information to investigators, health care providers should seek legal consultation.

Health care providers are typically asked by investigative personnel to provide medical and social histories on elderly patients who are suspected abuse victims. They may also be asked to conduct a forensically oriented examination in order to assist in investigatory data collection and to diagnose and treat any medical problems.

In a previously cited illustrative case, Dr. Willinger was contacted by Ms. Montgomery, an APS social worker. He was informed that his patient, Mr. Benson, was the subject of an abuse investigation as a result of the detection of multiple bruises on his body. Dr. Willinger had been Mr. Benson's primary care physician for a number of years. He had lengthy medical and social histories on Mr. Benson, and he had good rapport with his patient. At this point in the investigation, Ms. Montgomery was new to the case, had no history regarding Mr. Benson, and had established no relationship with him. Her investigation was greatly enhanced by Dr. Willinger's assistance and cooperation. Both Dr. Willinger and Ms. Montgomery were working in Mr. Benson's best interest. In the event that Mr. Benson had been physically abused (and perhaps remained in danger of ongoing abuse), he would benefit from the collaboration of the physician and social worker. Professional collaboration facilitates effective, thorough investigation and appropriate delivery of services.

Dr. Willinger practices in a state in which physicians are legally required to provide confidential patient information to authorities investigating suspected elder abuse. Dr. Willinger, therefore, did not need written informed consent from Mr. Benson or his guardian in order to provide information to Ms. Montgomery. Dr. Willinger revealed that Mr. Benson is a 78-year-old widower with Alzheimer's disease. Mr. Benson is lucid at times, but at other times he is confused and has memory impairment. He resides in his own home and has ample financial resources, which are managed by his son. The son has never married, is unemployed, and has resided with his father all of his life. Mr. Benson's son is his guardian and primary caregiver. Home health nursing assistants provide personal care three times weekly. Dr. Willinger last examined Mr. Benson 4 weeks earlier and noticed no evidence of abuse.

Ms. Montgomery apprised Dr. Willinger of his patient's condition. The home health nursing assistant reported that when she arrived to care for Mr. Benson, she was shocked to see bruising on his neck, face, forearms, and legs. In the past she had frequently observed bruising on his legs, but not on other areas of his body. The son had explained the previous bruising as self-inflicted because his father repeatedly kicked at the rails of his bed. The nursing assistant questioned Mr. Benson about the origin of the extensive bruises. He did not provide a coherent response. The nursing assistant was uncertain whether the lack of response was the result of the disease process or of the presence of the son, who regularly insisted on being in the room while his father was attended by the nursing assistant. Mr. Benson's son stated that he had heard his father thrashing about in his bed the night before, and surmised that banging into the rails had caused the bruises.

Ms. Montgomery recognized that Mr. Benson would be more comfortable being examined by his own physician, and that Dr. Willinger's relationship with Mr. Benson might facilitate disclosure if abuse had taken place. Ms. Montgomery asked Dr. Willinger to conduct an emergency examination of Mr. Benson. Dr. Willinger arranged to see Mr. Benson in the hospital emergency room. Ms. Montgomery and the home health agency arranged for ambulance transportation to the hospital. The nursing assistant who discovered Mr. Benson's injuries accompanied him to the hospital. Mr. Benson's son also drove to the hospital. Ms. Montgomery met the patient and the physician at the hospital to conduct her investigation.

Mr. Benson's son wanted to be present for his father's examination and interview. Dr. Willinger firmly informed him that his presence was inappropriate and would not be allowed. During the examination, Dr. Willinger observed multiple contusions about Mr. Benson's face, neck, shoulders, upper arms, and legs. Marks that resembled finger imprints were present on his neck and forearms. When asked about the origin of these injuries, Mr. Benson mumbled, "Sometimes my son shakes me, but he doesn't mean it. He's a good boy."

Mr. Benson's injuries were carefully documented via written notes, along with photodocumentation of the bruises. He was admitted to the hospital while the investigation continued. During the suspected offender interview conducted by Ms. Montgomery, Mr. Benson's son initially adamantly denied abusing his father. However, he eventually admitted to grabbing his father by the forearms and shaking him. He denied that this was abuse, and justified the action as being necessary to "calm dad down." During the hospital stay, nurses noticed symptoms of post-traumatic stress disorder in Mr. Benson. He cried out in his sleep and reported nightmares upon awakening. He tearfully confided to his night nurse that his son hit him, sometimes choked him, and occasionally blocked his breathing by placing a pillow over his face and saying, "Time to go to heaven now, Dad."

The outcome of the investigation was substantiation of physical abuse of Mr. Benson by his son and court action to remove the son as Mr. Benson's guardian. Mr. Benson was placed in a long-term care facility upon hospital discharge.

This case illustrates the important role of health care providers in assessing abuse suspicions and assisting investigating authorities.

Health care professionals functioning on an interdisciplinary elder abuse team may have additional responsibilities. For example, they may be required to conduct formal interviews of suspected victims and perpetrators. Guidelines for investigative interviewing have been developed (see, for example, Ramsey-Klawsnik 1993a, 1995).

CONCLUSION

Health care providers can deliver invaluable assistance to elder abuse victims, others concerned about abuse victims' safety, and collateral professionals involved in abuse assessment and investigation. Practitioners who are knowledgeable about elder physical and sexual abuse, aware of abuse indicators, and able to respond to suspicions of abuse in a clinically and legally sound manner will be of enormous benefit to their elderly patients who have been victimized.

REFERENCES

American Medical Association. (1992). *Diagnostic and treatment guidelines on elder abuse and neglect*. Chicago: Author.

American Psychiatric Association. (1987). *Diagnostic and statistical manual of mental disorders* (3rd ed. revised). Washington, DC: Author.

Berson, N., & Herman-Giddens, M. (1994). Recognizing invasive genital care practices: A form of child sexual abuse. *APSAC Advisor, 7*(1), 13–14.

Cartwright, P.S., & Moore, R. (1989). The elderly rape victim. *Southern Medical Journal, 82*(8), 988–989.

Chelucci, K., & Coyle, J. (undated). *Elder abuse acute care resource manual*. (Available from Elder Abuse Specialists, 3826 Martha Avenue, Toledo, Ohio 43612)

Groth, A.N. (1979). *Men who rape: The psychology of the offender*. New York: Plenum Press.

Herman, J.L. (1992). *Trauma and recovery*. New York: Basic Books.

Herman-Giddens, M., & Berson, N. (1989). Harmful genital care practices in children: A type of child abuse. *Journal of the American Medical Association, 261*(4), 577–579.

Kosberg, J.I. (1988). Preventing elder abuse: Identification of high risk factors prior to placement decisions. *Gerontologist, 28*(1), 43–50.

National Aging Resource Center on Elder Abuse. (1992). *Elder abuse: Questions and answers*. Washington, DC: Author.

Pillemer, K., & Finkelhor, D. (1988). The prevalence of elder abuse: A random sample survey. *Gerontologist, 28*(1), 51–57.

Ramsey-Klawsnik, H. (1991). Elder sexual abuse: Preliminary findings. *Journal of Elder Abuse & Neglect, 3*(3), 73–90.

Ramsey-Klawsnik, H. (1993a). Interviewing elders for suspected sexual abuse: Guidelines and techniques. *Journal of Elder Abuse & Neglect, 5*(1), 5–18.

Ramsey-Klawsnik, H. (1993b). Recognizing and responding to elder maltreatment. *Pride Institute Journal of Long Term Home Care, 12*(3), 12–20.

Ramsey-Klawsnik, H. (1995). Investigating suspected elder maltreatment. *Journal of Elder Abuse & Neglect, 7*(1), 41–68.

Reay, D.T., & Eisels, J.W. (1983). Sexual abuse and death of an elderly lady by "fisting." *American Journal of Forensic Medicine and Pathology, 4*(4), 347–349.

Tatara, T. (1993). Understanding the nature and scope of domestic elder abuse with the use of state aggregate data: Summaries of the key findings of a national survey of state APS and aging agencies. *Journal of Elder Abuse & Neglect, 5*(4), 35–57.

Wolf, R.S., Godkin, M.A., & Pillemer, K.A. (1984). *Elder abuse and neglect: Final report from three model projects.* Worcester, MA: University of Massachusetts Medical Center, Center on Aging.

5

Assessing Neglect

Terry T. Fulmer and Elaine S. Gould

Protective agencies have found that in compiling reports of elder mistreatment, clinicians most frequently select the category of "neglect" to identify aspects of elder mistreatment. The frequency of this selection is largely the result of the lack of a clear and consistent definition of elder neglect. This lack, in turn, leads to an absence of helpful protocol guidelines, which leaves clinicians to their own devices in assessing neglect in elderly patients.

As a construct within the broader framework of elder mistreatment neglect is confusing and often misunderstood. Problems in conceptualizing neglect are the result of several factors, including nonstandardized definitions for key terms, absence of empirically tested defining characteristics, and a paucity of good research (Fulmer & Ashley, 1986). This chapter focuses on defining neglect in a useful context in order to help clinicians better assess elderly patients for the presence of neglect.

TOWARD A USEFUL DEFINITION
FOR ASSESSING ELDER NEGLECT

Hudson and Johnson (1986) reviewed 31 of the major studies conducted in the area of elder mistreatment. Of the 27 studies that addressed neglect, 12 provided no definition of the concept. The remaining 15 studies used a variety of definitions. Some of the studies mentioned provided illustrations of the concept without actually defining it. As an initial step in exploring clinical perceptions of elder neglect, a pilot survey of visiting nurses working in the 27 protective services areas of Massachusetts revealed that all of the 17 responding agency representatives had observed elder neglect, yet 90% reported they had no training in assessing it (Fulmer, 1987). The definitions of elder neglect offered by this group varied widely and reflected a need for improved information.

Much of the research in the area of elder mistreatment has assumed that elder neglect shares a number of theoretical explanations with elder abuse; early theoretical work erroneously characterized neglect as a precursor or "lesser form" of abuse (Johnson, 1986). No evidence exists to suggest that neglect should be accepted as a subtype of abuse. Abuse is assault and battery, whereas neglect is a failure to provide some degree of minimal care. Cornell and Gelles (1982) criticized research approaches that consolidate all forms of physical abuse with neglect. They suggested that acts of commission (physical abuse) are conceptually different from acts of omission (neglect). Wolf, Godkin, and Pillemer (1986) conducted a community survey to compare various subtypes of elder abuse and found that the profiles of the victims and abusers differed according to the subtype of abuse. They concluded that some theories of abuse fit some of the typologies of abuse more closely than did others. Although the nonrandom sample of this study had limitations, its findings provide some validation that neglect is a separate phenomenon from abuse. Thus, in order to understand the construct of neglect more fully, it must be studied as a discrete event, apart from abuse.

Neglect has been conceptualized and defined in a variety of ways. Terms such as *caregiver neglect, self-neglect, passive neglect,* and *active neglect* are used in the literature and the law to help define elder neglect. Some states focus on one element; other states focus on a different element (Salend, Satz, & Pynoos, 1984; Thobaben & Anderson, 1985). Clinicians who are bound by state regulations for reporting abuse and neglect find the regulations inadequate to the task, for none of these terms when used alone clarifies appropriate methods for clinicians to assess neglect.

It is necessary to understand how these terms must interact in order to create a complete, useful definition of neglect. The varied terms associated with defining neglect need to be seen within two conceptual constructs. The first construct is the *presence of neglect*—positive identification of neglect distinguishable from the effects of age and disease (see top part of Figure 5.1, the age plus disease plus neglect continuum). The second is the *nature of neglect*—the interaction of passive, active, self-imposed, and caregiver-caused neglect in an "elder neglect chart." A single definition of neglect that is useful to the clinician is based on these two constructs in the elder neglect schematic (see Figure 5.1).

Construct 1: The Presence of Neglect

Understanding the intersection of neglect with the aging process and disease is a critical first step in assessing neglect. Clinicians are most comfortable in tackling this diagnostic aspect of neglect because of their education and the concrete, discernable nature of the physical diagnostic process. Determining the presence of neglect is the first step

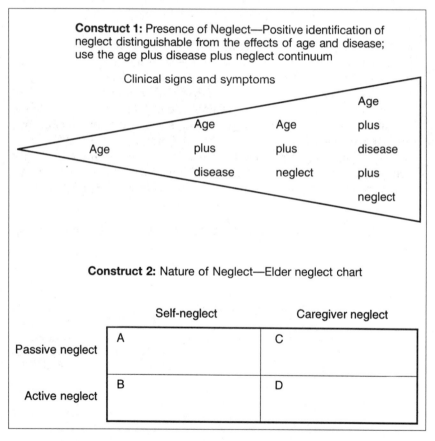

Figure 5.1.   The elder neglect schematic. Clinicians should use the top part of the figure, the continuum, to determine the presence of neglect (see text). Once the presence of neglect has been established, clinicians should address who is perpetrating the neglect and what is the level of intent to neglect. The elder neglect chart is a useful tool for clinicians in order to clarify the various natures of neglect. Indicators of neglect should be entered in the boxes, according to type. (Continuum adapted with permission from Fulmer, T., & Ashley, J. [1986].)

in assessing neglect. A useful tool for clinicians in this endeavor is the age plus disease plus neglect continuum (Figure 5.1, top) along with clinicians' familiarity with risk factors associated with neglect.

The clinician begins by addressing the following question: How does neglect intersect with the health of elderly people? When a child is referred for possible neglect, pediatricians use guidelines, such as the Denver Developmental Screen, that can provide useful markers for "normality." The guidelines may include the following: a baby should weigh within a certain range, a baby should demonstrate a specified range of motor activities, and a baby should present in a clean and healthy manner. This is not necessarily the case with elderly people. When older adults are assessed for neglect, clinicians must factor in the array of chronic diseases and functional limitations that have been acquired over a lifetime. Table 5.1 provides two examples of how clinicians may factor in these diseases and limitations to formulate a diagnosis of neglect (Fulmer & Ashley, 1986).

Clinicians must also be aware of the risk factors for neglect that differentiate it from abuse. Using Connecticut state guidelines, Fulmer, McMahon, Baer-Hines, and Forget (1992) studied the relationship between cognitive impairment and the diagnosis of "neglect" versus "abuse." Cognitive impairment was a risk factor for elder mistreatment in general, but when neglect and abuse were broken out, delirium, as a subset of cognitive impairment, was a risk factor for neglect,

Table 5.1. Two examples of indicators of neglect with possible causes of the indicator

Indicator of neglect	Possible causes of indicator			
	Age	Age plus disease	Age plus neglect	Age plus disease plus neglect
Fracture	Osteoporosis	Osteoporosis plus stress fracture	Osteoporosis plus inadequate assistance with ambulation	Osteoporosis plus stress fracture resulting from inadequate assistance with ambulation
Poor hygiene	Decreased visual acuity	Decreased visual acuity plus rheumatoid arthritis (pain)	Decreased visual acuity plus inadequate self-washing leading to poor hygiene	Decreased visual acuity plus rheumatoid arthritis (pain) leading to inadequate self-washing

Adapted with permission from Fulmer, T., & Ashley, J. (1986).

but not for abuse. Similarly, dementia was found to be a risk factor for neglect, but not abuse. Other risk factors for neglect identified in the study included being nonwhite, unmarried, and uninsured.

Some signs and symptoms that suggest an elderly person is at high risk for neglect are the following:

- Direct neglect—Listlessness, poor hygiene, evidence of malnourishment, inappropriate dress, pressure ulcers, urine burns, reports of being left in an unsafe situation, reports of inability to get needed medications
- Abandonment—Evidence that the elderly person has been "dropped off" at the emergency room or that the family does not intend to retrieve the older person
- Other high-risk situations—Drug or alcohol addiction in the family, isolation of the elderly person, history of untreated psychiatric problems, evidence of unusual family stress, excessive dependence of the older person on the caregiver

Construct 2: The Nature of Neglect (The Elder Neglect Chart)

Clinicians often prefer to let a multidisciplinary committee handle this portion of the assessment process because the assessment of the nature of the neglect has a critical impact on the interventions necessary once elder neglect is identified. It is important for clinicians to remember that although they are critical to the process of appropriate screening and identification of neglect, it is beyond their responsibility to correct the situation alone.

Once the physical presence of neglect has been established, clinicians must address who is perpetrating the neglect and what is the level of intent to neglect. Understanding the living arrangements of elderly people tells clinicians whether the neglect is self-imposed or perpetrated by caregivers. After the identity of the abuser is determined, clinicians must assess for intent and competence, which determine the passive or active nature of the neglect. The elder neglect chart (Figure 5.1) helps to clarify the various natures of neglect.

The American Association of Retired Persons (AARP) (Douglass, 1987) identifies two categories of neglect: passive neglect and active neglect. Passive neglect is the unintentional failure to fulfill a caretaking obligation and infliction of distress without conscious or willful intent. Active neglect is the intentional failure to fulfill caregiving obligations; infliction of physical or emotional stress or injury; abandonment; and denial of food, medication, or personal hygiene. These definitions are helpful only if used within the context of understanding the competence of the patient/client, caregiver, or both individuals.

Using the Elder Neglect Chart to Determine the Level of Neglect

Clinicians guided by state laws have assessed elder neglect using only one part of the elder neglect chart (see Figure 5.1). By using the chart in its entirety, clinicians can make complete, refined cases for elder neglect.

The following examples demonstrate how the chart in Figure 5.1 can be used to assess neglect. Note that these examples are rather simplistic; real-life situations are rarely so clear-cut.

- *Passive self-neglect:* An elderly person with dementia, living alone, with physical signs of neglect
- *Active self-neglect:* An elderly person, homeless throughout adult life, who willfully chooses to forgo socially accepted standards of hygiene
- *Passive caregiver neglect:* A caregiver overburdened with family obligations and financial constraints who feels unhappy that she cannot do more for her mother
- *Active caregiver neglect:* A caregiver who willfully withholds food and hygiene assistance

Interaction of Caregiver Neglect and Self-Neglect with Intent and Competence: Complicating Assessment

Caregiver Neglect Once caregiver neglect is determined, clinicians must address these questions: Was the caregiver a paid provider or an unpaid provider? Could the paid provider be held for malpractice, given the standard of care provided? (In cases of unpaid providers, intent becomes an important issue.) Did the caregiver possess the knowledge and background to deliver high-quality care, but fail to do so? "Inadequate care" (Fulmer & O'Malley, 1987) is a label that encompasses a wider group of elderly people who are at risk for harm, including intentional mistreatment. Fulmer and O'Malley focus on the outcome of the quality of care rather than the mechanism for how the victim came to receive poor care. Fulmer and O'Malley (1987, p. ix) described inadequate care as follows:

> There are differences between what a practitioner must do to manage a case of inadequate care that results from willful interference by a caretaker and in a case in which a similar degree of inadequate care results from a lack of a caretaker or caretaker's ignorance of proper technique. One difference is the need to assess the possibility of separating the elderly person from the source of [neglect] versus providing better homecare. In addition, in a [neglectful] situation, the practitioner must assess the need to engage the individual causing the neglect in a therapeutic relationship. However, the central concern of the practitioner is to identify and develop strategies to meet the care needs and ensure the safety of the elderly person.

Clinicians must be alert to the inadequate care of an elderly individual by a paid caregiver. In cases of neglect, the implied contract between the elderly person and the caregiver for provision of high-quality care has been broken and requires restitution. If the neglected older person is referred by a home health care agency, the older person's physician should speak to the agency, describe his or her concerns, and request a plan of appropriate care. This situation is potentially volatile because if the clinician is describing a possible case of malpractice, litigation may ensue. It is for this reason that some clinicians refuse to report elder neglect. They fear becoming involved in lengthy litigation as well as the possibility that they will be unable to justify their assessment. One reason for this doubt is that neglect is not always a certainty because of concomitant chronic disease in elderly people, such as arthritis, congestive heart failure, and cancer. These diseases may manifest signs and symptoms that can obscure signs of neglect. Elderly patients' temperaments may also influence outcomes. If an older person does not wish to be assisted by other people, harbors racial prejudice against a care provider, or simply has had lifelong poor hygiene, the outcomes may not be the fault of the paid provider.

Phillips and Rempusheski (1985) conducted a study from which a model evolved that described decisions of health care providers concerning elder abuse and neglect. They found that two sets of considerations helped providers make decisions about elder mistreatment. One set of considerations included structural factors (elements that form the background of the situation, including environment, finances, and the caregiver's resources) such as the caregiver's role performance. The second set of considerations included relationship factors, elder factors, caregiver factors, situational factors, cultural stereotypes, and personal and professional values. Clearly, clinical decision making relative to elder mistreatment in general and neglect in particular is a complex, multifaceted process.

Clinicians need to be made aware that it is not their responsibility to address each of these complicated features, but rather to refer the case at hand to the appropriate investigatory body. For example, at the Beth Israel Hospital in Boston, an elder abuse team accepts all internal referrals for suspected cases of elder mistreatment and works through the information before referring cases of suspected neglect to the state of Massachusetts. Although this process is expensive in terms of clinical time, ultimately it is the best practice in that fewer false positive referrals for elder mistreatment are made. This enhanced assessment process is especially helpful in eliminating the disruption a false positive report can cause in an elder–caregiver relationship. If a paid caregiver is accused of neglect without appropriate assessment, he or she is likely to leave the caregiving situation. It may be weeks before the elderly person finds a replacement, and months may pass until the elderly person forms a bond with a new caregiver.

In suspected cases of elder neglect in long-term care facilities, the implied contract between caregiver and care receiver is that the care delivered will be of high quality. If this is not the case, clinicians must determine whether the care provided was appropriate. All background information about the elderly persons' health, comorbid states, and personality must be explored. Here, too, it is essential that the clinician be prudent in the assessment approach. It may be that the care provided was inadequate, but the caregiver merely respected the elderly person's choices. In the case of an elderly individual who is competent, he or she may choose to return to the inadequate nursing facility because it is familiar, or because of its proximity to a son's or daughter's home, cost, or religious affiliation.

When the care provided in any agency or institution is judged to be poor and the elderly person is capable of making decisions, that capacity should be supported in every way possible. This support may include providing intensive social work services; using ethics teams or elder abuse teams, if available; and employing other mechanisms to support the elderly person through the decision-making process.

Self-Neglect   Assessment of self-neglect is a particularly thorny area for clinicians because the process is riddled with value judgments. For example, if an older adult chooses to live as a homeless person, is this self-neglect? Is it self-neglect if the adult is under the age of 65? Would a clinician institutionalize a 45-year-old person who chose to live in this manner? When elderly people make choices that cause discomfort for clinicians, age is sometimes used as a reason to diagnose incompetence or cognitive impairment. Thus, clinicians can substitute their judgment for patients' freedom of choice. Determining competence is crucial to determining the passive or active nature of self-neglect.

The issue of self-neglect has not been resolved for adults of any age in U.S. society. As members of society, we feel uncomfortable about individuals who live in squalor or who choose to ignore their disease, yet "freedom over safety" seems to take precedence for adults who are cognitively intact. This is a difficult issue for clinicians, who perceive that some elderly people may so neglect themselves that the consequences may be fatal. For example, an elderly man diagnosed with cancer refuses therapy. The best his clinician can do is to engage hospital administrators and legal counsel and attempt to marshal the necessary support for the older person and the clinician as they work through a difficult decision-making process.

The following case is an example of self-neglect in which the active or passive qualities of self-neglect are particularly difficult to define.

Mr. Murphree was a 68-year-old man who had lived for a number of years under a bridge in Newark, New Jersey. During a night of subzero temperatures, Newark police found Mr. Murphree and brought him to the local emergency room to have him treated for frostbite. The nurses, physicians, and social workers were faced with the implications of treating and releasing a self-neglecting individual. The health care team was uncomfortable with treating Mr. Murphree for frostbite and then releasing him to the community, but they were forced to comply with his choice to be released. The clinicians called the local unit of the State Office for Aging, and a case manager was assigned to investigate Mr. Murphree's case. The case manager determined that Mr. Murphree needed protective services. Mr. Murphree chose to refuse these services. The case manager had Mr. Murphree declared incompetent.

The clinicians who treated Mr. Murphree were caught in a quandary of defining his competence. Competence determines autonomy, which in turn influences the diagnosis of passive or active neglect, which in turn governs the nature of care for Mr. Murphree.

Assessing Incompetent Elderly People   Assessing incompetent elderly people adds another dimension to the assessment of elder neglect. When older people present with signs and symptoms of neglect, and they are incompetent by virtue of a cognitive impairment or some disease state, clinicians must identify the proxy or person who is authorized to act on behalf of others. If no proxy can be found, it is imperative that guardians or conservators be named as quickly as possible. Information must be shared with the proxy in order to determine *substituted judgment* (i.e., what the elderly person would want if he or she were legally competent). Legal counsel is essential in these situations. Clinicians must quickly refer the case to the appropriate individuals or agencies for resolution.

ASSESSMENT INSTRUMENTS

Creating appropriate assessment protocols is difficult. Clinicians are bound by state regulations that often are neither helpful nor comprehensive. For example, in Connecticut "neglect by others" is defined separately from "self-neglect," and both are reportable. In Massachusetts "self-neglect" is reportable, but an elderly person is not forced to accept services. New York State does not mandate reporting of elder mistreatment of any type; however, self-neglecting people are eligible for services from the state office of aging. It is important, therefore, that each institution be aware of and distribute the appropriate guidelines from its state.

No single, comprehensive assessment instrument exists on which clinicians can agree. Although a variety of assessment instruments for neglect are available, the American Medical Association (AMA) published a protocol entitled *Diagnostic and Treatment Guidelines on Elder Abuse and Neglect* in 1992. In the AMA document clinicians are encouraged to ask questions such as, "Has anyone ever failed to help you take care of yourself when you needed help?" or "Are you alone a lot?" Parameters that are generally considered by the AMA to be important in assessment include safety, access to the elderly person, cognitive status, emotional status, health and functional status, social and financial resources, and frequency and severity of mistreatment. Each domain needs to be reflected in whatever elder assessment instrument an agency chooses to use. A narrative flow sheet may suit one clinical need, whereas other clinicians may find an organized elder abuse assessment instrument more appropriate (see Appendix). Ultimately clinicians must rely upon good clinical judgment.

CONCLUSION

Neglect of older people is a complex phenomenon that requires careful scrutiny in order to avoid misdiagnosis. For too long, clinicians have attributed blatant signs and symptoms of neglect to the aging process, or have "forgiven" inadequate care when the life circumstances of caregivers or care receivers seemed too difficult to sort out. Health care providers can stem the tide of neglect by asking the simple questions, "Is this neglect?" and "Can the system do something to change it?" In order to answer the questions, clinicians must have a complete and useful definition of neglect. When they fully understand the presence and the nature of neglect, they will have a useful definition. Clinicians will then not be afraid to ask those simple, but important, questions because they will know the answers.

REFERENCES

American Medical Association. (1992). *Diagnostic and treatment guidelines on elder abuse and neglect.* Chicago: Author.
Cornell, C., & Gelles, R. (1982). Elderly abuse: The status of current knowledge. *Family Relations, 31,* 457–465.
Douglass, R.L. (1987). *Domestic mistreatment of the elderly: Towards prevention.* Washington, DC: American Association of Retired Persons.
Fulmer, T. (1987). Unpublished manuscript.
Fulmer, T., & Ashley, J. (1986). Neglect: What part of abuse? *Pride Institute Journal for Long-Term Care, 5*(4), 21.
Fulmer, T., MacMahon, D., Baer-Hines, M., & Forget, B. (1992). Abuse, neglect, abandonment, violence, and exploitation: An analysis of all elderly patients seen in one emergency department during a six-month period. *Journal of Emergency Nursing, 18,* 505–510.
Fulmer, T., & O'Malley, T. (1987). *Inadequate care of the elderly: A health care perspective on abuse and neglect.* New York: Springer Publishing.
Hudson, M.F., & Johnson, T.F. (1986). Elder neglect and abuse: A review of the literature. In *Annual Review of Geriatrics and Gerontology.* New York: Springer Publishing.
Johnson, T. (1986). Critical issues in the definition of elder mistreatment. In K. Pillemer & R. Wolf (Eds.), *Elder abuse: Conflict in the family* (pp. 167–196). Dover, MA: Auburn House.

Phillips, L.R., & Rempusheski, V.R. (1985). A decision making model for diagnosing and intervening in elder abuse and neglect. *Nursing Research, 34*(3), 134–139.

Salend, E., Satz, R.A., & Pynoos, J. (1984, February). Elder abuse reporting: Limitations of statutes. *Gerontologist, 24*(1), 61–69.

Thobaben, M., & Anderson, L. (1985, April). Reporting elder abuse: It's the law. *American Journal of Nursing, 85*(4), 371–374.

Wolf, R.S., Godkin, M.A., & Pillemer, K.A. (1986). Maltreatment of the elderly: A comparative analysis. *Pride Institute Journal of Long-Term Home Health Care, 5*(4), 10–17.

APPENDIX

ELDER ABUSE ASSESSMENT FORM

Patient Stamp

Date _____ Person completing form _____

Patient Information

Name _____

_____
Street address   City, State, Zip

Telephone ( )_____
Residence: Home ❑   Nursing facility ❑
W-10 form attached   Yes ❑   No ❑
Age _____   Unit # _____

Family Contact Person

Name _____

_____
Street address   City, State, Zip

Telephone ( )_____

Accompanied to ER by

Name _____

_____
Street address   City, State, Zip

Telephone ( )_____ Relationship to patient _____

Reason for visit (Check one)

Cardiac ❑   Orthopedic ❑   Fall ❑   GI ❑   Psychiatric ❑
Changed mental status ❑   Other (describe) _____

Current mental status

Oriented ❑   Confused ❑   Unresponsive ❑

Who provides home care? _____

General Assessment

	Good	Bad	Uncertain	Cannot obtain information
Clothing				
Hygiene				
Nutrition				
Skin integrity				

Additional comments _____

Possible Indicators of Abuse

	Yes	No	Uncertain	Cannot obtain information
Bruises				
Lacerations				
Fractures				
Various stages of healing of bruises or fractures				
Evidence of sexual abuse				
Statement by elderly person about abuse				

Possible Indicators of Neglect

	Yes	No	Uncertain	Cannot obtain information
Contractures				
Pressure ulcers				
Dehydration				
Depression				
Diarrhea				
Fecal impaction				
Malnutrition				
Urine burns				
Poor hygiene				
Repetitive falls				
Failure to respond to warning of obvious danger				
Inappropriate medications (under-/over-)				
Repetitive hospital admissions as result of probable failure of health care surveillance				
Statement by elderly person about neglect				

Possible Indicators of Exploitation

	Yes	No	Uncertain	Cannot obtain information
Misuse of money				
Evidence				
Reports of demands for goods in exchange for services				
Inability to account for money/property				
Statement by elderly person about exploitation				

Possible Indicators of Abandonment

	Yes	No	Uncertain	Cannot obtain information
Evidence that a caregiver has withdrawn care precipitously without making other arrangements				
Evidence that elderly person is left alone in unsafe environment for extended periods without adequate support				
Statement by elderly person about abandonment				

Summary

	Good	Bad	Uncertain	Cannot obtain information
Evidence of abuse				
Evidence of neglect Passive neglect/ self-neglect Active neglect/ self-neglect Passive neglect/ caregiver neglect Active neglect/ caregiver neglect				
Evidence of exploitation				
Evidence of abandonment				

Comments _____

6

Assessing Nonphysical Abuse

Mary C. Sengstock and Sally C. Steiner

Elder abuse and neglect encompass several categories of behavior that are nonphysical acts. As a result, many professionals and lay people tend not to define them as abuse or neglect. This chapter considers these behaviors, the reasons for characterizing them as abuse or neglect, and the actions that professionals should take in responding to them.

THE "OTHER" TYPES OF ABUSE AND NEGLECT

Since it was first researched and examined in the literature in the late 1970s, the definition of elder abuse was broadened to include psychological abuse. The original notion of abuse of either children or women excluded psychological abuse (Chen, Bell, Dolinsky, Doyle, & Dunn, 1981; Hudson, 1991; Hwalek & Sengstock, 1987; Johnson, 1991; Lau & Kosberg, 1979; McCreadie & Tinker, 1993; Pollick, 1987; Sengstock & Hwalek, 1987; U.S. Department of Health and Human Services, 1992). In general, these additional categories of abuse do not involve direct physical acts of abuse, but do entail psychological neglect, psychological abuse, and exploitation. The definition of exploitation includes both the violation of personal rights and material/financial abuse.

Psychological Neglect

Psychological neglect occurs when an elderly person is left alone without social stimulation for long periods of time. An example of this type of neglect is a caregiver who provides adequate food, clothing, medical care, and shelter, but who never engages in conversation with the older person, and does not permit or actively discourages other people from visiting or telephoning (Sengstock & Hwalek, 1986a). The following case history illustrates this example.

> Sophie is 72 years old and lives in a comfortable room in the home of her son, Casimir, and daughter-in-law. Her meals are brought to her room three times each day, but she eats alone and never has the opportunity to interact with other members of the family. Her loneliness is compounded by her inability to speak English, and she is able to converse only with members of her family and a few friends whom Casimir allows to visit infrequently. On the few occasions Sophie is able to leave the house, her loneliness often leads her to engage in inappropriate behavior, such as clinging to strangers.

Psychological Abuse

Psychological abuse is more overt than psychological neglect, because victims are subjected to verbal abuse and threats (Block & Sinnott, 1979; Sengstock, 1991; Sengstock & Liang, 1983). Some caregivers and family members are unaware of the harmful character of their words and demeanor toward elderly people. Others may deliberately use verbal assault in order to threaten elderly family members and coerce them into submission. Verbal assaults may include constant criticism or accusations about the problems the older person is perceived to create in the home: "Can't you hear anything?"; "You're such a bother"; "This is the third time I've had to take you to the doctor this month." Perhaps the most extreme threat that can be directed toward a frail elderly person is the reminder that he or she can be placed in a nursing home. To elderly people who already feel unwanted by their caregivers, these verbal assaults are an added reminder that others consider them useless and a hindrance.

Exploitation

Exploitation is the term used in many state laws to refer to behavior that manipulates an elderly person or his or her goods or property for the benefit of others. Exploitation can be divided into two categories, violation of personal rights and material or financial abuse (Sengstock & Barrett, 1993).

Violation of personal rights consists of forcing older people to act against their will or preventing them from making choices that adults should be free to make. Examples include preventing elderly people from marrying or divorcing if they choose to do so; forcing them to change residences against their will; or making key decisions, such as decisions involving financial affairs, for them. Invading the privacy of older people is also a violation of personal rights because it prevents them from maintaining the confidentiality of personal records (e.g., bank accounts) or enjoying the confidences of friends and family (Krasnow & Fleshner, 1979; Sengstock & Barrett, 1993). Health care facilities may violate the personal rights of older adults by allowing care providers or other family members to make decisions for an older person, rather than directly asking the elderly person to make a decision. Asking a family member to give permission for hospital admission is a clear violation of the right of an older person as a functioning adult to make decisions for him- or herself. Usurping personal rights can be depressing and debilitating for an older person (Sengstock, O'Brien, Goldynia, Trainer, de Spelder, & Lienhart, 1990).

Material or financial abuse is defined as utilizing the financial resources or property of an elderly person for the benefit of another without the older person's permission. *Material abuse* is the more general term, referring to the theft or misuse of either money or property. *Financial abuse* refers specifically to the theft or misuse of money (Quinn & Tomita, 1986; Sengstock & Barrett, 1993; Sengstock & Liang, 1983).

Material abuse often occurs when an older person holds considerable sums of money or a great deal of property, but it also may occur when little of either exists. In some households an elderly person may be the only individual with a regular source of income, such as a Social Security or Supplemental Security Income check (Wolf, 1986; Wolf & Pillemer, 1984). Family members may resort to abuse or intimidation to force an elderly relative to relinquish the benefit check to them.

IMPORTANCE OF NONPHYSICAL FORMS OF ABUSE

Nonphysical forms of abuse may appear to be less serious than more direct action. However, they may have important consequences for elderly people, and service providers should attempt to identify victims of exploitation and abuse for two important reasons.

First, nonphysical forms of abuse can have damaging effects in and of themselves. They can cause demoralization and depression in elder abuse victims, as has been found with battered wives (Campbell & Fishwick, 1993; Campbell, McKenna, Torres, Sheridan, & Landenburger, 1993) and with infants who exhibit "failure to thrive" (Humphreys & Ramsey, 1993). Like these infants, elderly victims may become so dehumanized because of the violation of their personal rights or the demeaning manner in which they are treated by relatives that they lose interest in living. Their appetites or sleeping patterns may be disrupted, or they may refuse or forget to take their medications (Sengstock, O'Brien, Goldynia, Trainer, de Spelder, & Lienhart, 1990).

In addition to depression and demoralization, material abuse can result in the lack or absence of the financial resources to provide for the older person's needs. Many elderly people whose sole source of income is Social Security or Supplemental Security Income benefits live marginally. Even the theft of a few dollars may prevent them from obtaining needed food or medicine or may cause them to be unable to pay rent or utility bills. Material abuse can reduce financially comfortable elderly people to a state of need and financially depressed elderly people into abject poverty. Thus nonphysical forms of abuse can have negative consequences for elderly people, extending even to the point of illness or death.

The second reason that service providers should attempt to identify victims of exploitation and psychological abuse is that nonphysical forms of abuse may signal subsequent, more life-threatening forms, such as direct assault or severe neglect. This is similar to a pattern found with victims of spouse abuse: A batterer may begin the cycle of abuse by psychologically demeaning the spouse, progress to destruction of the spouse's property, and complete the cycle in a direct physical assault on the spouse (Walker, 1984). Similarly, when family members are faced with the stress of caring for a dependent older person, the cycle of elder mistreatment may begin with occasionally ignoring or verbally insulting and taunting the elderly person, and may escalate gradually with a concomitant increase in caregiver stress. As the stress increases over time, family members may progress to theft or misuse of property or violation of the older adult's personal rights, and finally to physical neglect or direct physical assault of the elderly person. Consequently, health care and social welfare professionals who provide services to elderly clients should be alert to the signs and symptoms of exploitation or psychological abuse in order to identify elders who may be at risk for more severe mistreatment at a later date.

IDENTIFYING NONPHYSICAL FORMS OF ABUSE

As with victims of physical abuse, victims of the nonphysical forms of elder abuse and neglect may be identified by the observation of a number of symptoms.

Symptoms of Psychological Abuse and Neglect

Symptoms of psychological abuse and neglect include any indicator of depression in an elderly person, such as downcast eyes, an expressionless face, a tendency to lean away from others, or prolonged silences. Older adults who are slow to respond to questions or who provide monosyllabic answers to most questions may be exhibiting symptoms of depression. Other symptoms of depression include evidence of significant and often rapid weight loss, a tendency to withdraw from social interaction, and attempts to avert the gaze or to look down or aside when others try to communicate (Sengstock & Hwalek, 1986a).

Feelings of helplessness, loss of interest in activities, and a depressed mood are not part of "normal aging." These symptoms may indicate emotional distress, such as abuse or depression. Symptoms of depression include disturbed sleep (too much sleep, early morning awakening, or sleeplessness), diminished appetite, fatigue (lack of energy to perform routine tasks), and withdrawn mood. Depressive symptoms in older people often include complaints about body aches, vague pain, or digestive distress. Service providers should be aware that despite the debilitating effects of depression, it is treatable.

Although some older people experience depression, many more have dysthymia (Blazer, Hughes, & George, 1987). Dysthymia is a depressive mood disorder that is milder than clinical depression, and is prevalent in the medically ill. Service providers should be alert to the presence of mild depressive symptoms in older adults because the symptoms can indicate a mental or physical problem, including nonphysical abuse.

Health care professionals are often in a position to hear comments or observe the behavior of caregivers or other family members, which may provide clues to their treatment of the elderly person. For example, caregivers may make negative statements to nurses or doctors about their elderly relative, such as how great a burden the older person places on them. Health care professionals may note that family members speak in a harsh tone of voice or interrupt the older person. Family members also may make it difficult for nurses or doctors to speak to the older person alone. In particular, professionals should observe the style of interaction between the elderly person and members of his or her family. Observations should include both positive and negative signs, as follows:

Positive signs

- Touching the older person during conversation
- Including the older person in conversation
- Consulting the older person regarding decisions
- Allowing the older person to be alone with other people

Negative signs

- Withdrawal of the older person from the caregiver or other family members
- Appearance of anxiety or fear on the part of the older person
- Humiliation of the older person
- Threats to abandon the older person, establish a guardianship, or place the older person in a nursing home

Characteristics of the elderly person's lifestyle may also provide clues to the presence of nonphysical abuse. One characteristic may be that the potential victim is left alone for long periods of time without companionship. Everyone should have the opportunity to visit with friends and receive cognitive stimuli, such as reading materials or television programs (Sengstock & Hwalek, 1986a). The presence of any single indicator is not significant, but the accumulation of several indicators may mean that the elderly person is a victim of psychological abuse or neglect.

Symptoms of Exploitation

Symptoms of the violation of personal rights include indications that others are attempting to control an elderly person's actions. As in other areas, health care professionals are in key positions to observe the manner in which older adults are treated by their relatives. Professionals must become comfortable asking questions that encourage elderly people to report abusive behavior. If health care providers are uncomfortable asking potentially embarrassing questions, they should rehearse the interview process with friends or other professionals prior to interviewing an elderly client (Sengstock & Hwalek, 1986b).

Health care professionals may be in a position to observe directly actions that limit the personal rights of an abuse victim. For example, a nursing home administrator was aware that two residents wished to marry. However, the son of the husband-to-be was adamant that his father not remarry, and demanded that the administrator not allow the marriage to take place. The administrator contacted an attorney from Legal Aid, who assured the people involved that the father had the right to remarry, and that the son could not legally prevent the marriage.

Numerous queries can be used to determine whether personal rights are being violated. A simple method is to ask an elderly person who makes decisions about his or her life (Neale, Hwalek, Scott, Sengstock, & Stahl, 1991). For example, who decided where the older person would live? Who chose the doctor or decided whether medical treatment was necessary? If an attorney has been consulted, who chose this professional? Does someone live in the older person's home against his or her will? The service provider should note who has control over the elderly person's finances and who makes the decisions about how the money is to be spent.

Note also should be made about the provision of privacy for the older person. This includes a secure location for private papers, such as a will, financial documents, or even personal mementoes. The lack of privacy is a common complaint of residents of nursing facilities (Sengstock, McFarland, & Hwalek, 1990). Hospitals or other institutions often violate the right to privacy by asking relatives to obtain information from an older person's purse or wallet, which may contain documents the elderly person wishes to remain confidential (Sengstock, O'Brien, Goldynia, Trainer, de Spelder, & Lienhart, 1990). The right to privacy includes the right to a quiet place to have personal, uninterrupted social contact with a spouse or other adult (including a sexual partner), friends, and professional advisers, such as an attorney. If a nurse or social worker has difficulty separating the older person from family members for a private discussion, this may indicate that the elderly individual's privacy is also being violated in other instances. The client may seek assurances from the service provider that family members will not be told of the conversation. Professionals should watch for signs of fear while a client discusses issues of abuse because this may indicate that others try to control the client's behavior (Sengstock & Hwalek, 1986a).

Indicators of material abuse can be elicited by judicious questioning. One indicator may be a client's lack of money early in the month. This may be obvious if the professional knows the client well enough to recognize that poor money management is an unusual pattern for him or her. Medical personnel may notice that the older person has not been taking prescribed medications or is losing weight. Professionals should ask whether this is the result of a lack of funds and too many expenses, or whether someone has been taking money from the client.

Other aspects of the elderly person's financial affairs may provide indicators of material abuse (Sengstock & Hwalek, 1986a). Does someone else have control over the client's finances? Has the client been placed under a guardianship or conservatorship without sufficient cause? If the client has a guardian or conservator, is this person using the client's funds for his or her welfare, or are the funds being diverted to someone else's use? For example, a health care team became aware of a diversion of funds when an elderly person required 24-hour care, but his conservator refused to release the funds to provide this care.

A special problem occurs when a client's Social Security or pension check is sent to someone other than the entitled individual. A danger also exists when the resources of older people are controlled by others, such as placing the name of another person on a deed, bank account, stock certificate, or safe deposit box. Professionals should inquire as to whether the client personally makes withdrawals from bank accounts or whether he or she asks someone else to do so. Professionals should also determine whether the client's agents can be trusted to act in his or her best interest. A determination should be made as to whether the client has made any dramatic financial decisions in the last 6 months, such as making or changing a will or adding a name to a deed or bank account, and whether such decisions were made freely or under pressure. Care should be taken to ensure that the elderly person was capable of understanding the meaning of the document being signed. Many relatives have taken advantage of an elderly person's cognitive impairment in order to gain control of money.

Similar questions can be asked about the client's property. Relatives or other people who live with the client may take advantage of him or her in a variety of ways (e.g., tenants may refuse to pay rent, or people with access to the elderly person's home may remove items without his or her permission). Professionals should note whether any damage (e.g., broken dishes and furniture, defaced walls and grounds) has been done to the client's property. Such actions are not only damaging in themselves, but may foreshadow more serious assaults against the older person.

Researchers have reported that older people may jeopardize their health and welfare for the benefit of their adult children, who may be alcoholic, mentally ill, or drug addicted, and unable to manage life independently (Wolf & Pillemer, 1989). Parents may continue to feel responsible for their offspring, may feel guilt or shame at the behavior of their adult children, and may worry about the consequences of failing to assist their children. It is often difficult to determine whether the parents are acting of their own free will or are being coerced into providing assistance.

Financial exploitation is often regarded as a form of abuse that predominates among family members. However, the awareness of incidents of financial exploitation by strangers is growing. The following case histories are illustrative.

A stranger, representing himself as a case manager, was hired by the Y family to assist them in placing their mother in a nursing facility. The consultant informed the Y family that Medicaid would cover the nursing care costs, and advised them not to pay any bills received from the nursing facility. Only after the facility threatened to discharge Mrs. Y for lack of payment was it discovered that the consultant had not made the expected enrollment application to Medicaid. Fearing that the placement was in jeopardy, the Y family sought assistance from a legal services provider, who was able to intervene.

Mrs. C, who received supportive services through the local aging network, was referred to a benefits specialist for assistance in financial issues. The specialist discovered that Mrs. C had been sold several duplicative long-term care insurance policies by a single agent. Most of her monthly income was used to pay the premiums for these insurance policies. The agency that discovered the abuse took action on Mrs. C's behalf. The network was able to get the agent's license revoked for unethical practices.

These abusive situations are not easy to resolve and often require the participation of legal services providers, consumer protection agencies, and other professionals.

SERVICES AVAILABLE TO VICTIMS AND THEIR FAMILIES

Some services for elderly people and their families are suggested by the nature of the abuse itself; that is, cases of elder neglect require different types of services than do cases of direct abuse, and material abuse should be handled in a manner different from physical neglect. However, depending on the state of their health or other circumstances, elderly victims of a variety of types of abuse may require financial assistance, help with various activities of daily living, a change of residence, or other services. Overburdened caregivers may need respite care or other help.

The Use of Persuasion and
Legal Services Available to Victims of Nonphysical Abuse

Interventions in cases of nonphysical abuse are typically less intrusive than those that may be implemented in cases in which evidence of direct physical abuse or neglect is reported.

Dealing with material abuse and violations of an elderly person's personal rights demands that professionals be aware that abusive acts may be unintentional, intentional, or the result of misguided paternalism. Family members may assume control over some of an older person's affairs with the goal of providing support and maintaining the older person's independence, or they may use the elderly relative's health or mental status as a means to gain control of the older person's assets for the family members' benefit. Family members who become caregivers for a frail elderly person often take control of most aspects of his or her life, even areas that the older person can still handle effectively. Family members and others concerned about the elderly person may fail to understand that like other adults, older people need privacy and need to feel that they have control over their money and property.

Some family members may believe that they are acting in the best interest of their elderly relatives when they make decisions on the relatives' behalf. Professionals should assume initially that these actions reflect a lack of knowledge on the caregivers' part, and hope that an explanation of the client's needs can persuade family members to correct the problem. This course of action is always preferable because it is less intrusive, and family members are less likely to take offense. In such instances, additional assistance for the elderly client and his or her family may be appropriate.

When persuasion is not effective, more direct action may be necessary. Legal action is often an appropriate response when a client is the victim of material abuse (Sengstock & Barrett, 1986). People who steal or misuse the assets of another person, whatever the victim's age or the offender's relationship to the victim, have committed a crime. Although elderly people may be reluctant to charge their relatives or friends with theft, the client should be availed of the opportunity, which could result in either regaining possession of the property or, at the least, preventing further theft. Filing criminal charges may be useful in other instances as well, such as in forcing an unwanted tenant to move from a client's home.

Civil action, such as filing suit against the alleged abuser for return of the missing money or property, is another option available to victims of nonphysical abuse. For example, if the person responsible for misusing the older person's property holds legal status, such as guardianship of the older person or power of attorney, a change of guardianship or revocation of the power of attorney is in order. The assistance of an attorney in these cases is essential. The retention of an attorney and the threat of legal action may be sufficient to regain the missing property. Care should be taken, however, to ensure that the attorney selected has no connection to other members of the older person's family.

In cases in which an older adult's personal rights have been violated, criminal action is not usually appropriate. However, civil action may be useful. For example, if an older person has been prevented from marrying or divorcing, making or changing a deed or will, or obtaining access to financial records, the services of an attorney can ensure that the desired actions are carried out. In matters of coercion (e.g., an elderly person is forced or persuaded to make or to change a will or deed), an attorney may be able to correct the action. Many jurisdictions offer older people free or low-cost legal assistance in such matters. However, if an older person has freely chosen to relinquish control of funds or property to a child or another individual, there may be little that an attorney can do to correct the matter.

Psychological abuse and neglect are not amenable to the direct action that is appropriate in the more overt types of abuse. It is not possible to enforce laws that require family members to maintain cordial relations with each other. In such cases understanding the cause of the psychological neglect or abuse is useful.

A professional should observe how the members of the family treat each other—whether the offensive treatment of the client is part of a general pattern of verbal assault practiced in the family, or whether the client is ignored because members of the family often do not speak for long periods. These indicators may point to a generalized pattern of family communication rather than an intentional effort to exclude the elderly relative. Thus, guidance in order to alter the family pattern of interaction may be required.

When psychologically abusive behavior is directed only toward the elderly person, family members must be taught that older people require the same social stimulation as other family members. Family members who are stressed to the breaking point by the difficulties of caring for an elderly relative need assistance in alleviating the stress.

In summary, persuasion and the provision of legal services that the client and his or her family may require are the only appropriate responses in most instances of psychological abuse and neglect.

General Services Available to Victims and Their Families

Alleviating the problems of caring for elderly people and the stress of family members can help eliminate nonphysical abuse in many instances. Early intervention may prevent later, more serious, and perhaps life-threatening forms. One method of intervention is to establish a care management program for the victim of abuse and his or her family.

An important component of a care management plan is an analysis of the general problems of the older person and the family. The professional should ask the following questions in making this analysis:

- What kinds of needs does the client have?
- Are the needs of the client being met adequately?
- Have sufficient provisions for food, clothing, shelter, medical care, and social contact been made?
- Is caring for the client placing an exceptional demand on the caregiver?
- Is the client hostile or difficult to control?
- Is the client's family adequately equipped to deal with problem behavior?
- Do needs exist that could be met through outside sources, which may relieve the burden on the caregiver(s)?

Many caregivers, especially spouses, have physical limitations or have little knowledge of appropriate caregiving skills. For many older men, cooking, cleaning, and assisting another person with personal care are not routine activities. When the responsibility for these and other household tasks are thrust upon them through illness of the spouse, many elderly men are unable to prepare a balanced meal, to clean the house, or to provide personal grooming assistance to their ill wives. Older women may be accustomed to caring for others, but may lack knowledge of both simple and sophisticated care techniques required for many older people. These problems can be alleviated through in-home support services that assist as well as teach caregiving skills to caregivers. Home-delivered meals or personal or chore services may make the difference between a manageable and an unmanageable care situation.

Service providers often erroneously assume that people know the options and potential outcomes of various service choices. In fact, many older people are unaware of the range of aging services and other support services available, and misinformation about the nature of such services is rife. For example, many elderly people equate elder housing with nursing homes and Meals-on-Wheels with charity, or they may assume that chore or household services are costly. The ability to decide whether to accept such services assumes that the older person has received sufficient information about options to make an informed choice. When a person lacks an accurate understanding of chore services, adult day care, foster care, or respite care, he or she cannot make a decision as to whether it is desirable. Service providers are obliged to ensure that their clients make informed choices.

Finally, problems that may provoke elder abuse may be totally unrelated to the older person. For example, care providers may experience marital problems or be involved in disputes over child rearing. Unemployment, substance abuse, and other family difficulties may make caring for an older family member a more burdensome task than usual. Thus, assistance to the entire family may be necessary if an elderly person or another family member is not to be at risk for abuse. Indeed, some family problems may be so severe that it may be inadvisable for family members to undertake the care of a dependent older person. The safety of the elderly person may demand a change of care plans.

SPECIAL ISSUES OF CONSENT AND INFORMED CHOICE FOR ELDERLY PEOPLE WITH COGNITIVE IMPAIRMENT

The issue of mental competency of an older person is fraught with confusion for service providers who deal with all forms of elder abuse. This issue is particularly critical in assessing nonphysical forms of abuse. When signs of physical abuse are evident, the course of action is clear, but when faced with forms of nonphysical abuse, the appropriate intervention depends on the mental competency of the older person.

Mental competency is both a legal status and a social judgment. Competency refers to the ability to understand and the capacity to use that understanding to make informed decisions. The term applies not to the quality of the decision, but to the capacity of the decision maker. An older person who decides to give large amounts of money to questionable organizations or to make dramatic changes in his or her lifestyle may be "incompetent" according to the social judgment of friends or family, but the right to act foolishly or even against one's own best interests is not legally prohibited. The critical factor is whether the person understands the consequences of his or her actions. A person who has the capacity to make informed decisions has the right to make foolish or risky decisions.

Legal competency can be determined only in a formal hearing before a judge. In a guardianship hearing the judge must determine if the person is impaired to the extent that he or she no longer has the capacity to make informed decisions. A lack of capacity may be caused by mental illness, physical illness, disability, substance abuse, intoxication, or other conditions that impair a person's ability to understand or communicate informed decisions.

The varying dimensions of mental competency are only now being recognized. Historically, mental competency was viewed as existing or not existing. In many states, the courts now recognize that mental capacities vary, and that the remedy should fit the scope of the problem. People who are at risk for abuse or who actually experience abuse may be competent. They may recognize that abuse is occurring, and may even resign themselves to the situation. Older people in these circumstances may not need a legal remedy, such as guardianship, to protect them. They need information, support, and an intervention service. That these older people may not meet the state's definition for "vulnerable" or "incompetent" does not mean that they do not need assistance. Service providers must become familiar with the concept of competency and the complexities of informed consent in order to respond appropriately to the abusive or potentially abusive situation.

Informed consent, or the ability to understand a particular situation, the choices, and the consequences of a decision, is a key component of competency. People who have not been judged to be legally incompetent are assumed to have the ability to make informed decisions and conduct their personal affairs as they choose. However, some people may still lack the ability to make informed decisions in one or more areas of life. For example, some elderly people may lack understanding about how to arrive at medical or health decisions and other people may need assistance in deciding financial matters.

Assessing the competency of people with dementia, such as Alzheimer's disease, is a special concern. Many people with a diagnosis of dementia do not have a legal guardian because judges often prefer informal management of these cases, if a relative is willing to accept responsibility (Mental Health and Aging Advisory Council, 1993). Consequently, people with dementia are presumed to be mentally competent, although their ability to make important decisions is critically flawed. Persons with cognitive impairments are especially at risk for poor care, and service providers should determine whether poor care is the result of deliberate action, lack of knowledge, or undue stress on the caregiver. Appropriate action should be based on this assessment.

Competency and Noncompliance

Competency is often in the eye of the beholder. Service providers who associate frequently with an elderly person may view a situation differently from people whose contact with the client is limited. Many people with dementia can maintain an appropriate social demeanor for a short period of time. Only after considerable contact does their limited mental capacity become obvious. A service provider who sees the client frequently may be aware of the client's limitations, but the same client may appear to be functional to a protective services worker or a guardian *ad litem* on a brief visit. Subsequent or extended visits may be necessary to reveal the elderly person's lack of recognition or recall. Thus, assessments of competency should not be based on a single brief encounter.

Health and social services providers must take particular care not to engage in professional paternalism ("If you agree with my proposed plan, you are competent to make an informed decision; if you disagree, you must not be competent"). A legally competent client must consent to any recommendations for intervention. Furthermore, a client has a right to discontinue participation in the intervention program at any point. However, a client's refusal to accept a professional's recommendation on an important matter should not be interpreted as a lack of capacity to understand. Too often service staff label an elderly client "resistant" or "noncompliant," and use the refusal as the basis for pursuing a guardianship hearing or for discharging a client from a program. Service providers should explore the reasons for a client's refusal (e.g., what are the client's values? How serious are the consequences that may follow refusal?) Successful outcomes will recognize the values and feelings of the people being served.

Institutional Placement and Issues of Consent

The decision of family members to seek nursing home placement against the will of an older person raises many complex issues and engenders ambivalent feelings. Issues of autonomy, personal rights, caregiving burden, safety, guilt, blame, and responsibility are intertwined in the placement decision. Moody (1992) rejected the need for a commitment procedure for nursing home placement and argued for a consumer protection form of paternalism, which is a blending of an appropriate degree of paternalism with the advocacy of consumer protection. Paternalism is exercised when the elderly person cannot understand the consequences of a nursing facility placement and is unable to provide informed consent. The consumer protection aspect requires professionals to find the best available accommodation for the elderly person's care needs.

Using this model, professionals are challenged to acknowledge openly the conflicts and dilemmas they face and the power they exercise in placement decisions. Professionals are encouraged to determine the client's values and their own values and to seek to act on behalf of the client's autonomy rather than their own views of what is in the client's best interest. The ideal situation is a realistic and compassionate review of the client's care needs and the ability of others, both familial and formal caregivers, to meet those needs. An open examination of conflicting values, personal rights, and autonomy can lead to an accommodation that supports the client.

Once a client is placed in a nursing facility, care providers often face a "catch 22" situation. As Hashimi and Withers (1992) have noted, residents may not wish to participate in activities that are essential to their survival. If providers force the resident to participate, they violate the resident's rights and add to his or her loss of autonomy. If providers do not insist that the resident participate, they may be legally liable for failing to provide "life-enhancing care." The common reaction of staff when confronted with this situation, regardless of setting, is frustration with the uncertainty about the resident's ability to understand and make informed choices. Staff should review the person's needs, values, and capacity to understand the situation.

In-patient psychiatric services are provided to individuals who meet the rigorous criteria for mental health services. A person who is committed to a psychiatric facility for treatment is under the restrictions and requirements of the commitment order. Several methods of admission into a public psychiatric facility exist, each with its own set of rights. In Michigan, for example, a voluntary recipient of state inpatient psychiatric services can self-discharge after a period of treatment and has the right to withdraw consent to treatment. A person under an involuntary or court-ordered admission can be discharged only by court order or a doctor's orders, and may file complaints only about treatment.

The staff of a psychiatric facility must understand the whole range of types of elder abuse, from violation of personal rights to physical harm. At the same time, they must be clear about the mission of the facility as a treatment setting, and understand that conflicts with residents may arise regarding the necessity of participation in a treatment plan that was imposed as a condition of admission. In some cases the line between following a treatment plan and violating personal rights may seem blurred to some staff members. Staff and treatment teams must balance the resident's need to exercise control and make personal choices with the overall goals of the treatment plan. Accommodating a resident's lifelong routine as long as it does not conflict with the goals of treatment may be desirable. Thus, the determination of a violation of personal rights in a psychiatric facility should always be viewed within a clinical perspective.

CONCLUSION

Several types of behavior may be subsumed under the term *nonphysical types of abuse*, including psychological neglect and abuse, material or financial abuse, and the violation of personal rights. State laws often refer to the material or financial abuse and the violation of personal rights types as "exploitation." Impaired elderly people are at particular risk for exploitation, and special concerns may arise with regard to the issues of mental competency and informed consent.

Numerous methods of detecting nonphysical types of abuse are available but their lack of specificity makes the methods of detection more vague and ambiguous than those of physical abuse or neglect.

Dedicated service providers must take care to note such characteristics as depression in their clients, their clients' behavior, and the behavior of people surrounding their clients. Particular attention should be paid to excessive efforts to influence the behavior of a client.

Appropriate interventions in cases of nonphysical abuse are difficult to establish. Criminal or civil law may be invoked in some limited instances of material abuse. Civil action also may apply in some instances of the violation of personal rights. However, in general, informal interventions are more appropriate to nonphysical abuse cases. This is certainly true of psychological neglect and abuse, and it also may be true of material abuse or the violation of personal rights.

Although nonphysical types of abuse may be more difficult to identify and remedy, attention paid to these types of abuse is critical for the welfare of elderly people at risk. Victimization in and of itself can be damaging to older people, but many times, these types of abuse may be precursors for other, more life-threatening types of neglect or abuse. Dedicated professionals should note symptoms of the nonphysical types of abuse in order to prevent the development of more serious mistreatment of elderly people at a later point.

REFERENCES

Blazer, D., Hughes, D.C., & George, L.K. (1987). The epidemiology of depression in an elderly community population. *Gerontologist, 27,* 281–287.

Block, M.R., & Sinnott, J.D. (1979). *The battered elder syndrome: An exploratory study.* College Park, MD: University of Maryland Center on Aging.

Campbell, J., & Fishwick, N. (1993). Abuse of female partners. In J. Campbell & J. Humphreys (Eds.), *Nursing care of survivors of family violence* (pp. 68–104). St. Louis: Mosby/YearBook.

Campbell, J., McKenna, L.S., Torres, S., Sheridan, D., & Landenburger, K. (1993). Nursing care of abused women. In J. Campbell & J. Humphreys (Eds.), *Nursing care of survivors of family violence* (pp. 248–289). St. Louis: Mosby/YearBook.

Chen, P.N., Bell, S.L., Dolinsky, D.L., Doyle, J., & Dunn, M. (1981). Elderly abuse in domestic settings: A pilot study. *Journal of Gerontological Social Work, 4,* 3–17.

Hashimi, J.K., & Withers, L. (1992). Institutional care settings and self-neglect. In E. Rathbone-McCuan & D.R. Fabian (Eds.), *Self-neglecting elders: A clinical dilemma* (pp. 91–106). New York: Auburn House.

Hudson, M.F. (1991). Elder mistreatment: A taxonomy of definitions by Delphi. *Journal of Elder Abuse & Neglect, 3,* 1–20.

Humphreys, J., & Ramsey, A.M. (1993). Child abuse. In J. Campbell & J. Humphreys (Eds.), *Nursing care of survivors of family violence* (pp. 36–67). St. Louis: Mosby/YearBook.

Hwalek, M.A., & Sengstock, M.C. (1987). Assessing the probability of abuse of the elderly: Toward development of a clinical screening instrument. *Journal of Applied Gerontology, 5,* 153–173.

Johnson, T.F. (1991). *Elder mistreatment: Deciding who is at risk.* Westport, CT: Greenwood Press.

Krasnow, M., & Fleshner, E. (1979, November). *Parental abuse.* Paper presented at the 23rd annual meeting of the Gerontological Society of America, Washington, DC.

Lau, E.E., & Kosberg, J.I. (1979, September/October). Abuse of the elderly by informal caregivers. *Aging,* 10–15.

McCreadie, C., & Tinker, A. (1993). Review: Abuse of elderly people in the domestic setting: A U.K. perspective. *Age and Aging, 22,* 65–69.

Mental Health and Aging Advisory Council. (1993). *Changing systems for changing needs.* Lansing, MI: Michigan Office of Services to the Aging.

Moody, H.R. (1992). *Ethics in an aging society* (p. 106). Baltimore: The Johns Hopkins University Press.

Neale, A.V., Hwalek, M.A., Scott, R.O., Sengstock, M.C., & Stahl, C. (1991). Validation of the Hwalek-Sengstock elder abuse screening test. *Journal of Applied Gerontology, 10,* 406–418.

Pollick, M. (1987). Abuse of the elderly: A review. *Holistic Nursing Practice, 1*(2), 43–53.

Quinn, M.J., & Tomita, S.K. (1986). *Elder abuse and neglect.* New York: Springer Publishing.

Sengstock, M.C. (1991). Sex and gender implications in cases of elder abuse. *Journal of Women and Aging, 3*(2), 25–43.

Sengstock, M.C., & Barrett, S. (1986). Elderly victims of family abuse, neglect, and maltreatment: Can legal assistance help? *Journal of Gerontological Social Work, 9*(3), 43–61.

Sengstock, M.C., & Barrett, S. (1993). Abuse and neglect of the elderly in family settings. In J. Campbell & J. Humphreys (Eds.), *Nursing care of survivors of family violence* (pp. 173–208). St. Louis: Mosby/YearBook.

Sengstock, M.C., & Hwalek, M.A. (1986a). *The Sengstock-Hwalek comprehensive index of elder abuse* (2nd ed.). Detroit: SPEC Associates.

Sengstock, M.C., & Hwalek, M.A. (1986b). *The Sengstock-Hwalek comprehensive index of elder abuse: Instruction manual.* Detroit: SPEC Associates.

Sengstock, M.C., & Hwalek, M.A. (1987). A review and analysis of measures for the identification of elder abuse. *Journal of Gerontological Social Work, 10*(3/4), 21–36.

Sengstock, M.C., & Liang, J. (1983). Domestic abuse of the aging: Assessing some dimensions of the problem. In M.B. Kliman (Ed.), *Interdisciplinary topics in gerontology* (Vol. 17: *Social gerontology,* pp. 48–58). Basel: S. Karger.

Sengstock, M.C., McFarland, M.R., & Hwalek, M. (1990). Identification of elder abuse in institutional settings: Required changes in existing protocols. *Journal of Elder Abuse and Neglect, 2*(1/2), 31–50.

Sengstock, M.C., O'Brien, J.G., Goldynia, A.M., Trainer, T., de Spelder, T.G., & Lienhart, K.W. (1990). *Elder abuse assessment and management for the primary care physician.* Lansing, MI: Office of Medical Education, Research, and Development, Michigan State University College of Human Medicine.

U.S. Department of Health and Human Services. (1992). *Report from the secretary's task force on elder abuse.* Washington, DC: U.S. Government Printing Office.

Walker, L.E. (1984). *The battered woman syndrome.* New York: Springer Publishing.

Wolf, R.S. (1986). Major findings from three model projects on elderly abuse. In K.A. Pillemer & R.S. Wolf (Eds.), *Elder abuse: Conflict in the family.* Dover, MA: Auburn House.

Wolf, R.S., & Pillemer, K.A. (1984). *Working with abused elders: Assessment, advocacy and intervention.* Worcester, MA: University of Massachusetts Medical Center, Center on Aging.

Wolf, R.S., & Pillemer, K.A. (1989). *Helping elderly victims: The reality of elder abuse.* New York: Columbia University Press.

7

The Role of Risk Factors in Health Care and Adult Protective Services

Melanie Hwalek, Carolyn Stahl Goodrich, and Kathleen Quinn

Health care providers are frequent reporters of suspected elder abuse to Adult Protective Services (APS) programs. In making the decision to report suspected elder abuse, health care providers collect evidence that may suggest that an elderly person has been abused. In many states, once elder abuse is suspected, health care and other professionals are mandated by law to report their suspicion to the state APS system. One issue raised by these professionals is that they do not know what APS programs do once a report is made, or what happens to the alleged victim once suspected abuse is reported.

This chapter helps health care providers understand 1) how the "typical" APS process works, 2) how risk assessment in an APS pro-

This chapter was supported in part by Grant No. 90-AM-0447/02 and Grant No. 90-AM-0720 from the Administration on Aging, U.S. Department of Health and Human Services. Points of view or opinions do not necessarily represent official Administration on Aging policy.

gram differs from risk assessment in health care settings, 3) how case workers in one state (Illinois) used a risk assessment protocol in investigating and intervening with victims, 4) how APS providers and APS program managers can use risk assessment to promote high-quality services and to assess the outcomes of their interventions, and 5) how health care professionals can contribute to effective APS investigations and interventions.

The generic term *elder abuse* is used in this chapter to represent all types of elder abuse, including physical abuse, sexual abuse, neglect by another person, self-neglect, emotional or psychological abuse, and financial exploitation.

RISK ASSESSMENT IN HEALTH CARE SETTINGS

In health care settings, assessing the risk for elder abuse consists primarily of gathering facts about an elderly person that a professional can use to determine whether suspicion of abuse exists. The evidence gathered from an alleged abuse victim includes physical signs and symptoms such as bruises, wounds, broken bones, malnutrition, and dehydration. Information may be compiled regarding family dynamics, such as history of domestic violence or attitudes about caring for elderly people. Assessing risk also involves collecting information about the potential misuse of an elderly person's financial resources.

The meaning of risk assessment is that evidence gathered is sufficient for the health care professional to suspect that an incident of elder abuse has occurred. The final decision often is made by a team of health care professionals who have knowledge of the case. Once the decision is made that elder abuse is suspected, a decision to report the evidence to APS generally follows.

RESPONSE BY ADULT PROTECTIVE SERVICES TO REPORTS OF ELDER ABUSE

When a report of elder abuse is made, most state APS programs follow similar procedures in investigation and intervention. The report of suspected elder abuse is made by telephone, either to a local elder abuse agency or through an "800" line that is transferred to the local elder abuse agency. The individual taking the report at the agency obtains as much information as possible from the caller in order to determine the seriousness of the situation. At the completion of the call, the individual taking the report assigns a priority to the case, which establishes a deadline for the elder abuse case worker to begin an investigation. The priorities assigned include the following categories:

- *High priority*—Action must be taken immediately because the alleged victim's life is in danger.
- *Medium priority*—The situation is serious enough to warrant an investigation within 24 hours of the report.

- *Low priority*—The situation is not likely to worsen within the next 72 hours.

The investigation of elder abuse is a lengthy process that involves gathering information (i.e., substantiating) from many different sources. At a minimum, the elder abuse case worker talks with the alleged victim and the alleged abuser. Because talking about abuse is often personal and private, it may take several meetings over several days to collect information from the alleged victim.

Gathering information from other sources can be done only with the consent of a mentally competent victim. Friends, family members, or neighbors may provide testimony that validates or refutes evidence. Opinions may be sought from experts, such as the alleged victim's physician. Photographs may be taken of evidence of abuse such as the alleged victim's home or bruises on the victim's body. Records, such as police reports, bank statements, or medical files, may be reviewed by the case worker. In some instances, physical items, such as soiled clothing or canceled checks signed by the alleged abuser, may be used to substantiate abuse.

The elder abuse case manager, often in conjunction with the elder abuse program supervisor, determines when sufficient evidence is present to make a substantiation decision. The decision is rarely made easily because contradictory evidence is likely to emerge during the investigation. The case worker makes this difficult decision by weighing each piece of evidence. Only slightly more evidence in favor of abuse is needed in order for a case of elder abuse to be substantiated. The decision to substantiate is not made lightly, however. The case worker carefully documents every encounter as well as the reasons for making the decision to substantiate.

An analogy should not be drawn between a jury decision and a substantiation decision because it implies that the abuser is guilty of malicious wrongdoing, or that a second party is involved in the abusive situation. This is not always the case.

Although intentional physical abuse of elderly people does occur, in some cases abuse or neglect is unintentional. The alleged abuser may be a caregiver trying his or her best to cope with the highly stressful situation of caring for an older person with an impairment. Sometimes the stress becomes so great that the abuser lashes out in frustration, harming a loved one unintentionally. Other abusers may simply lack the knowledge necessary to properly care for the elderly person. In other situations, elder abuse is substantiated because the victim is neglecting him- or herself, with no second party present.

INTERVENTION BY ADULT PROTECTIVE SERVICES

Once a report of elder abuse is substantiated, the APS intervention process begins. Intervention aims to improve the quality of life of older people by linking them to needed services. If the abuse victim is willing to accept services, a care plan is developed, which lists service needs and resources available to fill the needs. The care plan may include informal services provided by family or friends as well as formal services provided by local agencies, churches, and volunteer programs. Based on the care plan, the case worker arranges for and monitors the delivery of formal services. The case worker periodically reassesses the situation to determine whether services need to be continued and whether any service changes are warranted.

The process of reassessment continues until the case is closed. Common reasons for closing elder abuse cases include the following:

- The victim is no longer at risk for future abuse.
- The victim dies.
- The victim moves away (usually referred elsewhere for services).
- The victim is placed into long-term care.
- The victim refuses further assistance.

Because elder abuse victims are often frail, closing a case of elder abuse can involve transferring the client into another program. This may mean placement of the victim into a case management program or institutionalization. In cases of institutionalization, if the victim permits, the state long-term care ombudsman program may be notified so that the safety of the victim can continue to be monitored in the institution.

Elder abuse interventions differ from case management in two important ways. First, in addition to maximizing the quality of life, elder abuse interventions aim to reduce or prevent future abuse. Second, elder abuse situations are frequently more volatile than other case management situations, making elder abuse interventions more difficult to institute. The case worker is not always a "welcomed guest" in an abuse victim's home. The victim rarely reports the abuse and, therefore, may not be aware initially of the reasons for the elder abuse case worker's presence in the home. Neither the elderly person nor family members may know who reported the alleged abuse, and the case worker is obligated not to reveal the identity of the person reporting. This may cause a stressful relationship to develop between the case worker and the family. Elder abuse interventions require the collection of personal, private information, which may result in the disclosure of negative feelings, behaviors, or family dynamics.

For these reasons and others, elder abuse interventions are not always successful. As with cases of child or spouse abuse, elder abuse cases are not often amenable to successful intervention when chronic domestic violence is involved. Unlike abused children, elderly victims have the right to refuse interventions, even if this means their lives are in danger. In cases of financial exploitation, the case worker may be able to end the abuse, but the chances of retrieving the stolen resources are slight.

Elder abuse interventions require that case workers have expertise in many areas. Not only must they understand the problems of normal aging and the network of services available to elderly people, they must also understand and be able to work within the court system. They must have investigatory abilities in addition to health and psychosocial assessment skills. They must be able to manage crisis situations, to cope with stress and ambiguity, and to protect themselves in dangerous situations.

RISK ASSESSMENT WITHIN
ADULT PROTECTIVE SERVICES SYSTEMS

The meaning of risk assessment within the context of an APS system differs greatly from its connotation within health care settings. In elder abuse programs risk assessment is the process of examining a victim's current circumstances to determine whether a risk exists that abuse will recur; it is not the documentation of whether an incident of abuse probably occurred, as it is within a health care setting. Risk assessment within APS determines the risk for repeated abuse; therefore, risk assessment is completed after abuse has been substantiated.

Because it is not the purpose of risk assessment to document substantiation, indicators in an APS risk assessment protocol differ from indicators in hospital risk protocols. Hwalek and Sengstock (1982) demonstrated that the indicators of risk for elder abuse in APS protocols describe characteristics likely to predict the occurrence of abuse, and not characteristics likely to describe the abuse itself. In Hwalek and Sengstock's study all elder abuse assessment protocols available to the researchers were dissected into their individual items. Professionals from health care, social, and legal services were asked to label each item from the protocols either as an "indicator" of elder abuse or as a "predictor" of situations likely to generate future elder abuse. These professionals made clear delineations between the two categories. Some examples follow:

Indicators

- Presence of bruises or wounds (physical abuse)
- Threatening remarks made by the abuser to the victim (emotional abuse)
- Malnutrition (physical neglect)
- Taking money from a victim against his or her will (financial exploitation)

Predictors

- Abuser unemployment
- Abuser does not cooperate with the investigation process
- Lack of knowledge of proper caregiving techniques

The indicators are similar to the items listed in hospital risk assessment protocols (Chelucci & Coyle, undated). The predictors describe the victim's situation rather than signs or symptoms of abuse. These are the types of indicators used, either implicitly or explicitly, by APS programs in assessing risk.

SAMPLE ADULT PROTECTIVE SERVICES
RISK ASSESSMENT PROTOCOL

A 1994 survey of state elder abuse programs showed that fewer than one third of the 38 states that participated in the study use a risk assessment process that meets the risk assessment definition stated earlier in the chapter (National Committee for the Prevention of Elder Abuse, 1994). Of the 38 states, Florida, Maine, and New York have been conducting formal risk assessments for the longest time. Florida APS created a risk assessment protocol that was adopted by Illinois. The Illinois APS program uses the Florida protocol to track the risk of victims for future harm or abuse (see Appendix). The Illinois APS risk assessment protocol uses five major categories consisting of 23 factors to measure risk. The factors are grouped as follows:

1. Client factors
    -   *Victim's age and gender:* This risk factor is based on the findings of previous research that victims tend to be older women. A high-risk rating is given to victims who are over age 75.
    -   *Victim's physical/functional health:* Data from the Illinois APS system indicate that a high percentage of functional impairment exists among victims. It appears that the greater the physical or functional limitations, the more vulnerable the victim is to future abuse. Thus, victims who are bedridden, are completely dependent on others, have chronic disabilities, or whose functional abilities are rapidly deteriorating are in the high-risk category.
    -   *Victim's mental/emotional health:* Victims with cognitive impairment may not be able to care for themselves or to contact someone if abuse recurs. Thus, victims with psychiatric limitations are at greater risk for future abuse. Psychiatric limitations include profound mental retardation, severe functionally limiting psychiatric conditions, confusion, or rapidly deteriorating emotional health. Victims who refuse needed services are also at high risk for future abuse.
    -   *Chemical dependency or other special problems of the victim:* Victims who are active alcoholics or substance abusers are placed in the high-risk category. This placement is supported by a 1993 study that found that victims are four times more likely to be

chemically dependent when their abusers are chemically dependent (Quinn, Hwalek, & Stahl Goodrich, 1993).

- *Income/financial resources of the victim:* Neglect is likely when victims do not possess the resources to support their health care or basic subsistence needs. Victims who are at high risk are totally financially dependent on others and are unable or unwilling to provide for their own necessities, regardless of their ability to pay.

2. Environmental factors

- *Structural soundness of the home:* When older people live in environments that are unsafe, a possibility exists that they are neglecting themselves or that others are neglecting their needs. High-risk situations include victims living in condemned structures or in environments in which safety problems are numerous.

- *Appropriateness of the environment to the victim:* When older people cannot move about the house, they cannot take care of their activities of daily living and are at risk for neglect. High-risk situations include nonambulatory victims living on an upper floor of a home without handicap access to the outside, victims living in neighborhoods in which they are repeatedly victimized by violent crime, and residences that cannot be made safe.

- *Cleanliness of the residence:* High-risk situations that suggest elder neglect include homes with serious health violations, such as severe pest infestation or the presence of human waste in the residence.

3. Transportation and support systems factors

- *Availability, accessibility, and reliability of services:* People at high risk are geographically isolated from needed community services and are living in areas where the waiting lists for services are long, where services are not reliable, or where services are not available when the victim needs them. These victims are likely to suffer continued abuse because their needs cannot be met by the existing service delivery system.

- *Adequacy of formal or informal supports:* Victims who are socially isolated and who have no one available, willing, or able to provide assistance are considered high risk, as are victims who lack knowledge of formal support systems available to them, who are unable to access available services, or who lack any willing or effective advocate.

4. Current and historical factors

- *Severity of the physical or psychological abuse that is perpetrated:* High-risk victims require immediate medical attention because of sexual abuse or injuries to the head, face, or genitalia. The victims experience escalating patterns of severe abuse or serious adverse psychological effects of abuse.

- *Frequency or severity of exploitation:* Any form of exploitation that threatens the health, safety, or well-being of the victim; that deprives the victim of the necessities of life; or that involves any systematic misuse of a victim's resources places an older person at high risk.
- *Severity of neglect:* High scores for this risk factor include situations in which the victim is at risk for death or serious harm because of the lack of adequate care or supervision. Such situations often require immediate intervention such as medical treatment or emergency services.
- *Quality and consistency of care:* Victims at high risk lack the ability to care for themselves, a responsible caregiver, or a caregiver with adequate knowledge of appropriate caregiving. Victims who live alone and who have diminished mental or physical capacity are also at high risk for this risk factor.
- *Previous history of abuse, neglect, or exploitation:* Victims with ongoing histories or patterns of increasing frequency of abuse, neglect, or exploitation receive a high risk score for this risk factor. Any previous report that was substantiated or that led to the prosecution of the abuser also would place the victim at high risk.

5. Perpetrator factors
   - *Access to the client:* High risk is present when the abuser has complete and unrestricted access to the victim.
   - *Situational response to stress or home crises:* Victims at high risk are those people whose abusers grossly overreact or present highly inappropriate reactions to stress or life crises. For example, abusers who display severe depression, who make remarks of hopelessness, or who have chronic fatigue would receive high-risk scores for this risk factor.
   - *Physical health:* Victims whose abusers have severe, functionally limiting physical conditions are at high risk. Functional problems, such as chronic or uncontrolled disease and rapid or recent deterioration of physical health, limit a caregiver's ability to provide adequate care.
   - *Mental/emotional health or control:* Victims whose abusers display bizarre or violent behaviors, are suicidal, or who demonstrate a desire to harm the victim are at high risk. These abusers may have severe and functionally limiting psychiatric conditions or a history of chronic psychiatric conditions. They may be unresponsive to the victim's needs, ask to be relieved from

caregiving burdens, threaten the victim, or demonstrate rapid deterioration in psychiatric or emotional health.

- *Perpetrator–victim dynamics:* High-risk situations are present whenever relationships between the victim and abuser cause the victim to tolerate abuse, neglect, or exploitation. These situations may involve a victim or caregiver who is emotionally dependent on the other, a victim obsessed with the perpetrator, a victim who fears the perpetrator, or a victim who has irrational desires to protect the perpetrator.

- *Cooperation with the investigation:* High-risk situations are those in which the abuser does not believe that a problem exists or in which the abuser refuses to cooperate with the case worker in order to resolve the situation. These situations suggest that the abuser is hiding or denying abuse.

- *Financial dependency on the client:* High-risk scores are given to victims whose abusers need and use the victims' financial resources to benefit themselves. These abusers have demonstrated a history of parasitic or opportunistic behaviors *vis à vis* the use of the victims' money or belongings.

- *Chemical dependency or other special problems:* Victims whose abusers are actively alcoholic or drug dependent or who have other, special problems that could result in abuse, neglect, or exploitation receive high-risk scores for this risk factor. Quinn, Hwalek, and Stahl Goodrich (1993) found that the risk for continued elder abuse increased when the abuser is chemically dependent. Other researchers (e.g., Anetzberger, Korbin, & Austin, 1994) found an association between chemical dependency and elder abuse.

In assessing risk, the elder abuse case worker determines whether the victim is at "low risk/no risk," "intermediate risk," or "high risk" for future abuse for each of the 23 factors. It is a clinical judgment that places the victim in these risk categories. A risk factor also can be coded "information unavailable" if no data are available to the case worker to help him or her assess the level of risk for the particular factor.

After assessing each of the 23 risk factors and the score for each (see Appendix; low/no risk is assigned a score of 1, intermediate risk is assigned a score of 2, and high risk is assigned a score of 3), the elder abuse case worker determines an overall risk score along the same continuum of low risk/no risk, intermediate risk, or high risk. No formulas are predefined and no relationships exist between the scores for each of the 23 risk factors and the overall risk assessment score because high risk in only one indicator category may suggest a situation so severe that the victim is judged to be at high risk for future abuse.

Very little research has been conducted to examine the reliability (i.e., accuracy with which each item is scored by APS staff) of the risk assessment protocol. Florida APS reported one study in which case workers completed a risk assessment protocol after they watched a videotape about a case and compared their ratings. According to Florida APS representatives, a high degree of agreement was noted among case workers on the presence or absence of each risk indicator (informal communication).

No research has been published on the validity (i.e., does the protocol actually measure risk of abuse) of the protocol for predicting future risk for elder abuse. However, the content areas covered in the risk assessment protocol were developed from case workers' reports and their experiences assessing victims. As such, the protocol appears to have "face validity."

USE OF THE RISK ASSESSMENT PROTOCOL IN ILLINOIS

In Illinois the risk assessment protocol is used to document the victim's level of risk at several points in time: 1) during the investigation to document the level of risk of the victims at the time the report was made, 2) during each 3-month reassessment until the case is closed, and 3) at the time of case closure.

Results from the 1994 National Committee for the Prevention of Elder Abuse survey of state APS representatives suggest that Illinois is the only state that uses a comprehensive risk assessment protocol to track elder abuse victims longitudinally. Florida uses the protocol only to initially assess victims during the investigation process. To the authors' knowledge, no other states use the risk assessment protocol described in this chapter.

CLINICAL USE OF THE RISK ASSESSMENT PROTOCOL

Although more research is needed to validate the risk assessment protocol, preliminary reports suggest that its value to case workers can be enormous. During the investigation process, the 23 factors can guide the elder abuse case worker in determining what information should be gathered. Factors scored as "information unavailable" can offer insights as to what information is still missing.

The protocol can be used to identify major treatment objectives in a care plan because those factors identified as high risk may be targeted for immediate intervention. For example, in situations in which the high-risk factors involve a highly stressed abuser or an abuser with physical frailties, respite care or in-home health services may be the interventions of choice. In other situations, in which the structural unsoundness of the home places the victim in danger, referral to a home repair program or relocation of the victim may be indicated.

Risk assessment results can be used to suggest when and which more comprehensive assessments are warranted. For example, a high-risk score for the victim mental health risk factor triggers the need for the case worker to refer the victim for a comprehensive psychological assessment. A high-risk score for the functional abilities risk factor triggers the same case worker to complete Illinois' standardized comprehensive functional and psychosocial assessment.

Using the protocol at various points in time can provide indicators of progress in reducing risk, such as what is changing, what is not changing, and what additional information is needed. The factors that have changed can be identified, as can the areas in which further investigation or intervention is needed. The protocol also helps case workers evaluate the effectiveness of interventions across many cases. Victims with similar risk scores at the beginning of each investigation can be identified. The various intervention strategies used in the cases can be compared so that case workers can delineate the interventions that may be more effective for certain high-risk situations.

MANAGERIAL USE OF THE RISK ASSESSMENT PROTOCOL

Managers of elder abuse programs can use information obtained from the risk assessment protocol to improve the quality of APS programs. Detailed information about the "typical" caseload of elder abuse case workers, which is obtained from data on risk factors, can be useful in determining service and resource needs. For example, an analysis of risk data from 500 closed cases demonstrated that abuser chemical dependency is a major factor affecting risk scores of victims. The study found that elder abuse victims are more likely to remain at high risk over time when the abuser is chemically dependent (Quinn, Hwalek, & Stahl Goodrich, 1993).

These data point to the need to establish linkages between APS and the substance abuse treatment network, and suggest that elder abuse case workers could benefit from training in how to identify substance abuse and where to obtain help for both the chemically dependent victim and abuser. The need for crosstraining of elder abuse and substance abuse clinicians is also indicated by these results. Such training would allow substance abuse treatment providers to share information on identifying and treating chemical dependency, and elder abuse case workers could inform substance abuse treatment providers about the dynamics of elder abuse.

Risk data can be used by APS administrators to help measure the effectiveness of agencies in intervention. For example, suppose an APS program establishes an expectation that 75% of cases will close at low risk. If the risk assessment data indicate that only 50% of cases close at this level of risk, questions should be raised, such as the following:

- Why are only 50% of the cases reaching low risk?
- Is the expectation too high?
- Are agencies less effective than they could be?

- Are any agencies meeting or exceeding the 75% level? If so, what are these agencies doing that can be shared with those that are less successful?
- Should more training in effective interventions be provided to case workers, or are the characteristics of cases handled by these successful agencies somehow different from the characteristics of cases handled by the less successful agencies?

Even the lack of data on risk factors can be meaningful. For example, if perpetrator risk factors are frequently scored as "information unavailable," this suggests the presence of barriers in the investigation process that limit what is learned about abusers. This finding also may indicate a need for further training for case workers in how to obtain information about abusers.

ROLE OF THE HEALTH CARE PROFESSIONAL IN ADULT PROTECTIVE SERVICES' RISK ASSESSMENTS

The health care professional can be a valuable asset to APS case workers both in investigating cases of elder abuse and in assessing victims' risk for future abuse. Knowing the risk factors that are important to APS can aid the health care professional in determining what information to provide when reporting elder abuse.

Health care professionals often know or have access to information about some of the risk factors that can maximize the efficiency of the risk assessment process. Documentation in the health care files may identify friends or relatives whom the APS case worker can contact. Medical details in patient files can help the case worker to determine scores on risk factors. Knowing the risk factors can help health care professionals target information that may be useful to the APS case worker. Health care professionals usually have longer and closer relationships with victims than do APS case workers and, therefore, may be familiar with the victim–abuser dynamics.

The health care professional who initially reported the abuse may be contacted by the APS case worker for this additional information. However, APS case workers may contact health care professionals or other sources of information only with the consent of the victim. If the victim is unable to give consent, case workers obtain APS consent from the legal guardian. If the legal guardian is also the suspected abuser, the courts can empower APS case workers to gain access to health care and other information.

CONCLUSION

Health care professionals must understand what happens when a report of suspected elder abuse is made to an APS system, and how health care professionals can assist in investigating abuse or assessing risk. An investigation into the alleged abuse is mounted. Information is gathered from numerous sources and a substantiation or nonsubstantiation of abuse is determined. Once this occurs, the APS investigation process begins, and this process includes risk assessment.

Risk assessment protocols can be used to aid both victims and their abusers. One risk assessment protocol that was developed in Florida is used in Illinois to track the level of risk of victims within the state's APS system. The assessment of risk was differentiated from the determination of substantiation and the documentation of specific signs and symptoms of elder abuse. The Illinois protocol includes 23 factors, along with definitions of the high-risk score for each factor.

The Illinois protocol has both clinical and managerial value. The protocol helps clinicians to guide investigations, generate care plans, track progress, and identify areas for further intervention. The value of the protocol for APS program managers is in guiding decision making regarding allocation of resources, program development, and training needs. Health care professionals must also understand their role in assisting APS case workers.

Assessing risk in APS settings can be valuable to both case workers and the statewide program. The authors propose that more state agencies consider instituting standard procedures for measuring and reporting risk levels of victims. More health care professionals should understand the APS system in their state and use the categories of risk to guide the collection and reporting of information when elder abuse is suspected.

REFERENCES

Anetzberger, G.J., Korbin, J.E., & Austin, C. (1994). Alcoholism and elder abuse. *Journal of Interpersonal Violence, 9*(2), 184–193.

Chelucci, K., & Coyle, J. (undated). *Elder abuse acute care resource manual.* (Available from Elder Abuse Specialists, 3826 Martha Avenue, Toledo, Ohio 43612)

Hwalek, M., & Sengstock, M.C. (1982). *Developing an index of elder abuse* (Final report to U.S. Department of Health and Human Services, Administration on Aging, Grant No. 90-AR-0040/02). Washington, DC: U.S. Government Printing Office.

National Committee for the Prevention of Elder Abuse. (1994). *National survey of adult protective services agencies's use of risk assessment.* Washington, DC: Author.

Quinn, K.M., Hwalek, M.A., & Stahl Goodrich, C. (1993). *Determining effective interventions in a community-based elder abuse system* (Final report to U.S. Department of Health and Human Services, Administration on Aging, Grant No. 90-AM-0447/02). Washington, DC: U.S. Government Printing Office.

APPENDIX

Illinois Risk Assessment Protocol

Client factors	1 = No risk/low risk	2 = Intermediate risk	3 = High risk
Client factors			
Client's age/sex	60-year-old female 60- to 74-year-old male	60- to 74-year-old female	75+-year-old male or female
Physical health/functional abilities	Ambulatory, minimal physical disability; capable of meeting activities of daily living	Diminished capacity; moderate physical disability; difficulty ambulating—requires prosthesis (e.g., cane, walker) or hands-on assistance to be ambulatory; occasionally nonambulatory	Severe and functionally limiting disability; bedridden; completely dependent on others; chronic disease; rapid deterioration of functional abilities
Mental/emotional health	None, or minimal/controlled mental or emotional disability; willingness to accept needed assistance	Moderate mental retardation; periodic confusion; impaired reasoning abilities; decompensated mental illness; resists accepting needed services	Profound mental retardation; severe functionally limiting mental illness; confusion; recent, rapid deterioration of mental/emotional health; refuses needed services
Substance abuse/other special problems (e.g., wandering, misuse of medication, noncompliance with physician's instructions)	No indication of substance abuse; no, or minor special problems	Periodic episodes of alcohol or substance abuse	Active alcoholic or substance abuser; any change that places the client at high risk
Income/financial resources	Adequate; able to provide for the necessities of life; financially independent of others	Partially financially dependent on others; marginal financial resources; barely able to provide for the necessities of life; must sometimes choose between necessities (e.g., medicine versus food)	Totally financially dependent on others or, regardless of income, unable/unwilling to provide for the necessities of life

Environmental factors

Structural soundness of the home	Sound structure with no apparent safety problems	Deteriorating structure, or safety problems that pose some degree of risk	Client living in a structurally unsound or condemned structure; serious safety problems
Appropriateness of residence to the client	Operating utilities (e.g., heat, power, water, ventilation) appropriate to climate and client's health; residence does not contribute to client's risk	Service temporarily terminated or periodic interruption of heat, power, water, ventilation (unvented heaters); residence poses special problems that place the client at risk (e.g., client wanders and lives near major highway)	Services terminated or utilities inoperative; residence poses special problems that place the client at immediate risk (e.g., nonambulatory client residing on third floor, client repeatedly victimized by violent crime, residence cannot be made safe)
Cleanliness of residence	Resident meets minimum standard of cleanliness; trash not exposed; no odors present	Trash and garbage not disposed of; animal droppings and some evidence of pest/insect infestation	Gross health violations (e.g., severe pest/rodent infestation, human waste present)

Transportation and support system

Availability of, access to, and reliability of services (e.g., transportation, home health, medical)	Adequate and reliable community resources available; client able to leave residence on a regular basis; transportation available	Limited community services available or short-term waiting list; service reliability is problematic; public transportation is unavailable; private transportation is problematic	Geographically isolated from community services; long-term waiting list; services unreliable or not available at frequency required
Adequacy of formal/informal support network	Family, friends, and neighbors available, willing, and able to provide or arrange needed services; has a well-informed, effective advocate; known to service system; already receiving services	Family somewhat supportive, but does not live in geographic area; limited support from family, friends, and/or neighbors; support is irregular in quality and/or frequency; limited or incomplete knowledge of available public or private resources	Client is socially isolated, no one available, willing, or able to provide assistance; no knowledge of formal support system; unable to access available services; lacks a willing/effective advocate

	1 = No risk/low risk	2 = Intermediate risk	3 = High risk
Current and historical factors			
Severity of physical/psychological abuse	No injury, or minor injury limited to bony parts (e.g., knees, elbows); no apparent adverse psychological effect on client	Minor or unexplained injury (limited to bony parts, buttocks, or torso) requiring medical treatment/diagnosis; pattern of increasing severity of abuse; client evidencing some adverse psychological effects of abuse (e.g., fear, anger, withdrawal, depression)	Client requires immediate medical treatment/hospitalization; any sexual abuse or injury to head, face, genitalia; escalating pattern of severe abuse; client evidences serious adverse psychological effects of abuse
Frequency/severity of exploitation of person/property	No exploitation, or exploitation with little, if any, impact on the client's health, safety, or well-being	A pattern of ongoing exploitation, which, if unchecked, could threaten the health, safety, or well-being of the client	Any exploitation that threatens the health, safety, or well-being of the client, or deprives the victim of the necessities of life; any systematic misuse of client's resources (e.g., fraud/forgery)
Severity of neglect	None; isolated, explainable incident, or neglect with little risk to the client	Deprivation of adequate supervision of basic needs (e.g., medical care, food, shelter), which if unchecked, will endanger the health and well-being of the client	Client requires immediate intervention (e.g., medical treatment, placement, emergency services); client at risk of death or serious harm for lack of adequate supervision or care

Quality/consistency of care	Client/caregiver is well informed, responsible, and provides the degree of care required	Client/caregiver provides care, but knowledge, skills, and abilities or degree of responsibility are problematic and may contribute to risk	Client is at risk due to irresponsibility or lack of knowledge, skills, and abilities of caregiving of self/caregiver; client lives alone and has diminished mental and/or physical capacity
Previous history of violence, abuse, neglect, or exploitation	No known history of violence, abuse, neglect, or exploitation	Any previous informal or formal report (e.g., law enforcement, medical) of violence, abuse, neglect, or exploitation	Ongoing history or pattern of increasing frequency of violence, abuse, neglect, or exploitation; any previous report that led to prosecution or was classified as confirmed or indicated

Perpetrator

Access to the client	Never or rarely alone with client; client has frequent, regular contact with others in or out of the household	Unpredictable presence of others in the home; limited opportunity to be alone with the client; despite allegations, uncertainty whether others will deny access to the client	Complete, unrestricted access to the client
Situational stress/response to home crises (e.g., the investigation, recent birth, death, marital difficulties, hospitalization, caregiving responsibilities, unemployment, financial problems)	Realistically adapts and adjusts to situational stress/life crises	Difficult, prolonged, inappropriate or unrealistic adjustment to situational stresses/life crises (e.g., frustration, fatigue, depression, anger)	Gross overreaction or highly inappropriate reaction to stress/life crises (e.g., severe depression, hopelessness, violation of societal norms); caregiver has chronic fatigue
Physical health	Good health or minimal but controlled or compensated physical difficulties	Physical disability and/or episodic physical difficulties; may be in poor health or have a poorly compensated or controlled chronic illness	Severe and functionally limiting physical disability; chronic or uncontrolled disease; recent, rapid deterioration of physical health

APPENDIX—*continued*

	1 = No risk/low risk	2 = Intermediate risk	3 = High risk
Mental/emotional health/control	None or minimal but controlled mental or emotional difficulties; responsive to client; realistic expectations of the client; can plan to correct problem	Periodic mental/emotional difficulties or problems of control; poor reasoning abilities; immature, dependent, or has unrealistic expectations; somewhat unresponsive to the client; periodic episodes of alcohol/substance abuse; parasitic/opportunistic behavior	Severe and functionally limiting mental disability; history of chronic or uncontrolled mental disease; desire to harm the client; overly concerned with client's "bad" behavior; bizarre or violent behavior; suicidal; unresponsive to the client; asks to be relieved; threatens client with hospitalization; recent rapid deterioration of mental/emotional health/control
Perpetrator/victim dynamics contributing to risk	Normal relationship; no apparent fear or reluctance to discuss allegation; no apparent special problems	Client makes excuses for or desires to protect the perpetrator because of blood relationship; concern over consequences, guilt, shame, or low self-esteem; victim guarded or reluctant to discuss allegations	Client fears or has irrational desire to protect the perpetrator; any bond that causes victim or caregiver (if not perpetrator) to tolerate abuse, neglect, and exploitation (e.g., victim or caregiver emotionally dependent or obsessed with perpetrator)

Cooperation with investigation	Aware of the problem; cooperates to resolve problems and to protect client	Minimal cooperation, with constant encouragement/support	Despite evidence, does not believe a problem exists; refuses to cooperate
Financial resources/dependence on the client	Financially dependent of, or not wholly dependent on, the client for income	Feels obliged to care for the client by financial necessity or blood relationship; victim or caregiver provides partial or supplementary support; some indication of parasitic/opportunistic behavior	Perpetrator is financially dependent on victim; history of parasitic/opportunistic behavior
Substance abuse/other special problems	No apparent special problems	Episodic substance/alcohol abuse or other special problems	Chronic substance abuse/alcoholism or special problems

Reproduced with permission from Illinois Department of Aging, Springfield.

III

Intervention

8

Documentation

Dorrie E. Rosenblatt

It is often a challenge to convince health care and mental health professionals that documentation is anything other than a dirty word. Most professionals recognize the necessity of documentation as a form of protection against lawsuits. However, documentation is also an extremely vital part of providing care. This chapter outlines the benefits of documentation and suggests models for documenting elder mistreatment.

WHY DOCUMENT?

Implicit in the concept of documentation is a process of gathering information to document. To document properly it is necessary to work through the processes of screening, assessment, and planning. Thus, the documentation process is crucial to current attempts to address the problem. Documentation is also essential to future attempts to track the clinical course and assess the value of interventions. Documentation, therefore, has value at both the case level and the policy level. Good documentation of what is effective, or of gaps in services, can serve as a basis for requests for funding to improve services. Finally, documentation is necessary for legal reasons. The fact that the abuse will be documented can often serve as a deterrent to an abuser. However, it may be necessary for Adult Protective Services (APS) to initiate legal intervention. This means that the documentation must stand up to legal scrutiny, as it must if it is used as defense against lawsuits.

WHO SHOULD DOCUMENT?

Most state laws mandate the reporting of suspected elder abuse, and many laws specifically require members of the health care professions to report (Ehrlich & Anetzberger, 1991). Elder mistreatment may be detected in many settings, such as the home, nursing facility, doctor's office, or emergency room. Therefore, all professionals (e.g., physicians, nurses, nursing assistants, home health aides, social workers) who interact with elderly people in these settings must know how to screen, document, and report.

Good documentation is a time-consuming process, and the time available to most health care providers is limited. Some professionals are concerned that if they engage in extensive investigation and documentation, it will undermine the anonymity of the report guaranteed by many state laws. This and other concerns that form a barrier to reporting are examined in Chapter 3. Some professionals may feel that the mandate to report is simply that and that they can fulfill their obligations by placing a telephone call to APS because APS is charged with the responsibilities of dealing with elder abuse. The responsibilities of APS include the following:

1. Determining whether enough evidence is contained in a report to warrant an investigation. Therefore, the reporter should ensure that adequate information is contained in the report.
2. Determining whether abuse or neglect has actually occurred.
3. Assessing the older person's ability to make decisions about his or her care.
4. Determining what services are needed to stabilize the situation.

APS agencies have been pressured because reports of suspected abuse have increased while federal, state, and local resources have lagged. One result has been a shift of the focus of APS agency personnel away from assessment and service provision to fact-finding, documentation, and intake (American Public Welfare Association [APWA], 1987). Another result is that social workers are being asked to assess many areas in which they have received little training, such as client competence, functional status, and illness burden. The paramount goals for both health care professionals and APS staff are to detect elder mistreatment and to ensure the safety and well-being of elderly people through interventions that provide all the needed services. Health care professionals must be a part of this process and cannot relegate it wholly to APS. Furthermore, because of their close contact with older people as clients or patients, health care professionals may be in a far better position to assess the needs of elderly people than the APS case worker. By providing APS with clear documentation of his or her professional assessment, the health care provider can increase the probability that mistreatment victims will receive all the services that are necessary for their well-being.

APS agencies substantiate only about one half of the cases reported to them as qualifying for their services (Tatara, 1993). This does not mean that these elderly people are not in need of services; it means that they do not fit the APS criteria (among these criteria is the oft-used "vulnerability") for receiving services. In this case the problem is usually referred back to the abuse reporter, which is often a frustrating experience for the reporter. This frustration may be lessened if assessment and planning have been completed prior to referral, and if both are well documented and available as a backup if APS cannot intervene.

STRUCTURES OF DOCUMENTATION

Documentation is facilitated when fact-finding has been organized through the use of assessment tools. Screening for elder mistreatment is examined in other chapters in this book, but it is relevant to reemphasize the value of screening and assessment tools in caring for older adults. Geriatric care has traditionally been both problem oriented and interdisciplinary. The approach to this type of care has been to screen for typical geriatric problems, assess needs, and provide coordinated care from all appropriate disciplines. To aid in screening, professionals involved in the care of elderly people developed screening tools and assessment instruments, such as the Mini-Mental State Examination (MMSE), used to assess cognitive function (Folstein, Folstein, & McHugh, 1975); the Geriatric Depression Scale (GDS), used to assess affective function (Yesavage et al., 1983); and the Activities of Daily Living (ADL) (Katz, Downs, Cash, & Grotz, 1970) and Instrumental Activities of Daily Living (IADL) (Lawton & Brody, 1969) indices, used to measure functional status (see Appendix).

Use of these standardized forms ensures adequate screening so that no common problems are excluded. The forms further ensure an assessment of what is needed to solve the problems that are uncovered, facilitates the development of a care plan, and provides a format in which to document the problem. Using standardized forms for documentation simplifies communication between all disciplines needed to provide comprehensive, coordinated care for older people.

In spite of the emphasis on the use of tools and the fact that elder mistreatment is a common geriatric problem, no universally accepted, standardized protocols exist for screening for or assessing elder mistreatment. This is in part because of the complexity of the problem. This complexity is multifactorial. Although all 50 states have passed elder abuse legislation and almost all mandate reporting of suspected abuse, definitions of elder abuse differ from state to state (Benton & Marshall, 1991). Definitions also differ among the professions of medicine, nursing, social work, and law enforcement, all of which deal with elder abuse (Valentine & Cash, 1986). These differing definitions of abuse have presented an obstacle to cooperative progress in the field. The paucity of research on elder abuse means that the understanding of risk factors for elder mistreatment is limited. This, in turn, has hampered the development of screening tools because it is not clear which markers must be screened. Finally, elder abuse encompasses multiple forms of mistreatment, which often overlap and which can be difficult to distinguish from common problems associated with aging. This complexity led to the conclusion that the use of instruments alone cannot provide an adequate assessment of elder mistreatment (Fulmer & O'Malley, 1987). Instruments do, however, provide a starting point and, as noted earlier, groundwork for good documentation.

Ashley and Fulmer (1988) reviewed some of the protocols published between 1980 and 1990, which include those protocols from Tomita (1982), Johnson (1981), Rathbone-McCuan and Voyles (1982), Ferguson and Beck (1983), and Fulmer and Wetle (1986). Hwalek and Sengstock (1986) and Costa (1993) also published screening protocols. The structure of these protocols varies from checklists to structured interviews. They take varying amounts of time and require varying amounts of skill on the part of the user. An APWA report (1987) stated that 14 APS agencies had developed assessment protocols for use by APS case managers. These instruments vary from 1 to 24 pages in length, and range from screening to assessment. None of these instruments has undergone validation studies, and none has been published in journals that are readily available to health care providers. The protocols developed by individual institutions, usually hospital emergency rooms, are not easily accessible to staff in other institutions. Several professional associations published guidelines for their members that suggest screening questions, and the American Medical Association (AMA) made specific suggestions about documentation (AMA, 1992), but these suggestions are not in the form of protocols. Because readers may be working in a variety of settings, it is impossible to recommend a particular tool. Therefore, the following section summarizes the recommendations from all these instruments on the information that must be collected and documented.

HOW TO DOCUMENT

Because a document can serve as both a care plan and a legal document, it is important to remember several points (Hwalek, 1989):

- Information should be well organized (hence the usefulness of a standard format) and systematically presented.
- The document should be legible and should not contain alterations of the text.
- The document should be clear, explicit, and comprehensive in content. Data selected for inclusion in the document should include pertinent negative and positive findings. For example, it is just as important to report that the patient or client has no history of alcohol abuse or depression (negative finding) as it is to report that he or she is frail because of arthritis and poor vision (positive finding).
- Facts should be reported objectively and behaviors described rather than interpreted. For example, it is better to report "the patient was crying" than to report "the patient was sad" because the patient may be crying as a result of rage, frustration, or an emotion other than sadness.
- It is useful to document the patient's or client's own words.
- It is important to document all the sources of information included in the report.
- For a document to withstand legal scrutiny, it must contain no changes, omissions, or time gaps.
- The document must show that the care plan is consistent with the assessment.
- The document must never reflect unprofessional statements, negligence, malpractice, failure to treat, or hostility toward the patient or client or the caregiver.
- The information in the document is confidential and to be shared only with individuals who have an appropriate role in meeting care needs.

Demographic Data

The collection of demographic data is simple and straightforward. The data include name, address, telephone number, sex, marital status, living situation, and insurance status.

Psychosocial Data

Cognitive status can be assessed and documented as an MMSE score, affective status can be recorded using the GDS, and functional status can be presented using the ADL and IADL formats. Use of these instruments should be a standard part of the care of any geriatric patient or client. Financial status must be documented, as must the fact that the patient or client has been questioned about possible exploitation or financial abuse. The health care professional should also ask questions about the patient's or client's living situation and his or her perception of the quality of the interactions with family (e.g., spouse, children) and document both questions and answers. The patient's or client's support system and dependency needs must be recorded, and it can be very useful to contrast the patient's or client's assessment of these needs with that of the caregiver. It is also important to investigate and document any history of mistreatment.

Caregiver Data

Frail elderly people at risk for mistreatment frequently are dependent on others for care, although they may also provide care for other dependent family members. Documentation on the caregivers or dependents should include name; age; sex; living situation (with or not with the patient or client); cognitive, functional, and affective status; financial status; history of psychiatric illness or substance abuse; and history of child or spouse abuse. Caregiver stress can be assessed and documented using caregiver stress scales (Kosberg & Cairl, 1986). It is also important to assess and document the caregiver's knowledge of the elderly person's care needs.

Medical History

It is not within the scope of this chapter to review medical history taking, which should be familiar to everyone in the health care professions. People in other professions can use a protocol such as the Health Status Questionnaire (Ware, Sherbourne, & Davies, 1992) to assess the medical burden. It is important to cull from and document items in the medical history that are suggestive of problematic care. These items are outlined in Table 8.1.

Patient/Client Observation

Assessments are routinely made based on patient or client appearance and behavior, but when a question of elder mistreatment arises, it is important to document observations that suggest that the patient or client is either at risk for mistreatment or is being mistreated. Table 8.2 lists physical findings that are suggestive of a problem and that should be documented, if present.

Table 8.3 lists observations of mood that are suggestive of possible problems and should, therefore, be documented. As noted by Hwalek

Table 8.1.   Items in a medical history that may suggest mistreatment

Doctor hopping

Missed doctor appointments

Repeated hospital admissions

Failure to respond to obvious disease

Duplicated medications

Under- or overmedication

Unexplained injuries

Previous similar injuries or history of similar injuries

Table 8.2. Physical observations that may suggest mistreatment

Cachexia (physical wasting and malnutrition)

Poor hygiene

Inappropriate dress

Mobility impairment

Sensory impairment

Absence of assistive devices (e.g., glasses, hearing aid, cane or walker)

Communication impairment (e.g., language barrier, sensory impairment, cognitive impairment)

Debilitation

(1989), both pertinent positive and negative observations should be documented.

Professionals whose role includes conducting a physical examination should examine the patient or client in a neutral setting; that is, without the caregiver's presence. The examination must be conducted with the patient or client fully undressed in order to improve the chances of finding signs of physical abuse (Table 8.4) or neglect (Table 8.5). When any of the visible markers listed in Tables 8.4 and 8.5 is present, the marker should be documented. An outline drawing of the front and back of the body on which findings can be noted (Figure 8.1) is helpful, particularly if a camera is not available. Photographic documentation can supplement written documentation and can serve as valuable evidence. In most states patient or client consent is required prior to taking photographs or x-rays. Photographs should be

Table 8.3. Behavioral observations that may suggest mistreatment

Depression

Agitation

Fearfulness

Cringing

Withdrawal

Confusion

Unresponsiveness

Inappropriate behavior

Aggressiveness

Obsession

Paranoia

Hallucinations

Suicidal ideation

Quality of interactions with caregiver

Table 8.4. Physical findings that may suggest abuse

Wounds

Lacerations

Burns

Bruises

Rope burns

Scalp hematomas from hair pulling

Fractures

Scars

Signs of sexual abuse, such as thigh bruising, genital itching and bleeding, and sexually transmitted disease

---

taken with color film using a color standard (familiar objects in primary [red, blue, and yellow] colors), before treatment if possible. Photographs should include full body shots, facial shots, and close-up shots of the injury. A ruler, coin, or other size standard should be included in the photograph to indicate the size of the injury. Signs of neglect also can be documented photographically. The AMA suggests that the photographs be marked with the patient's or client's name, the date, time of day, location of injury, and the name of the photographer and others present (AMA, 1992).

Laboratory Data

Laboratory data and x-rays may also form part of the documentation of abuse or neglect. Tests that may be useful are listed in Table 8.6. Patient or client consent is necessary in order to conduct these tests and should be documented along with the test results. If necessary, consent can be obtained from a surrogate at a later time.

Environment

Professionals who have the opportunity to make a home visit should be aware of environmental markers suggestive of mistreatment. Mark-

Table 8.5. Physical findings that may suggest neglect

Poor hygiene

Rashes

Parasite infestation

Edema

Bedsores

Contractures

Signs of untreated urinary or fecal incontinence

Fecal impaction

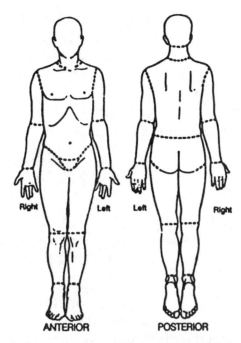

Figure 8.1. Template for notation of physical injury findings.

ers are listed in Table 8.7. Documentation of such findings provides strong support for making a case for elder mistreatment.

Assessment and Plan

Once data have been collected and organized, the health care professional must document his or her conclusions. The summary should contain one's best interpretation of the findings (e.g., probable physical neglect), and the evidence that supports the findings (e.g., poor

Table 8.6. Laboratory tests to support a diagnosis of mistreatment

Blood urea nitrogen (BUN), electrolytes, creatinine, urine analysis (used to measure hydration status)

Metabolic screen (used to detect nutritional or endocrine abnormalities)

Complete blood count and coagulation studies (used to detect easy bruising)

Drug levels (used to detect under- or overmedication)

Toxicology screen (used to detect substance abuse or use of unreported medications)

Radiologic screening (used to detect old or new fractures)

Cultures, wet mount, VDRL (Venereal Disease Research Laboratory of the U.S. Public Health Service flocculation test) (used to detect sexual abuse)

Table 8.7. Environmental markers that suggest elder mistreatment

Crowding

Dirt

Vermin

Broken locks or windows

Absence of food

Absence of medications or multiple medications

Lack of utilities

Loss of property

Poor or limited access

hygiene, poor nutrition, contractures). The document should also outline the care plan. If the care plan consists simply of reporting to the police or to APS, this should be documented, along with the name of the person to whom the report was made. If working under supervision, the professional should document that the case was discussed with his or her supervisor. If a possibility exists that the case will ultimately require legal intervention, the document should specify that the findings were made in "the regular course of business" and that a standardized procedure was followed.

If the professional will be providing ongoing care for the patient or client, the problem list outlining the concerns identified during the assessment which formed the basis for the document can provide the basis of the care plan. Documenting the care that is planned in order to address each of the patient's needs ensures that the care provided is comprehensive. Because documentation often serves as the basis for communication between the numerous agencies that may be involved in caring for a mistreated elderly person, clarity in documenting the plan can save time and prevent duplication of efforts.

Documentation should be thorough, not only at initial assessment, but also as care continues to be provided for the older person. Telephone calls, person-to-person encounters, and correspondence received by the professional should be incorporated into the document. The goal of thorough documentation is that anyone reviewing the documentation at any time, perhaps even several years after the alleged abuse occurred, can gain a clear understanding of what happened, how pertinent data were interpreted, what interventions were initiated over what time period and why, and of the outcome. Documentation should always be written as if it were being prepared for a lawyer's scrutiny. Detailed documentation of this caliber also enhances care provision.

CONCLUSION

Documentation is crucial to patient or client care. The goal of screening for elder mistreatment is to identify problems and ensure the safety and well-being of elderly people. Screening usually involves a complex assessment of psychosocial and physical problems and the combined efforts of a team of professionals from several disciplines. The use of standardized documentation procedures ensures that nothing is missed during the assessment process and helps the care provider to formulate a care plan. Documentation forms the basis of communication between disciplines and standardized documentation facilitates this communication. Good documentation of problems is essential for obtaining the services needed to carry out the care plan. On a policy level, thorough documentation of unmet needs can serve as the basis for funding requests. Documentation supports any legal interventions that may be needed to address a case of elder mistreatment. Indeed, the proof of the case is in the documentation. Good documentation protects the professional from legal problems that may arise from his or her intervention in a case of possible elder mistreatment, and may eventually result in an end to the abuse of the older person in question. Thus, although documentation may appear to take time from patient care and other preferred activities, good, clear, comprehensive documentation is the basis of good patient care. It will probably save time in the long run, and will result in a better outcome both for the older person and for the health care professional.

REFERENCES

American Medical Association. (1992). *Diagnostic and treatment guideline on elder abuse and neglect*. Chicago: Author.

American Public Welfare Association. (1987, June). *State strategies for assessing risk in elder abuse programs*. Washington, DC: Author.

Ashley, J., & Fulmer, T.T. (1988). No simple way to determine elder abuse. *Geriatric Nursing, 9*, 286–288.

Benton, D., & Marshall, C. (1991). Elder abuse. *Clinics in Geriatric Medicine, 7*, 831–845.

Costa, A.J. (1993). Elder abuse. *Primary Care, 20*, 375–389.

Ehrlich, P., & Anetzberger, G. (1991). Survey of state public health departments on procedures for reporting elder abuse. *Public Health Reports, 106*, 151–154.

Ferguson, D., & Beck, C. (1983). H.A.L.F.: A tool to assess elder abuse within the family. *Geriatric Nursing, 4*, 301–304.

Folstein, M.F., Folstein, S.E., & McHugh, P.R. (1975). Mini-Mental State: A practical method for grading the cognitive state of patients for the clinician. *Journal of Psychiatric Research, 12*, 196–197.

Fulmer, T.T., & O'Malley, T.A. (1987). The difficulty of defining abuse and neglect. In T.T. Fulmer & T.A. O'Malley (Eds.), *Inadequate care of the elderly* (pp. 13–24). New York: Springer Publishing.

Fulmer, T., & Wetle, T. (1986, May). Elder abuse screening and intervention. *Nurse Practitioner, 33–38.*

Hwalek, M.A. (1989). Proper documentation: A key topic in training programs for elder abuse workers. *Journal of Elder Abuse & Neglect, 1,* 17–30.

Hwalek, M.A., & Sengstock, M.C. (1986). Assessing the probability of abuse of the elderly: Toward development of a clinical screening instrument. *Journal of Applied Gerontology, 5,* 153–173.

Johnson, T.F. (1991). Elder mistreatment identification instruments: Finding common ground. In T.F. Johnson (Ed.), *Elder mistreatment: Deciding who is at risk* (pp. 85–115). Westport, CT: Greenwood Press.

Katz, S., Downs, T.D., Cash, H.R., & Grotz, R.C. (1970). Progress in the development of the index of ADL. *Gerontologist, 1,* 20–30.

Kosberg, J.I., & Cairl, R. (1986). The cost of care index: A case management tool for screening informal care providers. *Gerontologist, 26,* 273–278.

Lawton, M.P., & Brody, E.M. (1969). Assessment of older people: Self-monitoring and instrumental activities of daily living. *Gerontologist, 9,* 179–186.

Rathbone-McCuan, E., & Voyles, B. (1982). Case detection of abused elderly parents. *American Journal of Psychiatry, 139,* 189–192.

Tatara, T. (1993). Understanding the nature and scope of domestic elder abuse with the use of state aggregate data: Summaries of the key findings of a national survey of state APS and aging agencies. *Journal of Elder Abuse & Neglect, 5,* 35–57.

Tomita, S.K. (1982). Detection and treatment of elderly abuse and neglect: A protocol for health care professionals. *Physical & Occupational Therapy in Geriatrics, 2,* 37–51.

Valentine, D., & Cash, T. (1986). A definitional discussion of elder maltreatment. *Journal of Gerontological Social Work, 9,* 17–28.

Ware, J.E., Sherbourne, C.D., & Davies, A.R. (1992). Developing and testing the MOS 20-Item Short-Form Health Survey: A general population application. In J.E. Ware & T.A. O'Malley (Eds.), *Measuring functioning and wellbeing* (pp. 277–290). Durham, NC: Duke University Press.

Yesavage, J.A., Brink, T.L., Rose, T.L., Lum, O., Huang, V., Adey, M., & Leirer, V.O. (1983). Development and validation of a geriatric screening scale: A preliminary report. *Journal of Psychiatric Research, 17,* 37–49.

APPENDIX
Mini-mental state inpatient consultation form

Maximum score	Score	
		Orientation
5	—	Ask the patient or client what is the (year) (season) (date) (day) (month)?
5	—	Ask the patient or client where are we (state) (county) (town) (hospital) (floor)?
		Registration
3	—	Name three objects (1 second to name each). Then ask the patient or client to name all three. Give one point for each correct answer. Then repeat the objects until the patient or client learns all three.
		Trials
		Count trials and record.
		Attention and calculation
5	—	Serial 7s. Give one point for each correct answer. Stop after five answers. Alternatively, ask patient or client to spell "world" backwards.
		Recall
3	—	Ask the patient or client to repeat the three objects from "Registration." Give one point for each correct answer.
		Language
9	—	Hold up a pencil and then a watch. Ask the patient or client to name each (2 points). Ask the patient or client to repeat the following: No ifs, ands, or buts (1 point). Ask the patient or client to follow a three-stage command: "Take a paper in your right hand, fold it in half, and put it on the floor" (3 points). Ask the patient or client to read and obey the following: Close your eyes (1 point). Ask the patient or client to write a sentence (1 point). Ask the patient or client to copy the following design (1 point).

Total score _____

Assess level of consciousness
along a continuum (circle one)   Alert   Drowsy   Stupor   Coma

Geriatric depression scale

Choose the answer that best reflects how you felt this past week. (For all entries marked by *, the appropriate "nondepressed" answer is yes; all other answers are no. The total number of depressed answers is patient or client score. Normal, 5 ± 4; mildly depressed, 15 ± 6; very depressed, 23 ± 5.)

*1.	Are you basically satisfied with your life?	Yes	No
2.	Have you dropped many of your activities and interests?	Yes	No
3.	Do you feel that your life is empty?	Yes	No
4.	Do you often get bored?	Yes	No
*5.	Are you hopeful about the future?	Yes	No
6.	Are you bothered by thoughts you cannot get out of your head?	Yes	No
*7.	Are you in good spirits most of the time?	Yes	No
8.	Are you afraid that something bad is going to happen to you?	Yes	No
*9.	Do you feel happy most of the time?	Yes	No
10.	Do you often feel helpless?	Yes	No
11.	Do you often get restless and fidgety?	Yes	No
12.	Do you prefer to stay at home, rather than going out and doing new things?	Yes	No
13.	Do you frequently worry about the future?	Yes	No
14.	Do you feel you have more problems with memory than most?	Yes	No
*15.	Do you think it is wonderful to be alive now?	Yes	No
16.	Do you often feel downhearted and blue?	Yes	No
17.	Do you feel pretty worthless the way you are now?	Yes	No
18.	Do you worry a lot about the past?	Yes	No
*19.	Do you find life very exciting?	Yes	No
20.	Is it hard for you to get started on new projects?	Yes	No
*21.	Do you feel full of energy?	Yes	No
22.	Do you feel that your situation is hopeless?	Yes	No
23.	Do you think that most people are better off than you are?	Yes	No
24.	Do you frequently get upset over little things?	Yes	No
25.	Do you frequently feel like crying?	Yes	No
26.	Do you have trouble concentrating?	Yes	No
*27.	Do you enjoy getting up in the morning?	Yes	No
28.	Do you prefer to avoid social gatherings?	Yes	No
*29.	Is it easy for you to make decisions?	Yes	No
*30.	Is your mind as clear as it used to be?	Yes	No

Score _____

Adapted with permission from *Journal of Psychiatric Research, 17,* J. Yesavage et al. Development and validation of a geriatric screening scale: A preliminary report, 1983, Elsevier Science Ltd., Pergamon Imprint, Oxford, England.

Basic activities of daily living

	Independent	
1. Bathing (sponge bath, tub bath, or shower) Patient or client receives either no assistance or assistance in bathing only one part of body.	Yes	No
2. Dressing Patient or client retrieves clothes and dresses without any assistance except for tying shoes.	Yes	No
3. Toileting Patient or client goes to toilet room, uses toilet, arranges clothes, and returns without any assistance (may use cane or walker for support and may use bedpan/urinal at night).	Yes	No
4. Transferring Patient or client moves in and out of bed and chair without assistance (may use cane or walker).	Yes	No
5. Continence Patient or client self-controls bowel and bladder completely (without occasional "accidents").	Yes	No
6. Feeding Patient or client feeds self without assistance (except for help with cutting meat or buttering bread).	Yes	No

Score[a] _____

Adapted with permission from THE GERONTOLOGIST, 1, 20–30, 1970. Copyright © The Gerontological Society of America.
[a]Number of "yes" answers, out of possible six.

Instrumental activities of daily living scale

Ability to use telephone	
1. Operates telephone on own initiative; looks up and dials numbers	1
2. Dials a few well-known numbers	1
3. Answers telephone, but does not dial	1
4. Does not use telephone at all	0
Shopping	
1. Takes care of all shopping needs independently	1
2. Shops independently for small purchases	0
3. Needs to be accompanied on any shopping trip	0
4. Completely unable to shop	0
Food preparation	
1. Plans, prepares, and serves adequate meals independently	1
2. Prepares adequate meals if supplied with ingredients	0
3. Heats, serves, and prepares meals, or prepares meals, but does not maintain adequate diet	0
4. Needs to have meals prepared and served	0
Housekeeping	
1. Maintains house alone or with occasional assistance (e.g., heavy work, domestic help)	1
2. Performs light daily tasks such as dishwashing and bed making	1
3. Performs light daily tasks, but cannot maintain acceptable level of cleanliness	1
4. Needs help with all home maintenance tasks	1
5. Does not participate in any housekeeping tasks	0
Laundry	
1. Does personal laundry completely	1
2. Launders small items, rinses stockings, and so on	1
3. All laundry must be done by others	0
Mode of transportation	
1. Travels independently on public transportation or drives own car	1
2. Arranges own travel via taxicab, but does not otherwise use public transportation	1
3. Travels on public transportation when accompanied by another person	1
4. Travel limited to taxicab or automobile with assistance of another person	0
5. Does not travel at all	0
Responsibility for own medications	
1. Is responsible for taking medication in correct doses at correct time	1
2. Takes responsibility if medication is prepared in advance in separate doses	0
3. Is not capable of dispensing own medication	0

Ability to handle finances
1. Manages financial matters independently (budgets, writes checks, pays rent and bills, goes to bank), collects and keeps track of income   1
2. Manages day-to-day purchases, but needs help with banking and major purchases   1
3. Incapable of handling money   0

Score (out of possible 8)   _____

Adapted with permission from THE GERONTOLOGIST, 9, 179–186, 1969. Copyright © The Gerontological Society of America.

9

Hospital Response to Elder Abuse: The Adult Protective Team

Sue M. Parkins

Rosie arrived in the emergency department of St. Vincent Medical Center (Toledo, Ohio), unresponsive except to deep pain and dehydrated. Her clothing was soiled, her hygiene was poor, and her body was riddled with early pressure sores (bedsores). She had a 6-cm-wide circular bruise on her chest over the sternum (breastbone), multiple bruises of different ages over her lower legs, bruises and superficial skin tears on her arms, and bruising on the tops and soles of her feet (Figures 9.1 and 9.2).

Rosie was brought to St. Vincent by ambulance. Following behind in a car was Rosie's niece and her niece's son, a 20-year-old man with mental retardation, with whom Rosie lived. After supplying a minimum of information to the nurse, they left Rosie in the emergency department. Rosie was referred to the on-call internist.

Rosie was incapable of verbal communication when admitted, but after less than 24 hours of hydration she was alert and talkative, although disoriented. She had Alzheimer's disease, and was unable to provide a coherent medical history. Emergency room personnel were concerned about the number and location of the bruises and requested that photographs be taken. The staff found it worrisome that a nonambulatory person had a bruise on the center of her chest and on both the tops and soles of her feet. They felt that it was unlikely that Rosie could have incurred the bruises on her chest without falling on a round object while ambulating. The staff thought that it was possible that she could have dropped something on both feet, which would account for the bruises on the tops of her feet, but they could not find a plausible explanation for the bruises on the soles of her feet. The assumption was made that she had been struck with a blunt object. Perineal bruising was discovered when Rosie was bathed by the staff. She had suffered trauma to the labia and vagina, but any traces of seminal fluid had been washed away, making it impossible for the laboratory to identify the abuser. A confidential source subsequently informed the nurses that other family members were concerned that Rosie's great nephew was sexually abusing her; however, little direct evidence was found.

Rosie arrived at St. Vincent $2\frac{1}{2}$ months prior to the institution of Medicare Diagnostic-Related Groups (DRGs), which cap the reimbursement to the health care provider based on the diagnosis rather than on the actual cost of the service provided. Rosie was in the hospital 4 months. For the final 45 days of hospitalization, DRGs were in effect, and consequently, the Medical Center was not reimbursed for that portion of her stay. Rosie's husband had died less than 2 years earlier, leaving her the house, a modest monthly pension, and $150,000. The pension and Social Security checks were directly deposited in the bank. Rosie's niece, as legal guardian and heir, had unrestricted access to her funds. The $150,000 was missing. During Rosie's hospitalization, numerous items, including men's and women's clothing and household items, were charged to Rosie's credit card.

When Rosie was well enough to be discharged, the staff became concerned—where would Rosie go? Placement with her niece and great nephew was not an option. She could not be

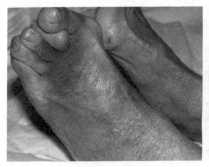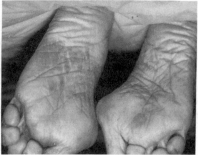

Figure 9.1. Bruises on the tops and soles of Rosie's feet are indicators of abuse because of the unusual distribution of the bruises. Bruises usually form on the tops and the soles of the feet from accidental injury, and usually only one foot is injured. Because Rosie was nonambulatory, the team felt it unlikely that she could have stepped on an object accidentally or could have had an object fall on her feet.

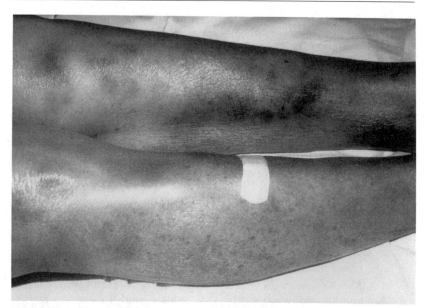

Figure 9.2. Rosie presented with bruises of various ages over much of her body, most notably on her shins. This "aging" of bruises is characteristic of elder abuse.

returned to the environment in which she had become dehydrated, malnourished, filthy, bruised, and possibly sexually assaulted. Rosie's niece, recipient of Rosie's pension and Social Security income, refused placement outside of her home. In fact, Rosie's niece and great nephew made attempts to remove Rosie from the hospital without authorization and discharge orders.

The state Adult Protective Service (APS) was notified of the suspected abuse. Attempts were made to stop direct deposit of the pension funds and Social Security checks, but many obstacles were encountered. As Rosie's legal guardian, her niece was the only person who had the authority to direct the funds. In an attempt to facilitate placement, the Adult Protective Team contacted the bank, the Social Security Administration, the local police, and the FBI, without clear resolution. St. Vincent Medical Center wrote off in excess of $40,000 of Rosie's hospital charges. Ultimately, the Medical Center hired an attorney to contest the guardianship by alleging misuse of funds. A neutral guardian was subsequently appointed by the court. Rosie's funds were then available to secure safe placement and to ensure ongoing care.

During the course of her hospitalization, Rosie provided challenges to many disciplines. At intake, the emergency department nurses and doctor, social services, and biomedical communication department (photographer) became involved. After admission, floor nurses, social services, enterostomal therapists (skin care specialists), nutrition services, and legal services became involved. When it became apparent that her family was attempt-

ing to remove her from the hospital illegally, the security department became involved. Among other actions taken, Rosie's room
was changed every 2–4 days.

Recognizing its complexity, the social worker involved with the
case felt that it would be advantageous to "staff" (assign personnel to provide care to Rosie) Rosie. The personnel who
staffed Rosie formed a loose multidisciplinary team that met to
discuss the various issues surrounding Rosie's care. These discussions helped resolve Rosie's case: Rosie was placed in a
long-term care facility, and the court appointed a guardian to
administer Rosie's estate.

ESTABLISHING THE ADULT PROTECTIVE TEAM

Because the team approach worked so well in Rosie's case, a permanent Adult Protective Team was developed using the St. Vincent Child
Protection Team as a model.

The Adult Protective Team developed the following mission statement in order to delineate its role in patient care:

> It will be the policy of St. Vincent Medical Center in compliance with
> the Ohio Revised Code, Section 5101.60 through 5101.71, to address
> the needs of those adults sixty years of age and older (or dependent
> or incapacitated adults eighteen years or older) who are unable to
> protect themselves from abuse, neglect and/or exploitation and who
> require protective intervention and/or services.

This mission statement is reflected in the premise and purpose of the
Adult Protective Team. The St. Vincent Medical Center Adult Protective Team is designated to respond to the complex problems facing
victims of adult abuse, neglect, and/or exploitation. The team collab-
orates with the attending physician in evaluating the patient's physical condition, investigating any injury, and assessing the patient's
strengths and deficiencies to determine what action the patient can
take on his or her own behalf. The team provides a supportive environment in which the patient can make decisions, and it makes appropriate referrals to available community resources. Figures 9.3–9.5
provide an overview of the team's reporting relationships, its reporting procedure, and its liasons with the community.

In order to fulfill the mission statement and to carry out its purpose,
the team outlined its goals as follows:

1. To develop multidisciplinary tools for systematic assessment,
   planning, and intervention
2. To describe the role of the individual health care provider as it
   relates to adult abuse
3. To develop hospital guidelines that address the medicolegal standards of protective services for victims of adult abuse
4. To develop specific hospital guidelines governing photography
   and documentation

5. To develop and coordinate posthospital evaluations and care
6. To strengthen relationships with community agencies and to identify the agencies most willing to provide emergency services
7. To become involved in local and national networking, statistics collection, and continuing public and professional education

The composition of the team was established and comprised a medical consultant (director of the team); a social worker (coordinator of the team); and representatives from each of the following disciplines: enterostomal therapy, legal services, nutrition services (clinical dietitian), the visiting nurse service, the credit department, medical outpatient services (head nurse), pastoral care (nun or chaplain), security, a nurse from the emergency/trauma department, a nurse from radiology, a nurse from the medical surgical unit, risk management, gerontological nursing (clinician), audiovisual services (manager), the hospital pharmacy, and other social workers and registered nurses ad hoc.

The expense to the hospital for the team is minimal. All team members perform their team-related functions during the course of the regular workday and are not financially compensated for their participation. The only deviation is attendance at the weekly or biweekly team meetings, if staffing is necessary, and an occasional in-service training session.

Each member of this multidisciplinary team reports to a departmental or division supervisor. If conflicts arise between a team member and a patient and his or her family, an attending physician, a co-worker, or an outside agency, a meeting of the complainant and

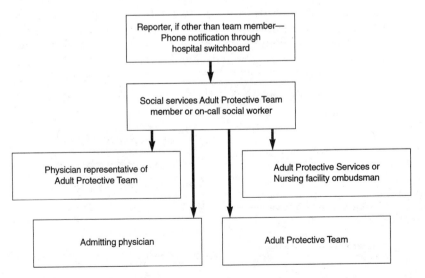

Figure 9.3. Adult Protective Team reporting procedure.

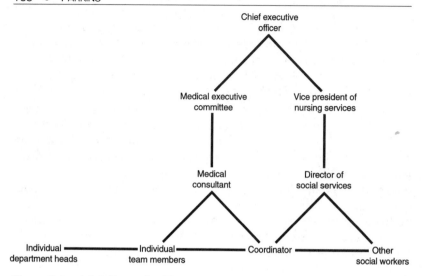

Figure 9.4. Adult Protective Team reporting relationships.

the identified team member, the team risk manager (an attorney or paralegal), the team physician, and, usually, the team coordinator should be arranged. The social services department head and/or the team member's department head may also be included. All such conflicts at St. Vincent have been resolved by clarifying the issues, identifying the team's duties and actions, defining the legal reporting responsibilities, and explaining the team's action and intent at a single meeting with the complainant.

The formation of the team was supported by St. Vincent Medical Center's administration because 1) the premise and purpose of the team was consistent with the Medical Center's mission, and 2) the cost reduction of facilitating referrals, expediting discharges, providing education, and preventing disabling conditions has been significant (the team was formed prior to the implementation of diagnostic-related groups [DRGs]). Abused elderly people are a

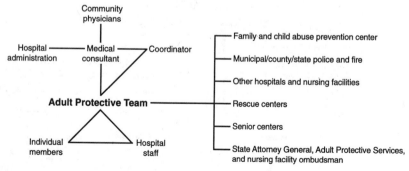

Figure 9.5. Adult Protective Team liasons with the community.

largely underinsured segment of the population. Thus, it is socially and financially responsible for hospital administrations to evaluate and treat abused elderly people in an efficient, coordinated fashion under the auspices of the Adult Protective Team.

The function of the Adult Protective Team can best be explained through detailed descriptions of each member of the team. Some case examples are included to enhance the descriptions.

Coordinator The team coordinator is most appropriately a social worker who works regularly with adults and who is frequently involved with the units (e.g., medical and orthopedic floors, emergency department) that care for the high-risk population. The coordinator is primarily responsible for compiling the agenda for the monthly meeting and for disseminating related information, such as reporting forms, intake information, and diagnosis of the treating physician. He or she collects reporting forms (see Appendix) and pertinent patient information on each case to be discussed at the weekly team meeting. The coordinator acts as a resource for social workers, nurses, and other staff in the management of their cases and makes the decision to call other members as needed on an urgent basis (i.e., in cases of imminent death or rapid discharge, there may not be time to wait for the next team meeting). In addition, the coordinator works with other team members on treatment and discharge plans, and facilitates communication. For example, if issues of probate or criminal reporting arise, the coordinator may make the appropriate contacts or may facilitate contacts between team members and probate or the police. The coordinator is expected to be familiar with both local reporting requirements and hospital policy. The coordinator ensures that documentation is in order and maintained, and monitors the need for in-service training for staff who are not team members. The total commitment of time to the team is approximately 8 hours per week.

Medical Consultant (Director) A physician acts as a consultant to the team, and attends the monthly organizational meetings and the weekly or biweekly staffing. Emergency department physicians have consulted to the team at St. Vincent; other institutions have used primary care physicians (family practitioners), internists, or geriatricians as medical consultants. The criteria for selecting a medical consultant are the physician's willingness to become involved in potentially hostile and disheartening situations, the physician's willingness to be certified competent in the identification and management of elder mistreatment, and the physician's willingness to be available for consultation 24 hours per day. A geriatrician is a particularly good choice for medical consultant because he or she is a specialist in the health care of elderly people. A family practitioner or an internist is also an appropriate choice because he or she may have the most insight into family dynamics and thus be able to identify early indications of elder abuse or neglect. Emergency department physicians work well for the following reasons:

1. The emergency department is a frequent point of entry into the health care environment for elder abuse victims. Having an Adult Protective Team physician working the emergency department helps to improve the level of awareness and the reporting expertise of the entire team.
2. Abuse or neglect cases require reporting suspected or actual abuse or neglect and the possibility of contact with the police and the court system. The emergency department physician is familiar with these representatives of the legal system because of similar responsibilities in cases of child abuse, firearms accidents, or rape.
3. The fact that many abusers are the victims' family members may create a conflict of interest for a primary care physician. He or she may have a long-standing relationship with the family, which makes it difficult to identify or accept the possibility of abuse and which may threaten his or her ongoing therapeutic relationship with other family members.
4. Court appearances can be inconvenient for a busy primary care physician. These appearances can be more easily accommodated by a physician who works specific shifts with "free" time between them.

It has been reported that elder abuse tends to be generational, which may either aid diagnosis or may more effectively mask clinical evidence and place the patient at increased risk for ongoing abuse. A physician who provides care to an entire family must maintain a high degree of clinical awareness of and sensitivity to the potential development of abusive situations within the family. Confronting abusers or self-abusers can be very threatening to the clinician, but it must be done. The team physician should contact the patient's private physician regarding his or her suspicions of elder mistreatment. The team physician should be aware that some private physicians and other health care providers and the community may consider the team effort to be "stirring up trouble" or they may feel that team members are "hysterical."

The team physician should educate the community about elder mistreatment and should be available to consult with team members, physician groups, and community associations. The total commitment of the physician's time averages less than 1 hour per week over 1 year's time.

Finally, the team physician should be diplomatic and be able to compromise as well as to recognize that many cases will have less than gratifying outcomes.

Nutritionist The nutritionist evaluates every admission to the Adult Protective Team for signs of malnutrition and dehydration and recommends the appropriate nutrition and hydration parameters for the patient.

Enterostomal Therapist An enterostomal therapist is an integral member of the clinical staff in any elder abuse case. Elder abuse victims commonly present with skin problems; many present with complications, including overwhelming infection or erosion into body cavities. The enterostomal therapist performs the initial assessment of the skin of a patient who has been referred to the team and distinguishes victims of elder mistreatment from patients who have been referred for skin care but have not been specifically referred to the Adult Protective Team.

The St. Vincent team enterostomal therapist is involved in discharge planning, instructing patients and/or caregivers in skin care needs, and facilitating the acquisition of skin care products through patients' medical insurance providers. The enterostomal therapist presents inservice training on skin care and pressure sore management and prevention to hospital nursing staff and to nursing facility staff. The therapist also documents progressive skin deterioration in recurrent admissions.

The enterostomal therapist may be the first point of contact for victims. When the enterostomal therapist identifies a potential victim of elder mistreatment the patient is staffed and, if necessary, the caregivers or professionals involved are contacted and education is offered. When the severity of skin breakdown is not acknowledged, the team files a report, and the physician (if any) involved at the time the lesion developed is notified of the team's decision to report abuse, neglect, or exploitation. Some people, even some physicians, mistakenly believe that all elderly people develop pressure sores and that these skin ulcers cannot be prevented. However, prevention is possible and should be a standard of care. Prevention requires proper nutrition and hygiene, elements frequently absent in the lives of elderly people who are victims of neglect. Prevention is also facilitated by the use of antipressure devices and other skin care products. The approach to prevention and to restoration must be aggressive. This view is not always shared by the lay and professional caregiving communities. The issues of skin care and nutrition and hydration are fraught with confusion about and inappropriate resignation to the inevitability of skin breakdown and nutritional deterioration. The Adult Protective Team at St. Vincent has been challenged by both the lay and professional communities in its refusal to accept skin ulcers and malnutrition as unavoidable. The team works aggressively to prevent and reverse the conditions and to document deterioration in recurrent admissions.

The following case provides an example of the contributions made by the team nutritionist and enterostomal therapist.

Brenda was transferred to St. Vincent Medical Center from a small community hospital in a neighboring state. She had been taken to the hospital by her elderly mother, reportedly for not having eaten Thanksgiving dinner the previous week. Brenda had a history of psychosis, but had not been in treatment for the last 3 years. She had a job, but had not worked for "a few months." In fact, Brenda laid on the couch day and night. She was 5'3" and weighed 87 pounds. She had pressure sores on her hips and buttocks and left chest. The chest wound allowed direct visualization of the ribs and intervening muscles (Figure 9.6). Brenda's mother claimed that the ulcers on Brenda's back and sacrum had developed over the few days before she took Brenda to the community hospital (Figure 9.7). Brenda responded only to irritating stimuli.

The team nutritionist was consulted about Brenda's case and ordered the appropriate laboratory tests for nutritional assessment. The grossly abnormal test results clearly reflected prolonged nutritional and hydration neglect. Recommendations to correct the nutritional deficiencies and to enhance wound healing were made by the nutritionist. As Brenda's nutritional and hydration status improved, she became more alert. However, she remained frankly psychotic.

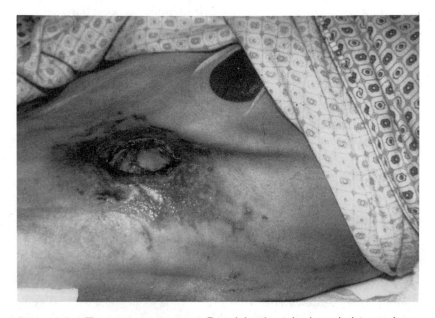

Figure 9.6. The pressure sore on Brenda's chest had eroded to such an extent that the contraction of her intercostal (between the ribs) muscles was visible.

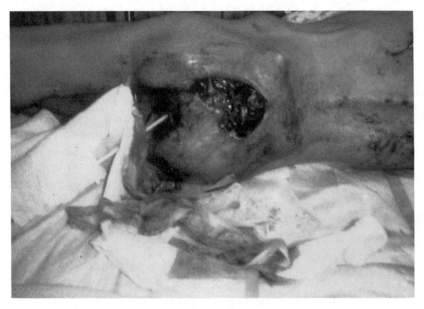

Figure 9.7. These pressure sores clearly had not occurred over "a few days," as Brenda's mother had claimed. These lesions required extensive care by the team enterostomal therapist and surgical care.

The team enterostomal therapist began a regimen of scrupulous wound cleansing and debridement with aggressive ongoing skin care. When Brenda's laboratory test results approached normal, skin grafting was performed. Ongoing mobilization of her contractures and steps to prevent further skin breakdown were initiated.

Radiology Technician   The radiology technician is integral to the team because many elderly outpatients are sent directly to the radiology department for x-rays (Figure 9.8). The technician looks for suspicious bruising, cuts, malnutrition and dehydration, and fractures or broken bones that are not consistent with the reported mechanism of injury. The technician asks the radiologist to evaluate and comment on his or her observations. The radiology technician regularly attends the monthly Adult Protective Team administrative meeting and he or she attends staffings on an ad hoc basis.

Hospital Pharmacist   The pharmacist originally was not a regular team member, but attended meetings only on an ad hoc basis. The pharmacist was added to the team because the team recognized that a pharmacist's knowledge of drug interactions and familiarity with the Medical Center's computer information services and data collection and retrieval were valuable. Knowledge of drug interactions is valuable to the team because it can be helpful in detecting patients

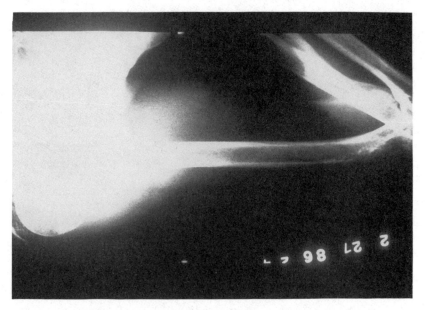

Figure 9.8.   This x-ray shows a break near the top of the upper arm (humerus) in an individual who presented without a history of a fall or other injury, but with a history of "not using the arm." The Adult Protective Team radiology technician brought this individual to the team's attention.

who are being inappropriately medicated, and because terminally ill people and people using controlled substances are at increased risk of being victimized.

Elderly people frequently become confused and restless during the night. In an attempt to keep an elderly person in bed and quiet at night, the caregiver may make frantic calls to the elderly person's doctor to request sleeping pills. Sedatives frequently cause confusion in the elderly patient, who then becomes more agitated and alarmed. The caregiver's impulse may be to sedate further, which often aggravates the situation to the point that the elderly person is unresponsive. The team pharmacist attempts to prevent these occurrences by monitoring medication usage.

John, a former employee of St. Vincent Medical Center, had cancer. All of his medication came from the hospital pharmacy. The team pharmacist contacted the team coordinator because John was purchasing enormous doses of narcotics from prescriptions written by three different physicians, but he still seemed to be in pain. The coordinator contacted the team physician, who agreed that the narcotic usage seemed excessive and contacted each of the three physicians. The physicians agreed that only one of them would continue to write John's narcotic prescriptions. The coordinator contacted the visiting nurse, who observed that two unrelated, much younger men were always at John's house when she arrived. The nurse copied the license plate number from their car, which was given to the police. The men had warrants for their arrest on drug charges. At John's next radiation therapy appointment, the team x-ray technician contacted the team coordinator, who met with John. He admitted to the coordinator that he was giving his medication to the two young men and that he had not used any of the drugs himself. John said that he had a dog about which he was worried because he did not think anyone would care for it when he died. The young men had promised to take care of the dog in exchange for the narcotics, which they were both using and selling. The metro police squad was called and arrested the two men. John continued radiation therapy at the hospital for a short time and received pain relief from the use of adequate doses of narcotics. He died within a few weeks. The visiting nurse had promised to, and did, care for his dog.

Risk Management/Legal Services Many cases of elder mistreatment involve issues of competency and/or guardianship. These cases tend to fall into the following categories:

1. Frank abuse or neglect of a psychologically competent elderly person who makes bad judgments, as assessed by the team, about issues such as finances, placement, and personal care. The team attempts to educate the victim about available options and to guide the victim toward the safest placement.
2. Borderline care of a competent elderly person not in imminent danger, but who is at significant risk for mistreatment. The elderly person and/or caregiver resist change. Both parties are targeted by the team for education. The team weighs the factors and proposes a safe discharge plan that allows the elderly person to exercise autonomy.
3. Frank abuse or neglect or self-neglect of an elderly person who appears incompetent, but who is not certified incompetent following a psychiatric examination.
4. Self-neglect in an incompetent elderly person with no guardian.
5. Frank abuse or neglect of an incompetent elderly person by his or her guardian.

The medical director, team coordinator, and risk manager of the Adult Protective Team at St. Vincent Medical Center have met with the probate court on a number of occasions in an attempt to address these problems. Generally, the hospital attempts to identify acceptable and receptive caregivers for incompetent elderly people. In the absence of an acceptable caregiver, the hospital occasionally hires an attorney to act as guardian, or the court appoints one from a list of attorneys who have agreed to serve as guardians. The guardianship proceedings can be a long, expensive process, as both medical and legal fees accrue. In emergency situations the court can expedite the process. The team has been selective in asking the court to do so.

Risk management plays a key role in the decision-making processes regarding placement and guardianship. Unfortunately, the competent older adult frequently makes personal placement decisions that are impractical and/or possibly dangerous. The team attempts to help the elderly person maintain autonomy to whatever degree is safe and financially feasible. A tremendous amount of physical and psychological abuse as well as financial exploitation is endured by elderly people because of their fear or misunderstanding of their perceived alternatives. In such cases the team invites the visiting nurse service and state Adult Protective Services (APS) case investigators to join the team meetings on an ad hoc basis. The visiting nurse or an APS case investigator can provide significant insight into the domestic situation. Both the visiting nurse service and APS act as the team's eyes on community-based elder mistreatment. They report and document squalor, limited or inadequate food, and heat and sanitation problems.

Biomedical Audiovisual Services   A photographer supports the team by taking photographs. Slides are made of direct injuries, pressure sores, wasting (dehydration and/or malnutrition), and occasionally, poor hygiene. Photographs have been invaluable in proving cases of elder mistreatment. Initially, prosecutors had difficulty believing the level of elder mistreatment documented in reports submitted by the Adult Protective Team. Presenting concrete evidence in the form of photographs convinced prosecutors that charges should be filed.

Prosecutors are not alone in their skepticism about the severity of mistreatment. The team has found that frequently victims are in denial about the severity of their mistreatment. Pressure sores generally are not painful and develop on surfaces that are difficult for the victim to see easily (e.g., sacrum, back), and thus, victims may not appreciate the severity of the injury. The photographs of wounds and pressure sores help to break down the defenses of the victims and their families in order to convince them that the victim needs help. The following case examples demonstrate the effectiveness of photographs in proving elder mistreatment.

Harold, age 79, lived with his granddaughter and her two young children. Her father, Harold's son, paid the rent for the shabby apartment in which they lived. Harold's pension and Social Security checks were directly deposited to his son's account. The son was Harold's legal guardian and controlled all of Harold's assets, most of which he used for his own benefit. The remaining assets, which were minimal, were used to provide for his father and daughter.

Before coming to the attention of the St. Vincent Adult Protective Team, Harold had been discharged from another local hospital, where he had been treated for pressure sores. He had been sent home with a topical ointment to help heal and prevent further breakdown of his pressure sores. The tube of ointment had been empty for an unknown period of time when Harold came to the team's attention. The paramedics had found Harold on a couch, where he had been lying for several days. His pressure sores had broken down considerably and were contaminated with dried urine and stool. The paramedics brought Harold to the St. Vincent emergency department on the couch cushions because his flesh had adhered to them. At the time of his admission, Harold was poorly responsive.

This graphic description of Harold's circumstances was shared with the prosecutor who seemed unmoved. The prosecutor felt that Harold's granddaughter probably did not understand that she was not providing adequate care. However, when the prosecutor was confronted with the photographs of Harold's pressure sores (Figure 9.9) and asked if he would be concerned if a dog had not moved from a couch for several days and had fouled itself, the prosecutor became outraged and wanted to move forward with prosecution. Because the state had no exploitation statute, Harold's son was immune from prosecution. Although Harold's granddaughter could be prosecuted for neglect, her children would be without a caregiver. Harold died within a few days of admission, therefore his placement was no longer an issue. As frustrating as it was for some of the team members, the decision was made not to move forward with prosecution.

Louella was reclusive and lived alone. She allowed her nephew to check on her every few days, but would not allow him, or

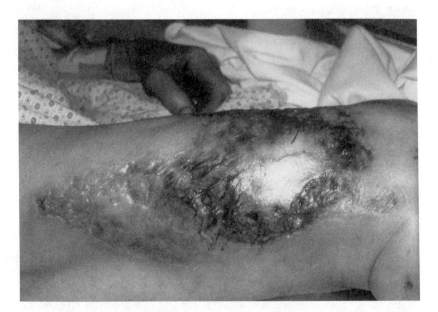

Figure 9.9. Harold presented with a number of pressure sores. The lesion in the photograph had adhered to the couch cushion and contained multiple fibers and hairs. The lesion was also contaminated with dried urine and stool.

anyone else, into the house. Her nephew could enter the house only as far as the vestibule; the inside door remained closed and locked. He would leave food and other supplies outside the door. Louella brought the supplies in only after he left. After one of her nephew's visits, Louella fell. She lay on the floor for several days until her nephew's next visit. Because she did not come to the inside door, Louella's nephew called the authorities to help him break in. They found Louella dehydrated and incontinent. She also had pressure sores (Figure 9.10) and a fractured hip, which was the result of the fall.

Upon arrival at St. Vincent, Louella was cleaned, rehydrated, and photographed. The team noted that she was bright and articulate, but paranoid. Louella was convinced that a group of people from the Caribbean was living in her attic. She "knew" they were from the Caribbean because they wore brightly colored clothing. The fact that the only access to the attic was through the house and that no one else had ever seen "the Caribbeans" made no difference to Louella. She was also convinced that she was fine physically and that she could easily and safely return home upon discharge from St. Vincent. Although she could be quite lucid, Louella had no insight into the danger of living alone at her home. She declined treatment of the pressure sores, insisting that they did not exist. The team suggested a psychiatric consult in order to find Louella incompetent. The team felt that this action would result in the appointment of a guardian and the completion of appropriate treatment and placement. They felt that because Louella was financially and medi-

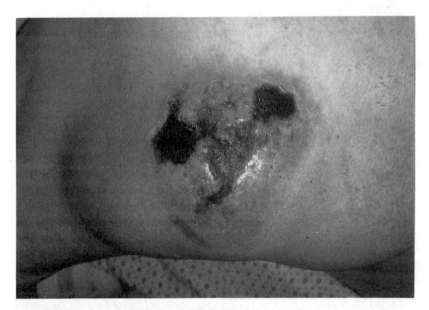

Figure 9.10. Louella presented with this pressure sore on her hip and sacrum. She had refused treatment because she did not believe she had a pressure sore. Only after repeated viewings of this photograph and seeing her lesion reflected in a mirror did Louella accept treatment.

cally stable, she could be readily placed. Unfortunately, the psychiatrist visited Louella during one of her lucid, articulate periods, and found Louella competent. The team was frustrated by its inability to treat Louella or make a safe placement. As a legally competent adult, she could decline both options. The team showed Louella photographs of her pressure wounds and used mirrors to show her the lesion. The team also talked with her frequently. The visual evidence finally convinced Louella to permit treatment. Once treatment was complete, the team convinced Louella to accept the weekly services of a visiting nurse. Her nephew could continue to visit her every few days. Louella did remarkably well with this solution. Although periodically obsessed with "the Caribbeans in the attic" she maintained her autonomy and her health fairly well.

Joseph, a frail man with a limited income, lived in a small apartment over a garage in an unsafe inner-city neighborhood. He had a friend who periodically checked on him and would take him shopping, to doctors' appointments, and on other errands. The nature of their relationship was never clear, but no abuse or exploitation was evident.

Joseph was admitted to St. Vincent Medical Center with several pressure sores. He had fallen and was unable to get up. He was dehydrated and his laboratory test values were consistent with those of malnutrition (Figure 9.11). Joseph's wounds were treated and he was discharged, even though the Adult Protective Team had misgivings about Joseph's ability to care for himself.

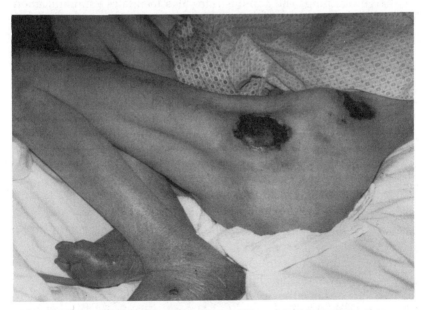

Figure 9.11. Joseph presented with pressure sores, which are typically located on bony prominences, such as the hip and the pelvic bones. The skin visible from the feet to the upper calf also showed early signs of breakdown as well as the color and tension frequently seen in malnutrition and dehydration.

He was quite frail and weak, but he was competent, financially able to maintain his independence, and stubbornly unwilling to acknowledge his inability to care for himself. Joseph's friend agreed to check in on him periodically and a visiting nurse was assigned to visit weekly.

Two days after discharge, Joseph was readmitted to the Medical Center. He had become wedged between his bed and the wall and was unable to free himself. His pressure sores had broken down and he was dehydrated. Joseph was still unwilling to acknowledge his inability to care for himself, and told the team that he would push the bed closer to the wall.

Joseph was again treated for pressure sores and dehydration. A home medical alert safety system was acquired for Joseph through a grant, and he was discharged. Joseph did well after discharge.

Pastoral Care   A representative from pastoral care is a key team member. This representative may be witness to or privy to a different profile of the victim and/or abuser from members of the medical team. The nun or chaplain is often able to provide insight into the victim's domestic situation, coping capabilities, and support systems.

Senior Programs Administrator   The Medical Center's Senior Programs administrator has knowledge of community resources that are available to older people, but that may not be considered in traditional discharge planning. The administrator also facilitates communication with community-based senior centers and has offered programs through the senior centers on the identification of abuse, medication safety, maintenance of health and safety, proper nutrition, and maintenance of financial independence and planning for medical emergencies. The Senior Programs administrator also is a source of information about the individual concerns, fears, priorities, and levels of awareness of elderly people.

Nurses   Nurses from each of the floors serving elderly patients, especially the teaching unit and the emergency department, are responsible for identifying potential victims and for ongoing evaluation of the patients and their support systems, or lack thereof. Many times, a family member, the caregiver, or the ambulance attendants are the only sources of information about the patient. On occasion, the caregiver stays only a brief time. Consequently, the contact with information sources while they are in the emergency department is critical for nurses in order to gain a historical perspective and insight into the patient–caregiver relationship.

Floor nurses have the opportunity to observe the patients and their relationships with visiting friends and family members. This is useful to the team for two reasons:

1. A clearer view may be obtained of both the elderly person's ability to live independently and the degree of support the caregiver

seems able or willing to provide. The elderly person and/or the caregiver may not realize that his or her estimate of the care required by the elderly person is unrealistically low. The Adult Protective Team at St. Vincent has found it instructive to allow the caregiver(s) to provide total 24-hour care of the elderly person in the hospital for 1–2 days.

2. The nurses supervise and act as backup to prevent injuries or other harm. (In an attempt to simulate the demands of home care of dependent elderly people, caregivers are provided with nursing assistance only if it is necessary to prevent the caregiver from injuring the care recipient.) This experience has helped our patients and their caregivers to make realistic decisions. It has also improved the ability of staff to judge their capabilities.

CONCLUSION

The spirit of the Adult Protective Team is a combination of compassion and reason. The team works with aging patients and their caregivers to help maintain or restore as much dignity, comfort, and autonomy as possible within the confines of the physical, psychological, and financial resources of the people involved. In order to achieve this goal a team member must be willing to be flexible, creative, and supportive of the patient and caregiver. Education and networking are important parts of the team's relationships with patients, caregivers, health care professionals, and the lay community, including citizen and government groups. The team must also maintain statistics in order to encourage the dedication of more resources to the growing national problem of elder abuse, neglect, and exploitation.

APPENDIX

Name of Institution
Street Address
City, State, Zip Code

ELDER ABUSE (NEGLECT) REPORTING FORM

Date: _____ Time: _____ A.M.   P.M.   Hospital no.: _____
Patient name: _____ Age: _____ Birthdate: _____
Address: _____ Phone no.: _____
Relative's/friend's name: _____ Phone no.: _____
Address(s): _____

History: _____
_____
_____

Physical findings (exam): _____
_____
_____
_____

Reason for suspected elder abuse/neglect: _____
_____

Persons notified: 1) _____ Agency: _____
                  2) _____
Date and time of notification: _____
Action taken: _____
_____

_____
(Reporting Person)

Name of Institution
Street Address
City, State, Zip Code

ADULT PROTECTIVE TEAM REPORT

Date of APT conference: _____ Name of agency worker: _____

Date of referral to SVMC social service: _____

Date of referral to APS or Ombudsman: _____

Patient's name: _____ Age: _____ Date of birth: _____

Unit no.: _____ Patient's address: _____

Relative's name(s): _____

Address: _____

_____ Phone no.: _____

Date and reason for admission or referral: _____

_____

Psychosocial evaluation of family situation: _____

_____

_____

APT's recommendations (include where patient is to be discharged, name, address, phone, and relation to patient): _____

_____

_____

_____

Additional comments: _____

_____

_____

_____

_____

Court action: Yes   No   If yes, explain: _____

_____

Statement of member(s) of APT who disagree(s) with APT recommendations:

_____

_____

_____

_____

_____

_____

Persons attending APT conference: _____

_____

_____

_____

10

Psychological Therapy with Abused and Neglected Patients

Bridget K. Booth, Audrei A. Bruno, and Robert Marin

Psychological treatment of elder abuse is a challenging process that depends on linking knowledge of elder mistreatment to the clinical skills and understanding that make up psychiatric care of elderly people. Elder mistreatment has many causes and many manifestations. The psychological causes of elder abuse may lie in the past or the present. The causes may be found in the history of a relationship that has been conflictual for decades, or in the interaction of present psychiatric, social, and medical factors that strain a relationship that has been satisfactory for a lifetime. The manifestations of elder mistreatment are also complex. For all these reasons, psychological treatment is a complex process that requires comprehensive assessment of the mistreated elder and the perpetrator of mistreatment.

This chapter offers a psychological profile of abuse victims. The psychological and physical circumstances of elder abuse often evoke powerful emotional reactions from professionals. Some of these emotional reactions are described, their potentially deleterious effects on treatment are illustrated, and suggestions are provided for their management. The major causes of elder abuse are then described and their implications for psychological management are indicated. An examination of the role of psychopathology and formal psychiatric evaluation follows. The final section describes primary, secondary, and tertiary interventions that apply to the circumstances of elder mistreatment. Throughout the chapter, examples are provided in order to emphasize that psychological interventions are directed not only at the identified victim, but also at the perpetrators, families, and communities that make up the victim's social environment.

PSYCHOLOGICAL ISSUES FOR VICTIMS

Elder abuse victims face numerous emotional problems. Profiles of victims and abusers have been developed by several authors (Table 10.1) (Benton & Marshall, 1991; Haviland & O'Brien, 1989; Kosberg & Nahmiash, Chapter 2, this volume; Quinn & Tomita, 1986; Steinmetz, 1988). The frequency of elder abuse is unknown, but a 1991 Congressional Subcommittee on Aging study estimated that as many as 2 million elderly Americans may be abused or neglected annually (U.S. House of Representatives, 1991). This number represents approximately 3.2% of the elderly population. Despite its prevalence, elder mistreatment is often unreported or denied. Older people are often

Table 10.1. Profiles of typical victims and perpetrators of elder mistreatment

Victim	Abuser
Female	Family member
75 years old	Mental illness
White	Substance abuse
Living with a relative	Poor self-image
Source of stress to the caregiver	Poor relationship with victim
Dependent on the abuser	Dependent on the victim for housing or financial support
Fear of nursing facility placement	
Unable to report abuse because of poor memory or communication skills	Poor self-control
	Ineffective coping skills
	Poor communication skills
Minimal social support	Burdened by caregiving
Exhibits problematic behavior	Life in disarray
Socially isolated	History of family violence
Unmarried, with financial management problems or with loss of spouse or other family member who managed finances	Ill-prepared or reluctant to provide care
	May be normally kind and caring, but abusive when pushed over the edge in moments of frustration, fear, or depression

ashamed because they have been mistreated by their children or spouses. Commonly, they fear reprisals if they disclose their mistreatment, and they may refrain from taking action because they feel ashamed of their dependency or their contribution to family pressures and tension. They may feel overly responsible and thus have difficulty asking for or accepting help. Loyalty to family can lead to a reluctance to admit abuse. Stoicism can lead to endurance of suffering without complaint.

PSYCHOLOGICAL ISSUES FOR HEALTH CARE PROFESSIONALS

Given the undisclosed and protean nature of elder mistreatment, health care professionals are confronted with the challenges of being alert to symptoms of abuse when none is reported and of being alert to situations in which abuse is likely to occur. Clinicians may be alarmed and overwhelmed when faced with elder abuse and neglect. Therefore, they must be cognizant of their coping mechanisms and methods of defending themselves psychologically. Each method encompasses unique strengths and vulnerabilities. Some clinicians are prone to intellectualize when empathy would be more helpful to the client. Some clinicians withdraw emotionally when emotional candor would be preferable. Some professionals feel pity or sympathy when the better course of action would be to confront clients in order to force the realization that their attitudes and behaviors may foster continued mistreatment (Marin & Morycz, 1990).

Providing psychological treatment in cases of abuse and neglect requires an awareness of the ways in which these emotional biases interact with the personal, social, and material circumstances of elder mistreatment. The physical circumstances of these cases—either the people themselves or their homes—may provoke intense emotional reactions. The personal values of victims or the actions of perpetrators may elicit moral repugnance or indignation. These circumstances make it a challenge to adhere to personal and professional ethics without becoming judgmental. Professionals must maintain a steadfast, confident, and humane approach with their clients. When professionals recognize that their approach is faltering, they must know their options. These options include curtailing an office session or home visit, venting feelings with colleagues, seeking supervision from coworkers who are more experienced or less involved emotionally, and asking advice from supervisors. Clinicians will at times confront limitations in what can be done to help clients, either because of personal constraints or constraints inherent in the clinical situation.

CAUSAL FACTORS IN ELDER ABUSE
AND THEIR TREATMENT IMPLICATIONS

Faced with emotionally complex and challenging clients, it is helpful for a clinician to know the causes of elder abuse. Awareness of the causes of elder mistreatment is useful because it provides clinicians with an organizational tool to evaluate new cases and helps them identify the different psychological interventions that are appropriate for individual cases. The causes of elder abuse are not mutually exclusive. In clinical practice multiple causal factors may be present in the same case.

Societal Attitudes Toward Aging

Societal attitudes toward aging provide the social backdrop against which elder abuse can be understood. These attitudes are expressed both directly and indirectly by the parties to elder abuse, and, in effect, serve as a precondition or justification for the unnecessary suffering inflicted on abuse victims. Recognizing ageist attitudes and the psychological purposes they serve may help professionals to develop a humane approach to these cases.

Many factors contribute to negative attitudes toward aging in the United States. These factors may be characteristic of American society as a whole or may reflect subcultural differences. Researchers find it convenient to define everyone 65 years old and older as "old," but no standard age exists at which an individual becomes "old." Prompted by concern for the rights and dignity of older people, the term *ageism* was coined in order to characterize the beliefs and practices that embody biased negative feelings toward older people (Nuessel, 1982). Central to ageism in the United States is the belief that elderly people are sick, isolated, useless, and pitiful.

Confronting ageist beliefs requires the awareness that these attitudes do not reflect the biological changes associated with aging. Instead, these beliefs are imposed by society. Comfort (1976) refers to these beliefs as "sociogenic aging." Thus, society teaches older people to become prejudiced against themselves (Comfort, 1976), and condones the oppression of older people (Butler, 1975). Elderly people are further devalued as a result of any physical or mental impairments. They are at an increased risk of seeing themselves as dispensable or undeserving of respect. These attitudes create a psychosocial context in which people tolerate mistreatment. In effect, mistreatment is seen as deserved and, thus, justifiable.

Knowledge of ageist attitudes helps in managing cases of elder abuse in several ways. First, this knowledge helps professionals to overcome their biases. Formal education helps to reshape these biases, but experienced professionals examine themselves continually for residue of any prejudice that older people are useless, needy, hopeless, or ungrateful. Second, sensitivity on the part of clinicians can help clients recognize and examine their own ageist beliefs. Professionals may, in some instances, directly correct misinformation and mistaken beliefs. Providing information such as written material, professional advice, and alternative explanations can help the parties to elder abuse reevaluate their beliefs about aging and about each other. This educational approach has a deeper psychological purpose. As people surrender their ageist attitudes, they make it possible to identify the defensive function of the attitudes. Armed with knowledge, abusers or caregivers are able to understand the shame, guilt, or fear that derives from their inability to relate humanely to the older people for whom they have responsibility.

Caregiver Burden

Caregiver burden is the experience of strain or distress resulting from caregiving, and entails complex interactions among the caregiver, the care receiver, and environmental factors. According to Steinmetz (1988), caregiver burden probably plays a major role in predicting the mistreatment of elderly people, in both families and institutions.

Family Caregivers Functional disabilities can cause older people to become dependent on others for mobility and/or activities of daily living. For the older person with moderate to severe impairment, this can mean becoming bedridden or housebound. The vast majority of care to elderly people with disabilities is delivered at home, not in institutions. Families provide up to 80% of care to functionally dependent elderly people. The burden of this effort is not evenly distributed among family members. The majority of caregivers of functionally impaired older adults are their adult daughters, daughters-in-law, or spouses. Caregiver burden affects all aspects of family life. Clinicians familiar with the caregiving experience are not surprised that between 46% (Gallagher, Rose, Rurena, Lovett, & Thompson, 1989) and 83% (Drinka, Smith, & Drinka, 1987) of caregivers may be clinically depressed. The financial, medical, and social health of caregivers also undergoes enormous disruption.

The interaction between the abuse victim's impairments and the caregiver's burden presumably accounts for the fact that spouses are responsible for nearly two thirds of elder abuse and children for one fourth of elder abuse (Pillemer & Finkelhor, 1988). These statistics sensitize clinicians to the role caregiver burden plays in elder mistreatment, and clarifies the implications for treatment. When elder abuse is perpetrated by the caregiver, reducing caregiver burden is often the primary treatment strategy. Doing so requires addressing all three components of the caregiver's strain: the abuse victim's impairments, the psychological state of the caregiver, and the environment in which the two people reside.

Offering treatment to the caregiver is straightforward when the caregiver is an open, devoted individual who acknowledges the strains of caregiving, recognizes his or her own limitations, and is willing to accept guidance and assistance. However, this is often not the case. Because of their own disabilities, caregivers may be unaware of having jeopardized the well-being of the victim. In other instances, caregivers are ashamed of their actions or feel justified in their abusive actions because the victim "is so demanding." Caregivers may feel overwhelmed, unappreciated, and isolated. They may also believe that the older person under their care is purposely creating undue work for them by being incontinent or stubborn. In such cases, caregivers may retaliate.

The caregiver's burden is often the result of his or her own needs and limitations. Clinicians should make every attempt to assess the caregiver for the presence of clinical depression or other psychiatric disorders (see "Psychopathology," pp. 193–197). Caregivers must be educated about their own needs as well as the needs of the older person. When caregivers understand that their well-being is a prerequisite for providing effective care, they are more likely to accept referrals for themselves. In particular, psychiatric care should be arranged for clinically depressed caregivers. Treatment of depression may make a decisive difference in the ability of caregivers to provide safe, appropriate care. If these psychiatric interventions are tied to a similarly comprehensive program of medical, psychiatric, and social interventions for the abuse victim, the risk of future abuse may be markedly reduced.

Psychological treatment for the caregiver also requires attending to his or her responsibilities outside of the caregiving relationship. Taking on responsibility for an older adult often occurs at a time when the caregiver is poorly prepared to provide the needed assistance, or is facing the challenges of mid- or later life. Innumerable social problems, such as poor health, job loss, childrearing, death of friends, moving, legal problems, pregnancy, marital difficulties, work demands, and financial burden, may contribute to a caregiver's burden. The following case illustrates caregiver burden in a woman who unexpectedly became responsible for her invalid mother.

Five years ago Laura and her two preadolescent children moved into Laura's mother's home. Laura, a secretary, was newly divorced. She moved in with her mother, Barbara, hoping to reduce her personal expenses while her mother took care of the children. A year ago Barbara had a stroke, which paralyzed the right side of her body and impaired her speech. When Barbara achieved the maximal benefit from professional rehabilitation, Laura was given instructions for at-home care. When the family's physician received a telephone call from Laura saying that her mother developed a large sore on her back, he ordered a home health nurse to make an evaluation.

The nurse's assessment revealed that Barbara was unkempt,

incontinent, malnourished, and dehydrated. She had an infected pressure sore on her coccyx and contractures in her legs. Barbara was also diagnosed with depression when she said to the nurse, "I'm no use to anyone; I wish I were dead." Barbara felt humiliated by her loss of independence and the role reversal with her daughter.

When the nurse shared her assessment with Laura, Laura cried. She explained to the nurse, "My mother was always so good to me. I need her so much but now I don't know what to do. I can't afford to stop working, I can't afford to place her in a nursing home, and my children are tired of helping me take care of her. The neighbor comes in twice a day while I am at work to check on her. I feel so guilty but I can't do it all."

Recognizing this as a case of neglect secondary to caregiver burden, the nurse developed a treatment plan for Laura and Barbara. The nursing evaluation of Barbara's physical problems was joined to an evaluation of Laura's problems, which were judged to be financial difficulties, fatigue, role overload, depression, role reversal, and grief. Barbara's physical problems were attended to in consultation with the physician. The mental health nurse from the home health care agency assessed Barbara for depression and arranged for a prescription for an antidepressant. The mental health nurse helped Barbara to express her feelings regarding her loss of health, independence, and self-esteem. She was encouraged to make some of her own decisions regarding her care, her health, and her home. Psychotherapy also addressed her relationships with her daughter and grandchildren.

The home health care agency social worker attempted to rally Laura's extended family to assist her in providing care to Barbara, and arranged for increased community supports, including respite care for Laura and adult day services for Barbara. Laura was referred to a local caregiver support group and to her community mental health center, where she received counseling to explore role changes in her life and to manage her grief at the loss of the mother she once knew. Over the next 1–2 years, Laura, her children, and Barbara gradually developed stable, supportive relationships with each other. Laura was able to support the household financially and at the same time reestablish a circle of friends. Her children accepted increased responsibility for their mother and grandmother. Barbara became more accepting of her physical limitations and of the help from her family and the community.

Institutional Caregivers   Elder mistreatment also occurs in institutional settings, where additional stresses may exist (Council on Scientific Affairs, 1987). The strain on professional caregivers in these settings may create frustrating working conditions, placing large numbers of elderly people at substantial risk for mistreatment.

Mistreatment of older adults can occur in nursing facilities, retirement centers, personal care homes, adult day services centers, community centers, hospitals, detention centers, and prisons. The residents of these environments are often frail or debilitated and thus their complaints are easily ignored. Mistreatment may become an insidious part of activities of daily living. One resident of a nursing facility commented, "They handle me so roughly in the shower. They always lift me by my sore arm." Institutionalized elderly people are a particularly vulnerable group because retaliation, or the fear of retaliation, may leave them feeling helplessly manipulated. Pillemer and Moore (1989) surveyed 577 staff members from 31 nursing facilities in order to determine the extent of physical and psychological abuse perpetrated by staff. In the year prior to the study, 81% of staff reported observing at least one incident of psychological abuse and 36% witnessed physical abuse within the preceding year. In addition, 10% admitted to committing acts of physical abuse and 40% committed at least one psychologically abusive act in this period.

The risk of elder mistreatment in institutions can be reduced. Sophisticated and humane approaches are needed in order to develop compassionate, accurate views of illness and death and their place in long-term institutions. Without these approaches, professional caregivers respond helplessly or callously in order to deny their opinions of residents' lives as empty and futile (Kinsey, Tarbox, & Bragg, 1981).

Administrative initiatives can play a major role in addressing institutional abuse. Administrators must continue to develop educational programs, institutional resources, and clinical policies that permit caregivers to view themselves as competent professionals carrying out valued work. Ensuring that these initiatives in turn shape residents' experience requires administrators to solicit and encourage the support and professional development of institutional staff. If supervisors or administrators conduct distant, aloof relationships with staff, it is likely the staff will conduct distant, aloof relationships with residents. If administrators rely excessively on the authority of their positions, it is likely the staff will rely on their authority over residents. As a result, staff morale and self-esteem will erode and the care of the most vulnerable residents will suffer.

A variety of psychologically oriented staff development projects can be implemented to support and empower professional caregivers. Role playing and videotaping offer useful means for clarifying values and modifying communication skills. The atmosphere in which staff development programs are carried out contributes directly to the treatment of residents. Reflecting on one's experiences and uncertainties, teaching in a lighthearted manner, and encouraging staff participation offer staff a model of a dignified, yet down-to-earth way of relating to residents' dependencies and frailties.

History of Family Violence

Elder abuse can be found in families that have a history of marital conflict, a history of using violence as a response to stress, or a history of poor relations between the caregiver and the elderly person. Experts on family violence (Bernard & Bernard, 1983; Fulmer, 1989; Straus, Gelles, & Steinmetz, 1980) describe violence as a learned response, with each generation modeling its behavior on that of the preceding generation. If a child observes abuse or is the victim of abuse by a parent, the probability of abusive behaviors surfacing in later relationships increases. Rathbone-McCuan (1980) identified the following seven factors as indicative of a pattern of elder abuse:

1. Family history of violence over several generations
2. Perpetrator's unconscious motivation to avenge his or her own abuse as a child
3. Abusive behavior associated with the consumption of drugs and alcohol
4. Reinforcement of perpetrator's behavior by other family members
5. Dependency of the older person and the perpetrator on each other
6. Stresses that confront multiple generations of family members
7. Unequal distribution of elder's resources among adult children

Psychological therapies are central to managing cases of elder abuse that occur in settings of longstanding family violence. These therapies are complex and likely ongoing. The examination of tertiary interventions later in the chapter looks at the various elements of therapeutic treatments. Although all psychological treatments may benefit from a focus on the family, this focus is of particular importance in cases of elder abuse.

PSYCHOPATHOLOGY

Understanding the ways in which psychopathology contributes to the causes and consequences of elder mistreatment plays an important role in determining an appropriate psychological treatment. For example, consider a self-neglecting woman with a diagnosis of schizophrenia. A mental health professional may expend enormous effort to persuade the woman to sell her home and to accept placement in a personal care home. However, a correct diagnosis and appropriate drug therapy may dramatically decrease the psychotic symptoms of schizophrenia and enable the woman to live independently. Similarly, effective treatment may enable a depressed caregiver to resume caring for a symptomatic spouse whom he or she has been mistreating.

The parties to elder mistreatment may suffer from a psychiatric disorder. Perpetrators or victims may have developmental disabilities or personality disorders that date from childhood or early adulthood, or they may experience recurring psychiatric disorders, such as chronic depression, bipolar disorder (more commonly known as manic depression), an anxiety disorder, or schizophrenia.

Serious mental disorders also may present for the first time in later life. As noted earlier in the chapter, caregivers are at high risk for developing depression, which in turn may decrease their patience and increase their risk for mistreating elderly relatives (U.S. House of Representatives, 1981, 1985). In particular, elderly people with treatable medical and neurological conditions may present with symptoms of depression, anxiety, psychosis, or cognitive impairment. In fact, medical illness, neurological disease, and medications can produce any number of psychiatric symptoms. These symptoms include symptoms of cognitive decline, which are typically attributed to irreversible dementing diseases, such as Alzheimer's disease or multi-infarct dementia, but which may signal numerous reversible medical or psychiatric conditions. The implication of this knowledge is that all psychiatric symptoms require thorough assessment. Health care professionals should learn to differentiate dementia from delirium because delirium signals the presence of a reversible medical condition. Intellectual and behavioral symptoms occur in both dementia and delirium. However, a delirious person is more likely to experience relatively abrupt onset of symptoms, marked fluctuation of symptoms, drowsiness, incoherent speech, impaired attention, hallucinations, and variability in emotional state, such as fluctuating sadness, irritability, or inappropriate cheerfulness, than people with dementia. Finally, drug and alcohol dependence, as well as medication misuse, may be factors contributing to elder abuse (Wolf, 1986).

Psychiatric disorders also may result from elder mistreatment. The experience of abuse is sometimes severe enough to cause post-traumatic stress disorder, an anxiety disorder in which severe psychological stress leads first to feelings of intense fear, terror, and helplessness, and then to a symptomatic state in which individuals are repeatedly disabled by recurring reminders and memories of the traumatic event. People with post-traumatic stress disorder avoid stimuli or people associated with the trauma and show symptoms of increased arousal, such as insomnia, irritability, and increased vigilance. The withdrawal, vigilance, distrust, and dysphoria of elder abuse victims may be a reflection of post-traumatic stress disorder.

Understanding the ways in which psychiatric disorders contribute to or result from elder mistreatment has obvious implications for clinicians and case managers. Clients must be carefully assessed for psychiatric symptoms, previous psychiatric histories should be obtained, and treatment should be arranged when significant symptoms are present.

Arranging for clinical assessment of abused or neglected elders is a great challenge to service providers. The number of symptomatic individuals is high, the need for intervention is great, and the accessibility of professional services is potentially low. Nevertheless, a knowledgeable, motivated mental health professional, supported by an agency or institution that appreciates the management implications of mental disorders, can provide appropriate treatment to most abused elderly people, as in the following case history.

> Seventy-seven-year-old Carl and his 50-year-old son, Harold, have lived together since Harold was born. Harold was diagnosed with schizophrenia when he was 25 years old. Carl worked in a local mill until it closed 15 years ago. Over the last several years, Carl has shown a decline in his ability to remember, often not recognizing friends or neighbors. He has become lost in the neighborhood and has wandered the streets. Having known Carl for many years and being aware that his mind was failing, members of the Ladies' Auxiliary from the local church visited Carl. On one of the visits the ladies noticed that Carl had black and blue marks on his arms and legs and smelled of urine. His right eye was swollen shut. When they spoke with Harold about his father's condition, Harold became anxious and said, "It's not my fault that old man can't take care of himself."
>
> Concerned for Carl's welfare, the ladies notified their local Area Agency on Aging. A protective services social worker, Ms. Benedetto, was sent to investigate. During the interview, Ms. Benedetto found that Harold smelled of alcohol and mumbled to himself. Carl was dazed and unable to answer questions appropriately. When questioned regarding his father's condition, Harold stated, "The voices keep telling me to hit him. He sleeps better when I hit him."
>
> Ms. Benedetto concluded that Carl was being abused by Harold, and that neither Carl nor Harold was in any condition to care for Carl. Ms. Benedetto called Carl's physician and reported her findings. The physician said, "What do you expect me to do? He's old. There's not much I can do for him." At Ms. Benedetto's insistence, the doctor arranged for Carl to be seen in the emergency room. Carl received a medical examination, followed by a psychiatric consultation. The psychiatrist found Carl incompetent and scheduled an emergency guardianship hearing. At the same time, Ms. Benedetto obtained a court order so that Carl could be placed temporarily in a personal care home. Ms. Benedetto arranged for an emergency involuntary commitment for Harold on the grounds that he was endangering others because of his command hallucinations. The outreach mobile crisis team of the local mental health center was contacted to help carry out the involuntary commitment procedures.

The preceding case history shows how an existing psychiatric illness in the caregiver led to the physical abuse of an elderly person. Ageist statements from both the son and the physician are revealing. This case illustrates how a social worker can use crisis intervention and community resources to manage the psychopathology of both the perpetrator and the victim.

Alliance Building and Basic Therapeutic Skills

The first and perhaps most important step in the psychological treatment of abused elders is to develop a trusting relationship. Building an alliance between therapist and client takes time, but it is a prerequisite for realizing the goals of secondary and tertiary interventions. Active listening, empathy, genuineness, and support are some of the techniques used to develop a therapeutic alliance with either the victim or the perpetrator. The following therapeutic principles are offered as a supplement:

- Do not judge and do not place blame.
- Communicate understanding and confidence.
- Encourage victims to vent their feelings and to tell their story repeatedly. Active listening and validating client feelings are important.
- Identify ambivalence. Make regular contacts to decrease it.
- Attend to the content and the emotionality of the communication.
- Provide help, comfort, and safety during periods of crisis.
- Allow clients and, when appropriate, other parties to participate in decision making; guard against impulses to rescue.
- Do not make decisions for abused elderly people without their knowledge or consent. Involve a protective services agency for older adults who cannot make their own decisions.
- Empower abuse victims to decrease their dependency by providing information on options and resources.
- Support client initiatives.
- Use negotiation, power of advocacy, and personal persuasion to engage and empower families.
- Ensure that interventions promote the least restrictive alternative.
- Respect the rights of elderly individuals.
- Remember that treatment depends on whether the clients and families accept help.
- Understand the unique and individual characteristics of each case in order to promote meaningful therapy.
- Educate caregivers about the older adult's illness and about behavior management strategies.
- Practice new behaviors by role playing problem situations; role playing promotes creative problem solving and minimizes blame placing.
- Educate all parties about the factors that escalate violence.
- Review strategies to use if an abusive situation recurs. These strategies can include who to call for help (e.g., a trusted neighbor, 911 or other emergency number, a woman's shelter).

Similar therapeutic principles apply when working with elder abusers. It may be helpful for clinicians to stress to the abuser that the clinician's role is to assist both the perpetrator and the victim of abuse. Because an accusation of abuse is usually denied when an abuser is directly confronted, the clinician may accomplish more by emphasizing his or her knowledge of the frustrations of caregiving. Normalizing actions that result from burdened caregiving may diminish the perpetrator's defensiveness. For instance, the clinician may say, "Other people in your situation have told me that they sometimes get so frustrated that they hit their mothers. Has this ever happened to you?"

Counseling the perpetrators can be hampered by the tendency of the abuser to minimize the seriousness of the abusive behavior, to blame others for the abuse, and to maintain a strong denial stance. Treatment of the perpetrator is sometimes controversial. Although some mental health professionals recommend counseling perpetrators, others support criminal prosecution and imprisonment, particularly for repeat offenders (Holmer & Gilleard, 1990).

Counseling the abuse victim can be hampered by the client's desire to protect the abuser. The presence of the mental health professional may increase the client's fear of further abuse and cause the client to present with symptoms of withdrawal or disorganization. It is important not to mistake these symptoms for those that result from mental illness (Rathbone-McCuan & Voyles, 1982).

The quality of the client–therapist relationship affects the client's degree of compliance with the therapist's suggestions. In general, neither the abuser nor the abused will follow through with suggestions or interventions without the continued assistance and support of the therapist. Therefore, it is usually important to follow these cases over time in order for change to occur.

INTERVENTIONS FOR VICTIMS AND ABUSERS

The effective treatment of cases of elder abuse and neglect incorporates a combination of primary, secondary, and tertiary components (Hackbarth, Andresen, & Konestabo, 1989). Primary interventions are concerned with prevention. Ideally, primary interventions would prevent the initial occurrence of elder mistreatment, but more practically, the aim of primary psychological interventions is to reduce the risk and frequency of elder mistreatment. Secondary interventions focus on identification and treatment of the immediate effects of elder abuse. Tertiary interventions are aimed at facilitating long-term recovery and rehabilitation after the trauma of the victimization (Curry & Stone, 1994).

Primary Interventions

Education of professionals and the public is the single most important primary prevention strategy. Seminars, public service announcements, media coverage, movies, magazines, newspapers, television, and research literature provide avenues for distributing educational messages. Legislative efforts are also used to prevent abuse. Legislation regulates care, establishes programs, provides penalties for perpetrators, and creates structures that protect the financial and personal autonomy of older adults.

Health care providers, such as nurses, social workers, and physicians, have a responsibility and an opportunity to identify high-risk situations for abuse. All evaluations of older adults need to consider the risk of abuse and neglect. Preventing the exposure of elderly people to high-risk home care environments is an important aim of hospital staff preparing to discharge a patient. This includes evaluating the family for risk factors such as a history of family violence, previous spouse abuse, financial stressors, dependency of family members on the elderly person, external stressors, and mental illness of family members. Kosberg (1988) developed a tool, the High-Risk Placement Worksheet, for identifying families at risk. The worksheet allows individuals who make placement decisions to assess the older person, the caregiver, and the family system. It includes questions on the quality of the past and present relationships between the older person and the caregiver and on each person's desire for the older person to be placed in the caregiver's care.

Potential offenders are usually unable to acknowledge their propensity to abuse. Therefore, primary prevention strategies usually focus on the abusive situation rather than on the abusing individual. Maintaining a long-term therapeutic alliance with the at-risk family helps to stabilize families. The strain of caregiving is reduced by providing information on stress reduction, respite care, physical and/or psychological care, community support, and in-home services. In addition, caregivers should be encouraged to seek help before becoming overwhelmed. It is crucial for them to avoid isolation by participating in recreational activities or support groups for caregivers. The value of having a confidante cannot be overstated.

When an infirm parent joins the household of an adult child, information should be provided about the impaired person's illness and functional limits. Caregivers should be trained in the management of difficult behaviors. Information should be provided about ways to access community agencies (e.g., legal services, private pay services) that could assist the caregiver.

In-home services such as homemakers, home health aides, and Meals-on-Wheels can help caregivers who are overwhelmed by the burden of caring for an elderly relative. Having the older person attend a day services program or making respite care available to the caregiver on a weekly or more extended basis are other options. Being able to anticipate problems with specific plans provides caregivers with a sense of control over difficult behaviors.

Secondary Interventions

The goals of secondary interventions are to treat promptly, to detect abuse early, and to minimize morbidity. Secondary interventions seek to limit the extent of physical, psychological, and social losses that occur because of elder abuse. Early detection through screening and assessment assists in preventing escalation or continuation of the mistreatment. Health care professionals must be sensitive to the vulnerability of the abuse victim. Medical and psychiatric assessment must be performed rapidly so that the necessity of emergency safeguards can be determined.

Professionals must be aware of their impulses to rescue so that the desire to protect the mistreated elderly person does not result in decisions being made without the older person's knowledge or consent. Professionals also must ensure that a competent victim is provided with sufficient information and that decisions are made without coercion (O'Malley, Everitt, O'Malley, & Campion, 1983). Abused individuals who are unable to make choices because of psychiatric illness or cognitive impairment need to be guided through the specific legal structures of their state and/or local protective agencies.

Crisis management techniques are often utilized during this stage of intervention. According to Aguilera and Messick (1982), the goal of crisis intervention is to resolve the immediate crisis and restore the client to the premorbid level of functioning. Clients will need to draw on past coping mechanisms or learn new methods. They also must identify and call on their natural support systems, if such systems exist. During this stage, medication, relaxation techniques, and exercise may help to decrease anxiety. At the end of this phase, a client may achieve an increased sense of control as the result of a reduction in helplessness and dependency.

Tertiary Interventions

The aim of tertiary interventions is to engage the victim and perpetrator of abuse in a treatment process that will prevent further abuse and enable optimal recovery from mistreatment. Assessment should characterize the type (e.g., psychological, physical) and severity of abuse, the risk factors for recurrence, and the characteristics of the participants that influence their motivation and ability to participate in treatment. As treatment proceeds, this initial assessment may be expanded or altered over a course of weeks or months (O'Malley, Everitt, O'Malley, & Campion, 1983). The competence of the individuals involved must be assessed and monitored. Legal steps, including establishing guardianship, may be initiated immediately or after the acute phase of treatment has passed.

It is helpful to distinguish between short- and long-term goals of treatment (Quinn & Tomita, 1986). From a short-term perspective, the aim of treatment is to terminate abusive acts, safeguard the victim, secure endangered property, and protect rights that have been violated. When indicated, the perpetrator will require clinical interventions as well. Treatment for psychiatric or medical illness is instituted.

From a socioenvironmental standpoint, personal and community supports should be implemented to relieve caregiver strain and the destructive aspects of mutual dependency. However, the central psychological objective of short-term treatment is to begin the process of identifying specific, concrete behaviors that predispose to, provoke, or reinforce abusive acts. As illustrations, both the abuser and the victim may be helped by discovering that incidents occur when the abuser is sleep deprived or intoxicated; or after a physical confrontation, the abuser may report, "She stops complaining and I have a few uninterrupted minutes to talk with my friends on the telephone." In these examples solutions may be easy to arrange: more sleep, treatment for insomnia, abstinence from alcohol, or time out of the house to be with friends. Other problems are more difficult to solve, particularly in the short run, but the involvement of a friend or a professional who will monitor the household and take specific actions in the event of recurrences may serve to stabilize the relationship.

Long-term treatment includes the monitoring and acute problem solving of short-term treatment, but adds interventions that address longstanding risk factors related to characteristics of the victim, the perpetrator, or family system. Trust and familiarity between client and professional becomes more profound in long-term treatment. This deeper relationship in turn serves as a foundation for overcoming resistance to change. For example, with treatment a dependent son may gradually take steps to increase his social or financial independence, thereby leaving him less vulnerable to the conflictual aspects of his relationship with his controlling mother.

In all stages of intervention, mental health professionals must be competent in general supportive therapy skills. They must be able to build relationships in which they are viewed as concerned, competent, knowledgeable professionals. They must be effective in communicating understanding through unqualified positive regard, nonjudgmental interpretation, and nonverbal affective responses. The ability to communicate empathy must be balanced by an ability to convey authority and a willingness to act decisively if abuse recurs. These general supportive therapy skills also form a foundation for a psychoeducational approach. Such an approach provides explicit information to clients about the nature and causes of their problems and the types of responses they can choose in order to end them. Psychoeducational approaches generally require an unambiguous acknowledgment by clients that a problem exists that warrants treatment. However, given this agreement, psychoeducational treatment provides new skills and a source of competence that reduces stress and the risks of further abuse. For example, burdened caregivers benefit from learning how to interpret the abnormal behavior of a parent with dementia. They also benefit from knowledge of community resources, such as in-home services or respite care, and from education about the treatability of their own depressive symptoms.

More complex psychotherapeutic strategies are required when the victim or perpetrator denies the significance of mistreatment or fails to appreciate the behaviors or attitudes that lead to it. Such cases generally require the intervention of mental health professionals with considerable psychotherapy experience. Individual, interpersonal, or family-oriented approaches must be considered, depending on the circumstances. Much effort is often invested in developing a shared understanding of the nature of a problem. Therapists must help clients first to accurately label the problem behaviors or attitudes, and then to recognize the way in which the behaviors or attitudes contribute to conflict. Particularly challenging are instances in which character-based or attitudinal issues were once perceived as sources of strength or accomplishment, but now function as impediments to treatment. For example, stoic or rigidly independent abuse victims resist acknowledging a need for help. The therapist gradually helps the client to recognize that independence is counterproductive in this situation. Achieving this recognition may be accomplished directly by raising the client's awareness of the negative consequences of independence. Recognition also may be accomplished indirectly by identifying the client's emotional resistance to accepting treatment (e.g., dealing with the emotional pain of acknowledging helplessness or of accepting that a child is unable to live independently).

CONCLUSION

Psychological treatment for elder abuse is complex and challenging. Treatment of abuse cases is based on a comprehensive psychiatric, medical, and social assessment. The victim and, when possible, the perpetrator or family system should be evaluated. Diagnosis and treatment of psychiatric disorders are important components of case management because mental illness may figure prominently as either a cause or a consequence of elder abuse. Because of the profound psychological meaning of elder mistreatment, mental health professionals must consider their own psychological responses as well as those of their clients.

Primary interventions are aimed at preventing elder mistreatment and may be readily integrated into the practices of professionals offering services to older people. Secondary interventions are aimed at minimizing harm and distress related to acute events. Social and environmental resources figure prominently in secondary interventions, but supportive psychological measures are an integral part of the interventions used to stabilize abusive relationships. The aim of tertiary interventions is to reduce the risk of subsequent incidents and to ensure the best possible recovery from the psychological, physical, or material injuries that were sustained. Psychoeducational approaches to working with the victim and perpetrator of abuse are most helpful when clients agree on the nature of the problem and on the need for professional help. When character-based or attitudinal traits prevent constructive problem solving, long-term psychotherapeutic interventions may be helpful. At all phases of treatment for elder abuse, supportive therapeutic skills are necessary in order to establish and develop an effective working alliance.

REFERENCES

Aguilera, D.C., & Messick, J.M. (1982). *Crisis intervention: Theory and methodology.* St. Louis: C.V. Mosby.

Benton, D., & Marshall, C. (1991). Elder abuse. *Clinics in Geriatric Medicine, 7,* 831–845.

Bernard, M.L., & Bernard, J.L. (1983). Violent intimacy of the families as a model for love relationships. *Family Relations, 32,* 283–286.

Butler, R. (1975). *Why survive? Being old in America.* New York: Harper & Row.

Comfort, A. (1976, November/December). Age prejudice in America. *Social Policy,* 3–8.

Council on Scientific Affairs. (1987). Elder abuse and neglect. *Journal of the American Medical Association, 257,* 966–971.

Curry, L.C., & Stone, J.G. (1994). Maltreatment of older adults. In M.O. Hogstel (Ed.), *Nursing care of the older adult* (pp. 500–518). Albany, NY: Delmar Publishing.

Drinka, T.J., Smith, J.C., & Drinka, P.M. (1987). Correlates of depression and burden for informal caregivers of patients in a geriatric referral clinic. *Journal of the American Geriatric Society, 35,* 522–525.

Fulmer, T. (1989). Mistreatment of elders: Assessment, diagnosis, and intervention. *Nursing Clinics of North America, 24,* 707–716.

Gallagher, D., Rose, J., Rurena, P., Lovett, S., & Thompson, L.W. (1989). Prevalence of depression in family caregivers. *Gerontologist, 29,* 449–456.

Hackbarth, D.P., Andresen, P., & Konestabo, B. (1989). Maltreatment of the elderly in the home: A framework for prevention and intervention. *Home Health Care Practice, 2,* 43–56.

Haviland, S., & O'Brien, J. (1989). Physical abuse and neglect of the elderly: Assessment and intervention. *Orthopaedic Nursing, 8,* 11–19.

Holmer, A.C., & Gilleard, C. (1990). Abuse of elderly people by their caregivers. *British Medical Journal, 301,* 1359–1362.

Kinsey, L.R., Tarbox, A.R., & Bragg, D.F. (1981). Abuse of the elderly—the hidden agenda. I: Caretakers and categories of abuse. *Journal of the American Geriatric Society, 29,* 465–472.

Kosberg, J. (1988). Preventing elder abuse: Identification of high-risk factors prior to placement decisions. *Gerontologist, 28,* 43–50.

Marin, R.S., & Morycz, R.K. (1990). Victims of elder abuse. In R.T. Ammerman & M. Hersen (Eds.), *Treatment of family violence* (pp. 136–164). New York: John Wiley & Sons.

Nuessel, F.H. (1982). The language of ageism. *Gerontologist, 22,* 273–276.

O'Malley, J.A., Everitt, D.E., O'Malley, H.C., & Campion, E.W. (1983). Identifying and preventing family mediated abuse and neglect of elderly persons. *Annals of Internal Medicine, 98*(b), 99–105.

Pillemer, K., & Finkelhor, D. (1988). The prevalence of elder abuse: A random sample survey. *Gerontologist, 28,* 51–57.

Pillemer, K., & Moore, D.W. (1989). Abuse of patients in nursing homes: Findings from a survey. *Gerontologist, 29,* 314–320.

Quinn, M., & Tomita, S. (1986). *Elder abuse and neglect: Causes, diagnosis, and intervention strategies.* New York: Springer Publishing.

Rathbone-McCuan, E. (1980, May). Elderly victims of family violence and neglect. *Social Casework: The Journal of Contemporary Social Work,* 296–303.

Rathbone-McCuan, E., & Voyles, B. (1982). Case detection of abused elderly parents. *American Journal of Psychiatry, 139,* 189–192.

Shanas, E. (1979). The family as a social support system in old age. *Gerontologist, 19,* 169–174.

Steinmetz, S.K. (1978, July/August). Battered parents. *Society,* 54–55.

Steinmetz, S.K. (1988). Elder abuse by family caregivers: Processes and intervention strategies. *Contemporary Family Therapy, 10,* 256–271.

Straus, M., Gelles, R., & Steinmetz, S. (1980). *Behind closed doors: Violence in the American family.* Garden City, NY: Anchor Press / Doubleday.

U.S. House of Representatives. (1981). *Elder abuse: An examination of a hidden problem.* Select Committee on Aging, 97th Congress. Publ. No. 97-277. Washington, DC: U.S. Government Printing Office.

U.S. House of Representatives. (1985). *Elder abuse.* Select Committee on Aging, 99th Congress. Publ. No. 99-516. Washington, DC: U.S. Government Printing Office.

U.S. House of Representatives. (1991). *Elder abuse: What can be done?* Select Committee on Aging, 102nd Congress. Publ. No. 102-808. Washington, DC: U.S. Government Printing Office.

Wolf, R.S. (1986). Major findings from three model projects on elderly abuse. In K.A. Pillemer & R.S. Wolf (Eds.), *Elder abuse: Conflict in the family* (pp. 218–238). Dover, MA: Auburn House.

IV

Some Solutions
to the Problem

11

Discharge Planning

Lisa Nerenberg and Susan W. Haikalis

Discharge planners play a pivotal role in reducing the risk of abuse to victims once they leave the protected hospital environment. The timing of the discharge, the environment into which patients are released, and the arrangements that are made for follow-up can have a critical impact on patients' future safety and security.

The discharge planner's task is difficult because he or she is often under intense pressure from a variety of sources (Goldberg & Estes, 1990; Wood & Estes, 1990). Under Medicare's reimbursement system and managed care plans, planners are under increasing pressure from plan administrators and third-party payors to discharge clients as soon as it is medically possible. This is particularly difficult when a patient has been mistreated because abuse cases do not often lend themselves to rapid resolution. Often, victims are ambivalent about accepting help or are reluctant to take action against abusers. They may need extended periods of time to consider their options and work through their ambivalence. Many of the legal and protective interventions that are employed in abuse cases involve a significant amount of time. As a result, discharge planners may feel pressured, by community agencies as well as by their own concerns for the patient's safety, to postpone discharge while legal interventions are completed or while support networks are put into place. Finally, because abuse cases often involve conflicts or disputes within families, successful discharge planning may include lengthy assessments of the competing interests, rights, and motivations of all of the parties involved. The discharge planner must carefully balance all of these complex ethical, financial, legal, and clinical considerations in developing a successful plan.

DISCHARGE PLANNING

Discharge planning is a complex series of functions that combine to produce a timely and effective plan for a patient's release from the hospital (American Hospital Association, 1985). These functions usually include an assessment of the patient (who he or she is, where he or she came from, who is available for support, and how he or she coped in the past); an assessment of how disease or illness has affected and will continue to affect the patient's life; the development of a plan to provide necessary interventions and counseling in order to help the patient cope with necessary changes; an assessment of alternative placement options (e.g., home, skilled nursing facility, residential care facility) and a list of the services that are needed to support the placement (e.g., Meals-on-Wheels, attendant care, home health care); and referrals to postacute community resources. Discharge planning should involve the patient, his or her support system, the attending medical personnel, and postacute resource staff.

Although medical treatment planning depends entirely on the patient's medical condition, discharge planning addresses the broad psychosocial needs of a patient and his or his family while the patient is hospitalized and afterward. The aim of discharge planning has traditionally been to achieve maximum independence for a patient after he or she returns home.

Hospital discharge planning falls within the domain of clinical social work. The social worker is viewed as the health care professional who develops the bridge between the hospital and "home" for the patient (Volland, 1988). The clinical perspective is that discharge planning embodies many of the characteristics of crisis intervention because hospitalization usually represents a crisis that requires reorganization of the patient's life following discharge.

Hospital licensing regulations require that discharge plans be completed for all patients, but the delivery of discharge planning services varies from hospital to hospital. Ideally, discharge planning begins at the time a planned admission is considered. The planning process involves close monitoring of the patient's medical status, the patient's wishes, the thoughts and diagnoses of the physician, and the involvement of the family and other caregivers throughout the hospitalization.

DISCHARGE PLANNING IN A
CHANGING HEALTH CARE ENVIRONMENT

The field of discharge planning is rapidly changing. This change can be attributed to a great extent to the incentives created by new health care financing systems (Falck, 1989). Under capitated medical care plans, profits depend on the point at which patients are discharged in relation to specified breakeven points. Medicare, for example, has defined diagnosis-related groups (DRGs), which establish reimbursement rates for various diagnoses. Elderly people are also increasingly giving up their Medicare cards and enrolling in health maintenance organizations (HMOs) (Manton et al., 1993), which also set caps on the amount of money paid for hospital stays (QualMed, 1994). The average length of stay (ALOS) has been moving steadily downward, even for elderly patients on Medicare. For example, in southern California, the ALOS for Medicare-age patients in 1994 was 3.5 days.

Under these systems, if patients stay longer than the ALOS, the hospitals lose money. The consequence is that significant pressure exists to discharge patients as early as possible. These developments have propelled hospital discharge planning in a new direction. Within the managed care environment the goal of discharge planning becomes the discharge of patients from hospitals with the proviso that their medical progress is sufficient to ensure a safe discharge; that is, that nothing will happen to require readmission for essentially the same medical problem (Oktay et al., 1992).

The role of effective discharge planning in cost containment has led health care providers to disagree as to which group is best qualified to undertake discharge planning. Many hospitals are transferring the responsibility for discharge planning from social workers to other professionals, such as case managers (usually nurses), in the hospital setting. Consequently, medical considerations are taking precedence over social considerations in discharge planning. Many hospitals, however, continue to employ social workers to provide discharge planning. The most effective discharge planning programs seem to use teams of social workers and nurses to provide comprehensive discharge planning services, thus capitalizing on the skills of both types of professionals (Haddock, 1994; Haikalis, 1994).

The movement toward capitated plans has also meant that it is increasingly the insurers (i.e., plan administrators), rather than hospital personnel, who are making decisions about discharge. Corporate headquarters or third-party payors are assuming prominent roles in discharge planning.

DISCHARGE PLANNING IN ELDER ABUSE CASES

Although abuse is likely to be discovered by hospital personnel (e.g., emergency room staff, attending physicians, nurse case managers), abuse cases are usually referred to social workers in order to develop follow-up plans.

Discharge planning for victims of elder abuse involves developing plans that reduce the risk of revictimization and subsequent readmission. When victims of abuse are released into high-risk situations or when the problems that led to the abuse remain unresolved, the abuse is likely to recur. Thus, successful discharge planning in abuse cases often addresses the root causes of abuse, which are interpersonal rather than related to medicine or health. Although the time spent with clients by the discharge planner is becoming shorter (as a result of reduced LOS), particularly in light of the lengthy process that may be needed to effect lasting change, the victim's hospitalization creates an opportunity for the discharge planner to reduce the risk of future abuse.

Reducing the risk of revictimization entails counseling victims and family members and making referrals to community agencies for follow-up. Counseling may focus on helping victims explore and assess their options, work through their ambivalence or apprehension about seeking help, and develop safety plans or coping strategies. Community agencies to which victims are frequently referred include the police, legal aid programs, public guardians, social services agencies, and support services.

COUNSELING

Professionals who work with victims of abuse have noted that seeking help is a process rather than a discrete event, and that the process may be time intensive. Counseling techniques, such as those listed below, were developed to provide support to victims as they seek help. The techniques, many of which were developed by domestic violence professionals, reduce the risk of future injury and enhance the likelihood that victims will seek help. Although many of these techniques were developed to assist younger victims of domestic violence, they hold promise for elderly victims of abuse, neglect, and exploitation.

Educating Victims About Domestic Violence

Many victims believe that abuse will end spontaneously if certain conditions are met. For example, victims commonly believe that the abuse will end if they make fewer physical and emotional demands on the abuser. The research on domestic violence, however, belies this common belief. Experience shows that abuse often escalates in frequency and intensity over time (Walker, 1984). Many professionals believe that educating victims about this trend may negate false assumptions and motivate them to seek help, although changing such deep-seated beliefs probably will require considerable time.

Developing a Safety Plan

During periods of crisis, victims may be unable or unprepared to take action to protect themselves. Developing safety plans in advance may prepare them to avoid revictimization. A safety plan may include provisions for what the victim will do if the abuse recurs, such as staying with a friend or family member. Making these decisions in advance increases the likelihood that the victim will follow through on seeking help.

Options Counseling

Options counseling is the systematic assessment of available services and the ways in which victims can access those services. It acknowledges and addresses victims' apprehension and emotional confusion about making changes in their lives and their need to consider and reconsider options over time.

REFERRALS TO COMMUNITY RESOURCES

Discharge planning also matches the individual with appropriate community services. In order to be effective, discharge planners must be familiar with a wide variety of community resources and how to access them, and they must fully understand the mandates, procedures, information needs, and perspectives of the agencies with which they interact. For example, if the discharge planner has a basic understanding of the evidence required to substantiate the need for public guardianship, he or she is better equipped to provide the needed information and to facilitate the referral.

The following sections detail the community-based services with which discharge planners are most likely to interact (Aravanis et al., 1993).

Adult Protective Services

The function of Adult Protective Services (APS) is to protect individuals who are endangered because of unsafe or hazardous living conditions, physical abuse, neglect, or exploitation. APS services are voluntary and the client must agree to the provision of services.

APS has been designated by most states as the agency that receives the reports of elder abuse that are mandated under state elder abuse prevention law. Depending on the state law, APS may be required to investigate all cases of abuse or only certain types of abuse. Reporting laws may dictate that APS cross-report with law enforcement, or may suggest that APS cross-report under certain circumstances, such as when the APS investigator is denied access to investigate or when it would be unsafe for the APS investigator to visit the client alone.

When APS investigators receive reports of abuse and neglect, they must investigate to substantiate the claims and evaluate the client's capacity to consent to services. If the case is opened, a service plan is developed with the participation of the client, caregivers, and other family members. APS then implements the plan and monitors the case.

APS investigators also are charged with protecting clients' civil liberties and autonomy. This includes respecting their right to make decisions for themselves, even when those decisions jeopardize their health or safety. Exceptions to this rule include situations in which the older person has a cognitive impairment and lacks the mental capacity to give or deny consent and situations in which the abuse constitutes a crime.

Long-Term Care Ombudsman

The Long-Term Care Ombudsman Program is a federal program that was created to receive and investigate complaints by and on behalf of residents of nursing facilities and residential care facilities. The program employs paid staff and volunteers to provide regular visitations at these facilities. In many states the long-term care ombudsman also investigates allegations of abuse and neglect in nursing homes, residential care facilities, and adult day health centers under abuse reporting laws.

Law Enforcement

Some forms of abuse constitute criminal conduct and must be reported to law enforcement. For example, abuse may be classified as assault, battery, domestic violence, theft, fraud, larceny, or neglect. Some states have special criminal elder abuse statutes, which extend the range of conduct that is covered, enhance penalties for crimes against elderly victims, or make cases easier to prosecute.

In addition to punishing abusers for their conduct, the criminal justice system offers a variety of options for victims. In some states criminal courts can order abusers into drug or domestic violence counseling, order restitution, or place restrictions on abusers' conduct (e.g., restraining orders) (Plotkin, 1988).

The criminal justice system operates on the principle that society has established a code of conduct for all citizens, and that abusers must be held accountable when their actions exceed these boundaries. Thus, criminal proceedings can be undertaken in cases of serious abuse without victims' consent or cooperation. In situations in which victims do not want to take legal action against their abusers, service providers must balance their responsibilities to promote client autonomy with their obligation to uphold the law.

Medicaid Fraud Control Units

Under federal law, state attorney generals' offices are required to investigate and prosecute fraud and patient abuse or neglect in health care facilities that participate in Medicaid. These units have been designated Medicaid Fraud Control Units.

Area Agencies on Aging

The federal Older Americans' Act (OAA) of 1978 established a national structure for providing services to older people. Under the act, every state established a state unit on aging. Within each state Area Agencies on Aging (AAAs) serve smaller geographic areas. They may cover cities, counties, or groups of counties. AAAs coordinate the delivery of aging services that are supported by federal funds. Many of these agencies also coordinate services that are supported by state and local funds. AAAs also serve as information and referral sources for older people and their families, although some AAAs contract with other agencies to provide this service. AAAs provide a point of access to the numerous health and human services that can be employed to reduce the risk of abuse or treat its effects.

Legal Services

The federal OAA established a network of free legal services for people over age 60. These programs are becoming adept at handling abuse cases, assisting with obtaining civil restraining orders, initiating lawsuits to recoup misappropriated funds or property, and helping older people establish financial plans that reduce their vulnerability.

Victims Services

Victims services are available for victims whose cases have advanced to the criminal justice system. Victims services units, which are usually located within prosecutors' offices, provide victims with information about the court process and the status of their cases. They advocate for victims and convey to the court victims' preferences about jail time, plea bargaining, or the need for restraining orders. They also provide victims with information about special victims' compensation programs and community services.

Domestic Violence Programs

The benefits of domestic violence programs are increasingly being recognized in the field of elder abuse prevention. Domestic violence services include shelters, counseling for victims and abusers, and crisis lines.

Although battered women's shelters are found in most communities, the facilities are not always appropriate for elderly women or men. Many shelters are unable to accommodate victims with serious disabilities who require special care. Those shelters that can accommodate victims with disabilities do so with the proviso that clients' care needs are thoroughly explained to shelter staff and that special assistance is arranged for the victims. Some communities have special shelters or temporary housing for elderly people that can be accessed in emergencies. Numerous communities have "safe houses," which offer emergency shelter in private homes with foster families until alternative housing options can be located (American Association of Retired Persons, 1992).

Financial Management

Financial abuse frequently occurs when elderly or dependent adults lose the ability to manage their financial affairs. When this ability is lost or impaired, elderly people may voluntarily place authority in the hands of untrustworthy individuals, or they may be coerced or tricked into signing away home ownership or property. Discharge planners can arrange for the services of trustworthy people or agencies to provide financial management.

Financial management may be informal—an appointed individual or agency simply helps an older person to pay bills or make transactions, or it may be formal—lawyers set up legal transfers of authority such as representative payeeships, powers of attorney, or guardianships.

Mental Health Services

Mental health services that are often required in abuse cases include crisis intervention and counseling for victims, abusers, and families, and assessment of victims' or abusers' mental health status. Mental health assessments determine whether victims possess the mental capacity to consent to or refuse services, to comprehend transactions they have made, and to provide legal testimony. Abusers may be assessed to determine whether they constitute a danger to others as a result of mental illness. Violent abusers who are found to be mentally ill may be detained involuntarily for further assessment or treatment.

Family and Caregiver Support Services

In situations in which abuse or neglect is related to the stresses associated with caring for an older person, the risk of abuse can be reduced by providing the family with support services that reduce the older person's dependence on the caregiver and provide temporary respite from caregiving tasks for family members. Support services include a home-delivered meal, transportation, and attendant care.

Support Groups for Caregivers Since approximately 1985 support groups for caregivers have proliferated. These groups address and ease the emotional demands and stresses that are associated with providing care to older people with disabilities and impairments. They also provide instruction and guidance in meeting the needs of these older people and in handling difficult behaviors. Support groups reduce the tensions, resentments, and stresses that may trigger incidents of abuse and neglect.

Respite Care Respite care programs are designed to relieve the stress of caregiving by providing caregivers with "time off" from their responsibilities. Some respite care programs assign attendants, nurses, or volunteers to visit older people's homes for a few hours to spell caregivers; other programs transport older people to special facilities, such as an adult day services center. Some respite programs provide care and supervision of older people for a few hours a day or for several days or weeks, allowing caregivers to take extended breaks or vacations. Respite programs reduce the risk of abuse and neglect by relieving the stresses that prevent caregivers from providing adequate care or that cause them to lash out at the older people to whom they are providing care.

Dependency Reduction Situations in which abusers are dependent on their victims for money or a place to live can often be improved by reducing the abuser's dependency on the victim. This may be accomplished through job training or job placement, financial assistance, or counseling in independent living. Although it is more difficult to induce abusers with substance abuse problems to seek treatment voluntarily, treatment can be mandated as a condition of probation or as an alternative to prosecution.

DOCUMENTATION
Good documentation is essential in all medical and social work practice, but particularly in elder abuse cases in order to effect needed changes (see also Chapter 8) (Hwalek, 1989). For example, ending abuse may require legal interventions, in which compelling evidence of abuse must be presented to criminal or civil courts. Hospital personnel may be called upon to provide evidence or testimony about injuries or conditions related to the abuse or about the impact of those injuries or conditions on the victim. Staff may also be asked to provide evidence or testimony about a victim's mental capacity or medical history. Documentation ensures accurate recollection of events and their aftermath.

Documentation of the abuse should be collected by all attending personnel, but the discharge planner usually compiles, organizes, and maintains the documentation and is likely to be asked to provide or interpret the information contained in the documentation to other community agencies. The discharge planner may need to instruct attending medical personnel as to what signs or symptoms may suggest abuse. For example, the discharge planner may instruct physicians to note that a patient's or family member's explanation of an injury is inconsistent with the medical evidence. The discharge planner may also need to instruct other hospital personnel in preparing evidence and testimony for court. Finally, the discharge planner may be responsible for collecting and safeguarding evidentiary materials and obtaining patient consent in order to release information to the proper authorities.

The following case example demonstrates what can be accomplished by a discharge planner in a relatively short time to reduce the risk of revictimization and to set the stage for future interventions.

Mrs. Giordano, a 79-year-old widow, was brought to a hospital emergency room with a cut on her head. Although the injury was not serious, the attending physician noted that Mrs. Giordano was in extremely poor health and appeared to be malnourished. He admitted her and ordered laboratory tests that revealed an electrolyte imbalance and dehydration.

The case was referred to the social services department, and a social worker was assigned to develop a discharge plan. The discharge planner interviewed Mrs. Giordano and learned that she lived with an adult grandson and several of his friends in a home that she owned. The grandson and his friends frequently used drugs in the home. He pressured Mrs. Giordano into giving him most of the limited income on which she lived. He threatened her verbally at first, but the confrontations escalated and he soon became physically abusive. As the abuse escalated, Mrs. Giordano began spending most of the day in her room and she stopped eating regularly.

The discharge planner reported the abuse to APS. An APS investigator interviewed Mrs. Giordano about the abuse, counseled her about her options, and instructed her as to how she could obtain a restraining order against her grandson, which would force him to move out of her home. Mrs. Giordano refused this option because she said she did not wish to have her grandson or his friends removed. She expressed concern that her grandson would become homeless if she forced him to move out. She refused all other services that the APS investigator offered. Because APS services are voluntary, and because Mrs. Giordano refused to accept help, APS closed the case.

Although the discharge planner acknowledged Mrs. Giordano's right to refuse services, she was convinced that Mrs. Giordano was denying the seriousness of her situation. She felt that if she could develop a trusting relationship with Mrs. Giordano, she could help her to acknowledge the danger she was in and to recognize that the abuse would likely worsen.

The discharge planner obtained Mrs. Giordano's consent to notify a daughter who lived in another city about the situation and encouraged the daughter to become involved. With the discharge planner's support and the encouragement of her daughter, Mrs. Giordano informed her grandson that he and his friends could continue living with her only if they stopped using drugs and if he stopped physically abusing her.

The grandson agreed to these conditions, but the discharge planner believed that the abuse would likely recur. She helped Mrs. Giordano develop a safety plan. The plan was that Mrs. Giordano would call her daughter immediately if the abuse recurred or if she became frightened of her grandson. The daughter agreed to allow her mother to stay with her temporarily if needed. The discharge planner gave Mrs. Giordano and her daughter phone numbers for the APS unit and a legal assistance program and encouraged them to contact these services if the abuse continued. She also made a referral to the hospital's home care program, which would provide follow-up and monitoring. Finally, the discharge planner carefully documented the physical abuse, Mrs. Giordano's physical condition, and all actions that were taken.

OBSTACLES TO RESOLUTION

Despite the numerous community agencies that offer services that intervene in abuse, discharge planners may encounter a variety of obstacles in trying to resolve abuse cases effectively, including the following (Nerenberg, 1995):

- Limited community resources for investigating and documenting abuse. Investigating abuse can be extremely complex and time consuming. It may involve collecting medical records, testimony, or legal documents that cover extended periods of time and many sources. Many communities lack sufficient resources to meet the demands of a protracted investigation.
- Lack of coordination among agencies. The need for coordinated interagency responses to elder abuse is becoming recognized in the United States. However, the lack of coordination and cooperation among agencies for sharing information, conducting collaborative investigations, and developing care plans continues to inhibit abuse prevention efforts.
- Difficulties in defining mental incapacity. Many decisions regarding the appropriate course of action in abuse cases are based on assumptions about victims' mental capacity. For example, agency personnel must determine when victims are capable of consenting to services. Courts must determine when victims are in need of surrogate decision makers. Substantiating abuse also often involves determining whether victims understood the documents that they signed. Service providers who work with victims frequently disagree about victims' capacity. Discordant judgments may lead to subsequent disagreements about appropriate courses of action.
- Lack of training in the identification, documentation, and treatment of elder abuse. Because the field of elder abuse prevention and treatment is still relatively new, many professionals lack skills in abuse intervention techniques. Consequently, discharge planners may find that other professionals in the community are reluctant to accept referrals, lack skills in working with elderly people or in dealing with abuse, or disagree with the discharge assessments.

The following case example demonstrates how these obstacles can lead to repeated readmissions and discharges, which can result in exorbitant and wasteful expenditures.

Mr. Ostrowski, a 67-year-old widower, was admitted to the hospital with difficulty breathing and cardiac symptoms. After a physical examination and laboratory tests, he was diagnosed with endstage cardiac disease, which was attributed to heavy cigarette smoking. He lived in public housing with an unemployed 35-year-old son and friends of the son. Mr. Ostrowski received Social Security and Supplemental Security Income benefits and was covered by Medicare and Medicaid.

Over a period of 4 years, Mr. Ostrowski was admitted to four different hospitals. The lengths of the hospitalizations ranged from 2 weeks to almost 1 year. He stayed for 6 months in an acute care unit and more than 6 months in a hospital-based skilled nursing facility. He was admitted to the public long-term care unit three times.

During the hospitalizations Mr. Ostrowski rarely received visitors, except for the monthly visits from his son or the son's friends, who came to have him sign over his benefit checks. Each time Mr. Ostrowski's condition stabilized to the point at which he could be discharged, discharge planners were unable to find family members who were willing to assist him at home. Each time he was released, follow-up nursing staff found him at home alone, asleep on a couch, or smoking while taking oxygen. No one was present to monitor his medications or his cardiac condition. Multiple, but futile, attempts were made to educate the son and his friends about the dangerous combination of smoking and oxygen as well as the seriousness of Mr. Ostrowski's medical condition.

During several of his hospitalizations, Mr. Ostrowski was examined by psychiatrists, who initially did not find him gravely disabled. By the 12th admission, however, hospital staff determined that he lacked the mental capacity to make decisions. A referral was made to the Public Guardian, but Mr. Ostrowski's son appeared at the hearing and promised to provide care to his father. The neglect continued, and Mr. Ostrowski was hospitalized several more times before he was finally transferred to a hospital-based skilled nursing facility, where he lived for 6 months. Mr. Ostrowski's numerous hospitalizations at multiple institutions resulted in costs that approached $1 million.

CONCLUSION

Discharge planners face many challenges in handling elder abuse cases. Pressures are exerted by hospital administrators and third-party payors to release clients as soon as it is medically feasible, and obstacles are encountered in working with other community agencies, such as inadequate interagency coordination, lack of professional understanding and competency, a shortage of services, and an absence of consensus in handling cases.

Because discharge planners are the hospital's link to community agencies, they can contribute to overcoming these obstacles by participating in efforts to improve the community's response to elder abuse. Their participation on planning and problem-solving councils, on multidisciplinary case review teams, in cross-disciplinary training programs, and in advocacy efforts can have a significant effect on a community.

The trend toward managed care plans and capitated health care financing has also created special challenges for discharge planners in the field of elder abuse prevention. Professionals in the field need to provide information to insurers, managed care providers, doctors, and nurses on the patterns, dynamics, and effects of elder abuse. They must also convey the message that an aggressive and proactive approach to abuse prevention can be cost effective. The failure of communities and institutions to develop effective intra- and interagency responses can result in repeated, inappropriate, and costly hospitalizations as well as undue hardship and suffering for victims.

REFERENCES

American Association of Retired Persons. (1992). *Abused elders or older battered women?* Report on the AARP Forum, Washington, DC: Author.

American Hospital Association, Society for Hospital Social Work Directors. (1985). *The role of the social worker in discharge planning: Position statement.* Chicago: Author.

Aravanis, S.C., Adelman, R.D., Breckman, R., Fulmer, T.T., Holder, E., Lachs, M., O'Brien, J.G., & Sanders, A.B. (1993). Diagnostic and treatment guidelines on elder abuse and neglect. *Archives of Family Medicine, 2,* 371.

Falck, H.S. (1989, April). *Discharge planning as clinical social work.* Paper presented at the annual meeting and educational conference of the Society for Hospital Social Work Directors of the American Hospital Association, St. Louis.

Goldberg, S.C., & Estes, C.L. (1990, March). Medicare DRGs and post-hospital care for the elderly: Does out of the hospital mean out of luck? *Journal of Applied Gerontology, 9*(1), 20.

Haddock, K.S. (1994, September). Collaborative discharge planning: Nursing and social services. *Clinical Nurse Specialist, 8*(5), 248–252.

Haikalis, S.W. (1994). Workshop presentation at the annual meeting of the American Hospital Association's Society for Hospital Social Work Administrators in Health Care, Philadelphia, 1994.

Hwalek, M. (1989). Proper documentation: A key topic in training programs for elder abuse workers. *Journal of Elder Abuse and Neglect, 1*(3), 17–30.

Manton, K.G., Woodbury, M.A., Vertrees, J.C., & Stallard, E. (1993, August). Use of Medicare services before and after introduction of the prospective payment system. *Health Service Research, 28*(3), 269–292.

Nerenberg, L. (1995). *Building partnerships: A guide to developing coalitions, interagency agreements and teams in the field of elder abuse.* San Francisco: Mount Zion Institute on Aging.

Oktay, J.S., Steinwachs, D.M., Mamon, J., Bone, L.R., & Fahey, M. (1992). Evaluating social work discharge planning services for elderly people: Access, complexity, and outcome. *Health and Social Work, 17*(4), 290–298.

QualMed. (1994). *Annual report.* Los Angeles: Author.

Volland, P.J. (1988). Evolution of discharge planning. In P.J. Volland (Ed.), *Discharge planning: An interdisciplinary approach to continuity of care* (pp. 1–20). Owings Mills, MD: National Health Publishing.

Walker, L. (1984). *The battered women's syndrome*. New York: Springer Publishing.

Wood, J.B., & Estes, C.L. (1990). The impact of DRGs on community-based service providers: Implications for the elderly. *American Journal of Public Health, 80*(7), 840.

12

A Model Abuse Prevention Training Program for Long-Term Care Staff

Beth Hudson Keller

According to the 1994 Pre–White House Conference on Aging forum, *Silent Suffering: Elder Abuse in America,* elder abuse is beginning to gain a place in the minds of the populace and policy makers (Watson, 1994). The abuse and neglect of elderly people represents a potentially life-threatening problem that may affect 1–2 million elderly people per year (Anetzberger, Lachs, O'Brien, Pillemer, & Tomita, 1993). The elderly people most vulnerable to abuse are frail, impaired, and dependent on others for their care. No national prevalence data exist for domestic or institutional elder mistreatment; development of the knowledge base has been hindered by disbelief, misinformation, underdetection, and a scarcity of well-designed research (Anetzberger et al., 1993). Only since the mid-1980s have researchers begun to examine the nature and correlates associated with abuse that occurs at the hands of paid caregivers.

As public awareness of this issue has grown, incremental improvements have been made in the content of training curricula for care providers. Training programs across the health care continuum incorporate basic information regarding the recognition and identification of the various forms of abuse. However, research from institutional settings shows that health care staff require intensive training in subtle forms of abuse and neglect, strategies to cope with challenging residents, and methods to monitor their feelings and reactions to the elderly people under their care and their own caregiving practices.

Paid caregivers from nursing facilities, board and care homes, and home health care agencies are faced with the task of providing the physical mechanics of care as well as the emotional, psychological, social, and spiritual needs of vulnerable long-term care consumers. Care providers perform these tasks under stressful working conditions, receive little or no support from supervisors, and are often the targets of abuse from the residents/clients and family members. Rosalie Wolf, speaking at the Pre–White House Conference on Aging, stressed the need for training in violence reduction and conflict resolution for professional caregivers (Watson, 1994).

The most recent information from the nursing facility, personal board and care home, and home health care industries documents the need for training in abuse prevention. The training should educate care staff about the types of abuse and their indicators, and it should educate staff members about strategies that defuse potentially abusive situations with residents and clients.

The information in the following section accentuates the lack of adequate training for direct care staff in nursing facilities, board and care homes, and home health care. Feldman (1994, p. 7) summarizes the challenges facing paraprofessionals:

> low wages and poor benefits, compounded by the emotional and physical strain of the work, . . . the lack of sufficient organizational training and support, and the absence of opportunities for advancement [are] factors contributing to difficulties in recruiting frontline workers, to high staff turnover, and to quality problems in long-term care.

This chapter reviews a training program that was designed to ensure high-quality care by raising staff awareness of elder abuse and by providing abuse prevention strategies. Although the language used throughout the chapter pertains to institutional settings, the topics covered may be easily adapted to the home health care industry.

TRAINING IN THE LONG-TERM CARE ENVIRONMENT

Nursing Facilities

Although nursing facilities have received more attention from researchers on elder abuse than other long-term care settings, very few statistics are available to provide a clear picture of why abuse happens and how often it occurs. Gannett News Service's special investigative project on criminal care in nursing facilities reported that 613,000 nursing assistants are working nationwide and that most are "caring, industrious people—paid about $12,000 a year to be the workhorses of the business" (Eisler, 1994, p. 1). Anecdotal information portrays nursing assistants, who provide 90% of resident care, as condescending, indifferent, insensitive, and cruel to residents. Tellis-Nayak and Tellis-Nayak (1989) describe care provided without commitment, often with a cheerless attitude and an unsympathetic touch. After completing 8 months of field work in a New York City nursing facility, Foner (1994) concluded that most nursing assistants are neither saints nor monsters. She states that the daily mixture of "compassion and exasperation is a powerful reminder that aides' relations with patients cannot be reduced to simple all-or-nothing evaluations—and [is] a reflection of the complex tangle of attachments, obligations, and antagonisms involved in nursing home care" (Foner, 1994, p. 250).

Two quantitative studies have shed some light on the nature and scope of resident abuse. Pillemer and Moore (1989) conducted the first random sample survey of staff to specifically assess the prevalence and correlates of abuse in nursing facilities. A total of 577 registered nurses, licensed practical nurses, and nursing assistants were surveyed in nursing facilities in New Hampshire. The survey encompassed two major components: staff reports of abuse by other staff and staff reports of their own abusive actions. The researchers analyzed the data and concluded that abuse is sufficiently prevalent to merit public concern. Several factors related to abusive behavior were identified: Staff who experienced low job satisfaction, who treated residents as childlike, and who had stressful personal lives were more likely to abuse residents. Based upon their findings, the researchers highlighted the need for increased attention to the quality of interactions that staff have with residents because this interaction may be the single most important variable in a resident's quality of life in a nursing facility. Pillemer and Moore also recommended staff be trained in coping with and avoiding confrontational situations with residents.

In April 1990 the Office of Inspector General (OIG) issued its study of abuse in nursing facilities, which corroborated the New Hampshire results (U.S. Department of Health and Human Services, 1990). The OIG interviewed 235 people from 35 states who were involved with either receiving or investigating complaints of abuse in nursing facilities. All respondents reported abuse was a problem in their facility, and that staff, other residents, and family members contributed to the problem. Other factors were inadequate supervision of staff, high staff turnover, and lack of staff training in handling difficult situations with residents. The OIG report recommended staff training in conflict resolution, abuse awareness, and reporting responsibilities.

Industry advocates and regulators advise that the best way to recruit and retain good staff is to provide good training, a properly staffed work environment, and administrators who believe that the work performed by nursing assistants is important and worthwhile (Eisler, 1994). Nursing assistants who have good skills, such as insight into the conditions of aging and behavior management strategies, are apt to pay attention to and reinforce the strengths and competencies of residents (Abeles, Gift, & Ory, 1994).

Board and Care Homes

Elderly people who reside in board and care homes are isolated and susceptible to improper care practices. The 1989 Senate Special Committee on Aging report, *Board and Care: A Failure in Public Policy,* found that many homes provide grossly substandard care that endangers the health and well-being of residents. One reason is the lack of education and training among caregivers. The development of meaningful training materials is a solution that can directly affect the care of residents by supplying caregivers with sound tools for providing high-quality care.

According to a 1993 American Association of Retired Persons (AARP) report the total number of board and care homes is unknown. An industry survey conducted in 1990 identified over 500,000 beds in 36,186 licensed homes serving elderly people, people with illnesses, and people with mental retardation in the United States (Lewin/ICF Inc. & James Bell Associates, 1990). However, the actual number of board and care homes is probably significantly higher because of confusion over the numerous definitions of board and care. Although these facilities represent a significant portion of the long-term care services available to older people and people with disabilities, little attention has been paid to understanding the nature of these facilities, researching the needs of staff and residents, or assessing the quality of care provided. Information about the extent and scope of abuse and neglect in board and care homes and training programs that address these issues are almost nonexistent.

The AARP's 1989 report, *The Board and Care System—A Regulatory Jungle,* reveals that older women and older people with functional limitations make up the largest categories of residents in board and care homes. The vulnerability of these older adults is often exacerbated by the absence of family members, limited resources, and the lack of alternative housing arrangements. The care required to support older people with mental and physical impairments is both physically and emotionally taxing. Serious problems have been identified regarding resident care, including physical and sexual abuse, neglect, and death of residents (U.S. General Accounting Office, 1989).

The stress and frustration inherent in caregiving requires that board and care home staff be adequately trained to recognize their own levels of stress and to use strategies to control stress. Down and Schnurr (1991) advise that the staffs of board and care homes need continuous on-the-job training and counseling: "Employees can be trained with specific job skills, but the quality of being sensitive and caring toward persons who are among society's most vulnerable is an important one that is not easily instilled" (p. 39). The hard, often disagreeable work board and care home staff perform can cause caregivers to become frustrated, angry, abusive, and neglectful. Training requirements that are in place for staff do not adequately address the issues of abuse and neglect. However, providing meaningful options for board and care home staff to use when encountering conflict or frustration will help staff members to negotiate a balanced approach to tasks, co-workers, and residents.

Home Health Care

In response to the growth of the old-old segment of the population, the increasing limitations of family members to provide necessary care for their elderly relatives, and the movement toward health care cost containment, the home health care industry has grown to meet the needs of a dependent population who want to remain in their own homes. This segment of the long-term care industry is the fastest growing health care sector in terms of employment (National Association for Home Care, 1995). Reports of abuses have ranged from incompetent care to the murder of homebound clients. However, as a result of decentralization of the industry, statistics on incidents are difficult to collect. America's fastest growing health care industry is one of the least regulated, and that fact has sparked debate over how best to protect consumers in what can be a life-and-death business (*Philadelphia Inquirer*, April 30, 1992).

In their in-depth study of home care industry employees, Feldman, Sapienza, and Kane (1990, p. 29) describe the inherent stresses associated with home care work:

> The aide is isolated from her peers and rarely ever sees a supervisor on site. She is usually alone with an old woman who is ill, possibly in pain, perhaps disoriented or abusive. Apart from her client, the aide's most frequent contact is with the client's family, which often treats her as a domestic servant.

The problems in care delivery reported by home health care aides involve client behavior that is abusive, angry, bizarre, stubborn, depressive, forgetful, and fearful. Caregivers report that clients' families can be overly demanding and critical. Feldman, Sapienza, and Kane also cite abuse of clients by family members. Home health aides report being sexually harassed, the most threatening situation being when family members or neighbors with greater physical strength harassed aides, who are vulnerable to assaults in their isolated settings.

Compounding these difficult working conditions is the lack of training and support given to direct care staff. Organizational support systems are not often available to help caregivers cope with difficult clients or with personal problems that affect job performance and job satisfaction. This lack of support further detaches caregivers who are trying to cope with the isolation of their work. The small amount of research available recommends training that provides caregivers with opportunities to become familiar with one another and with their supervisors and to identify with the agency (Cantor & Chichin, 1989; Feldman, Sapienza, & Kane, 1990). Education should be interactive; that is, the caregiver should participate in his or her own learning process (Kaye, 1992). How caregivers feel about job training affects their job satisfaction. Adequate training is seen as a method for reducing job-related stress and preventing "burnout" in highly tense or difficult job environments (Cantor & Chichin, 1989). Feldman, Sapienza, and Kane (1990) believe that training should "minimize didactic teaching methods, maximize interactive techniques, and emphasize role-playing and other hands-on methods for building worker confidence and competence" (p. 196).

GOALS OF THE PROGRAM AND RECOMMENDATIONS FOR IMPLEMENTATION

The abuse prevention training program increases staff awareness of abuse, neglect, and the potential for abuse in long-term care facilities; equips staff with appropriate conflict intervention strategies; and reduces abuse in long-term care facilities, thus improving residents' quality of life. The key to avoiding potential abuse is to address the issues that can precipitate abusive or neglectful behavior and to provide proactive, preventive solutions. Therefore, this curriculum is designed to be interactive, dynamic, and practical. The concepts should be presented to staff in a straightforward manner, and the majority of training time should be used for group discussion and the practice of intervention techniques. Throughout the training, participants should be encouraged to share specific, day-to-day examples of challenging caregiver situations. The group should then work together to generate possible interventions based on information acquired from each training module. The use of role play should provide learners with opportunities to test newly acquired knowledge and skills, foster their ability to "think on their feet," and promote creative approaches to potentially difficult situations.

A safe learning environment should be established for participants in order for them to feel comfortable discussing their work, their backgrounds, and their frustrations, and to test newly acquired skills. Some knowledge of the participating caregivers is important for successful training implementation. Brannon and Smyer (1994) describe frontline caregivers as "the underclass of the health services delivery system . . . grappling with the conflicting institutional goals of providing healthcare and providing a home for residents" (p. 34). Staff members must be allowed to vent their frustrations before they can effectively develop coping strategies. The trainer should be a skilled group facilitator with an easygoing style that invites discussion.

Training is unlikely to revolutionize the quality of care provided without a substantial change in management systems. Investment in staff training must be supported by supervisors who model the behaviors and approaches to care that are expected of direct care staff. However, few managers in long-term care facilities have received training in the roles and skills of managing people and processes. "Without this professionally guided personal growth, paraprofessional . . . staff are more likely to be frustrated in their efforts to implement new approaches, to experience symptoms of burnout and to leave their jobs" (Brannon & Smyer, 1994, p. 37).

Management sets the tone for the facility and shapes its culture. Staff members take their cues from the daily gestures, actions, and words of their supervisors. Effective managerial strategies set clear priorities, provide a working structure, and encourage creativity and innovative problem solving. A paycheck may motivate, but does not necessarily inspire people the way a good supervisor does. Regular and careful supervision, as well as praise when the job is well done, are important elements of a facility's culture (Tellis-Nayak, 1993). As a method of judging a facility's "quality culture," Ammentorp, Gossett, and Euchner Poe (1990, pp. 51–52) suggest that the stories told throughout the facility reflect the character of the facility:

> Think about how staff talk about residents. If their stories about attempts to deal with difficult residents or superiors reflect a feeling of hopelessness or futility, extra work on management's part is required to find out more about these sentiments in order to convince staff that there is power in a focus on quality. If the stories are about ideas, successful approaches to problems, and positive relationships with residents, you have a staff in tune with the quality culture.

Once the groundwork is laid for the management of daily life in the nursing facility, and staff members feel consistently supported in their work, the abuse prevention training program empowers staff to become resident advocates by raising their awareness of the nature and scope of mistreatment and by equipping them with the skills necessary to provide high-quality, abuse-free care.

Good training begins with hiring good staff. It is critical to screen out potentially abusive employees. However, screening out potentially abusive staff members is difficult because even caregivers with the best intentions can become involved in abusive situations. The first line of defense is to check for the person's name on the state's abuse registry and to check references from past employers. However, checking references often does not yield enough information to judge the capabilities of the applicant. The interview process is crucial to collecting important information about the prospective employee's skills. Questions should be asked of the candidate about his or her attitude toward nursing facility residents and elderly people. An example might be, "Do you agree with the following statement: 'Most nursing home residents are like children; they need discipline from time to time.'?" Also, a job candidate should be asked to provide an example of how he or she handled a recent stressful situation. The employer can describe a conflictual situation with a resident or other staff member and ask the candidate how he or she would handle the situation. Using role play during an interview can demonstrate whether the applicant can think quickly and can use creativity to solve problems. Assessing the applicant's ability to handle stress and conflict and his or her ability to solve problems will help the employer to judge the applicant's potential on-the-job performance. Once hired, a comprehensive orientation program and regular in-service training on abuse awareness and prevention will help to foster a therapeutic working environment for staff members. The training program described in the following section addresses these issues.

THE ABUSE PREVENTION CURRICULUM

This section describes the eight training modules that constitute *Ensuring An Abuse-Free Environment: A Learning Program for Nursing Home Staff*, the curriculum developed by the Coalition of Advocates for the Rights of the Infirm Elderly (CARIE, 1991). Each section of the curriculum begins with a role play scenario that depicts the subtle types of abuse that occur almost daily in most long-term care facilities. Staff should use these vignettes to practice intervention strategies.

Module 1: An Overview of Abuse in Nursing Facilities

It is 10:45 A.M., and Nancy, a nursing assistant, enters Miss Warner's room to help her get dressed. Miss Warner's closet contains only slips. Nancy knows that everyone is supposed to be up and dressed by 11:00 A.M. She takes a dress from Mrs. Long's (Miss Warner's roommate) closet and puts it on Miss Warner. Knowing that Miss Warner is confused, Nancy feels it is unlikely she will realize that the dress is not hers. As Nancy is walking with Miss Warner down to the dining room for lunch, Mrs. Long passes by. She realizes that her roommate is wearing her favorite dress. Mrs. Long, not one to complain or to make trouble, feels very angry, and decides to spend the rest of the day in her room, looking after her belongings to prevent any further "borrowing."

The world of a nursing facility resident is often reduced to what one can fit into half a room. The material exploitation illustrated in the vignette can be devastating to both residents, and yet, the staff member involved is only trying to do her job, unaware of the impact of her actions. Module 1 provides an opportunity to acknowledge the crucial role of staff in the long-term care industry by validating the difficult work they perform in a sometimes stressful setting. To begin the discussion of abuse in long-term care facilities, staff are asked to step back and view their facility, the residents, and their work from a larger perspective as a means of "setting the stage" for this training program. The question "What percentage of people age 65 and over live in nursing homes?," elicits interesting responses from direct care staff. Many participants believe that more than half of people over age 65 live in nursing facilities, are incontinent, and live on their floor. Most staff who complete this program remark that they do not stop to consider how or why residents are placed in the nursing facility. Characteristics of residents are reviewed and events that usually precipitate placement are discussed. This validates for participants the difficulties of caring for frail, sick residents, some of whom have dementia, and reminds them that living in a nursing facility is usually the "last resort" for residents.

Learners are urged to recall their views of nursing facilities before they began working in the health care field. The negative publicity about long-term care facilities is generated by the media, who often broadcast only the sensational horror stories of life in nursing facilities; stories about facilities that provide good care are judged by news executives not to be newsworthy. Learners often welcome the opportunity to discuss their feelings about working in a field that most of society would like to avoid. They speak of the feelings of guilt and unfulfilled expectations of the residents' family members and how these feelings can lead to conflicts with staff. A review of nursing facility legislation, including resident rights and nursing assistant certification, provides a reminder that strides are being made to improve the industry and professionalize staff members' work.

Module 2: Identification and Recognition of Abuse

> Mrs. Waltrip, a resident with Alzheimer's disease, wanders the halls, often asking, "Have you seen my mother?" Marcie, a nursing assistant, observes a group of nursing assistants making fun of Mrs. Waltrip. They point her in the direction of the administrator's office and say, "We saw your mother down there." They walk away, laughing, while Mrs. Waltrip hurries toward the administrator's office.

Many learners are not aware that the behavior of the group of nursing assistants in the scenario constitutes psychological abuse. All staff members need education in the definitions, examples, and indicators of the different types of abuse and neglect. Although no universal definition of elder mistreatment has been developed, this curriculum delineates six categories of abuse and neglect based on the state of Pennsylvania's definition (see Appendix). For each category, training participants are asked to define the abuse in their own words, offer specific examples of each type, and list indicators that are the warning signs for each category. Psychological abuse and active and passive neglect are highlighted because they are the more subtle types of abuse that manifest in most facilities. Active neglect (the willful deprivation of goods or services necessary to maintain physical or mental health) and passive neglect (the deprivation of goods or services without conscious intent to inflict physical or emotional distress) are the categories with which most participants identify, and discussions about specific examples and personal stories involving these types of neglect are enlightening for the entire group. This module raises awareness of the broad spectrum of abusive behavior, provides a solid background of the warning signs of abuse and neglect, and helps learners recognize behaviors that are abusive or neglectful.

In conjunction with reviewing abuse definitions in this module, the videotape *Incident Report* can be shown (Massachusetts Department of Health Care Quality, 1984). The videotape skillfully illustrates an abuse scenario from the perspective of the resident, the charge nurse, the director of nursing, the nursing assistant, the administrator, a family member, and a state investigator. The conflict that develops between the nurse and the resident that leads to abuse is an insightful example of the ways in which abuse is influenced by every level of nursing facility staff. The videotape also underscores the need for control by both residents and staff. *Incident Report* is an important tool that helps learners recognize when a negative caregiving situation is becoming uncontrollable and it validates the fact that even the most well-meaning staff member can find him- or herself in an abusive situation.

Module 3: Possible Causes of Abuse

Mrs. Keefe is a recent admission to a nursing facility. She is 87 years old and had a stroke that left her left side paralyzed, although she manages very well with some assistance. Mrs. Keefe's daughter, Arlene, feeling guilty because she could not care for her mother at home, visits for several hours each day. Arlene constantly gives direction concerning her mother's care, and makes most of the staff feel as though they do everything incorrectly or that they are not doing enough for her mother. The nursing assistants steer clear of Mrs. Keefe's room, even when Arlene is not visiting.

Factors that place residents at risk for abuse include behavioral problems (e.g., aggressiveness, physical or verbal abusiveness toward staff, difficult personality); the effects of physical, mental, and social impairments; and communication deficits (e.g., speech impairments, deafness). In the scenario described here a misunderstood family member contributes to the possible neglect of her mother. The potential for abuse is evident when caregivers react negatively to the challenges of difficult resident care situations. Examples of negative reactions from staff include the following:

- Ignoring: Not responding to a resident with a speech impairment who is attempting to talk to a staff member. The caregiver is very busy, and does not have time to decipher what the resident is saying.
- Indifference: Not caring if a resident with dementia receives an incorrect meal tray because the caregiver is sure the resident will not know the difference and will not be able to ask for another tray, which would delay the caregiver's work schedule.
- Neglect: Avoiding a resident's room during the work shift because he or she always needs something, but has trouble finding the right words to ask. The caregiver is tired of trying to decipher what she needs. Sometimes the caregiver closes the door to the resident's room so that she will not see the caregiver walk by and call for her.
- Acting as though the resident is invisible: Walking by a resident who is sitting in her wheelchair in the hallway, yelling and waving her arms. The caregiver finds that it is much easier to behave as though he or she does not see the resident rather than to become involved in ensuring the resident's safety.

Other factors that place residents at risk for abuse include problems specific to the facility or a staff member. Inadequate supervision and training, insufficient staffing, previously learned inappropriate response patterns, and caregiver stress all contribute to the quality of care provided by direct care staff. It is important to note that the description of possible "causes" of abuse does not excuse the abusive acts.

Module 4: Understanding Feelings About Caregiving

> Barbara and Joan go into Mrs. Wooley's and Mrs. Poole's room to awaken them and ready them for breakfast. As Barbara tells Joan about the hectic morning she had at home with her children, Barbara pulls down Mrs. Poole's covers and sees that she has soiled the bed. Barbara says loudly, "Oh, look what you've done! You know better than that, Mrs. Poole! Now I have to change the whole bed! I'll probably be behind for the rest of the day!" Both Joan and Mrs. Wooley look over to see the soiled bed. Mrs. Poole hangs her head and quietly says that she rang the call light earlier but that no one came to help her.

This module provides frontline staff with the opportunity to talk about the frustrations in their jobs and the difficult situations in their personal lives that influence their ability to deliver care. In order to manage stress effectively, staff must be able to identify their own areas and levels of stress inside and outside the workplace. Individual symptoms of stress (e.g., headache, stomachache, pounding heart, shaking, crying, anger) should be taken seriously and controlled as quickly as possible. The signs that stress is escalating (e.g., losing one's temper, raising one's voice, "forgetting" to do important things, losing one's patience, becoming numb, acting indifferent) are clear indicators that a staff member should relieve the cause of the stress before making further contact with residents.

During abuse prevention training, participants explore methods of stress management in order to develop healthy responses to on-the-job stressors. Direct care staff have limited options for stress reduction because they are usually on the floor or in residents' rooms. Participants are urged to pay attention to their stress warning signs and to identify immediate methods for "cooling off" (e.g., sit down, count to ten, take several deep breaths, ask for help, remove self from the stressful situation after the resident's safety is ensured). Staff should also be aware of the stress warning signs of co-workers. As one training participant urged, "We need to rescue each other by offering to help or suggesting a break. It hurts all of us when someone gets out of control." Supervisors can assist direct care staff by recognizing when an individual appears to be frustrated and by offering their office as a private space in which to calm down.

Module 5: Cultural and Ethnic Perspectives and Implications for Staff–Resident Dynamics

> Today is Mrs. Scardino's bath day. She would like to take her bath, but she does not like the nursing assistant, Rita, who is assigned to her. Mrs. Scardino says, "That thick Jamaican accent makes it impossible for me to understand her!" Rita is tired of the unkind treatment she receives from Mrs. Scardino. Mrs. Scardino refuses to go with Rita to the bathroom, and Rita exclaims, "No wonder nobody around here likes you!"

This module helps participants to eliminate the "us versus them" mentality of residents and staff by focusing on three important concepts: autonomy, self-direction, and self-esteem. Resident control is often compromised in an institution; residents are told when to get up, what to eat, what to wear, when to bathe, and when to go to bed. Participants are asked to explore ways to encourage autonomy and decision making by residents, which can lead to enriched self-esteem. Offering residents what may seem like simple choices about daily events (e.g., time of day they want to take their bath, which dress to put on) may provide them with some feeling of control.

An open discussion of the various cultural backgrounds and ethnic diversity of the facility's residents and staff provides participants with the opportunity to share their feelings about how these differences sometimes lead to conflict with residents. Participants have a forum in which to discuss the frustration of maintaining a positive, caring attitude in the face of racial slurs or poor treatment by residents. Learners also become aware that many residents spent much of their lives in a segregated society and in ethnically homogenous neighborhoods. A nursing facility may represent their first close contact with people who are different from themselves. Residents may find being dependent upon people who share no common bonds frightening.

As a way of educating each other about their diversity, staff and residents can develop an ethnic profile orientation program for the entire facility, including residents' families. Facility-wide meals that celebrate the different cultures of both residents and staff may help to reduce conflict. Personal timelines or life histories of residents and staff also are helpful in gaining a better understanding of the people who make up the facility community. If the race, culture, and ethnic backgrounds of staff and residents do not differ or do not present conflicts, trainers may explore gender and/or generational differences and differences between urban and rural backgrounds.

Module 6: Abuse of Staff by
Residents—Understanding Versus Personalizing

> Mr. Astarte has been in a bad mood all day. Now it is time for the resident council meeting, which Mr. Astarte usually attends. Olive, the nursing assistant who cares for Mr. Astarte, comes into his room to remind him about the meeting. He refuses to go. Olive asks why. She knows that usually he is very enthusiastic about the council and helps to motivate other residents to attend. She also knows Mr. Astarte has not been himself today, and she feels the meeting will lift his spirits. Mr. Astarte becomes increasingly agitated as Olive stands over him asking questions. Finally, he barrels into Olive's shins with his wheelchair, yelling, "Leave me alone!"

The rate of resident aggression toward staff is alarming, according to the nursing assistants who participated in this program's pilot test. Of the 211 nursing assistants who completed the training program, only 8% had not been sworn at by a resident in the previous month; only 14% had not been pushed, grabbed, or shoved by a resident in the previous month; and 58% had been kicked or bitten by a resident in the previous month (Pillemer & Hudson, 1993). Module 6 explores the causes of resident anger as a means of understanding why and how resident aggression toward staff occurs. Confusion, loneliness, pain, incontinence, living in a nursing facility, having no visitors, not being in control, and having no freedom of choice are a few of the many reasons for resident anger. Nonviolent approaches to defusing anger and minimizing resident aggression include the use of voice tone and volume, body posture, and distance. In the scenario described here, Olive could have paid more attention to Mr. Astarte's mood and taken the time to explore the reasons for his agitation, rather than pressing him about the council meeting. A simple question such as, "I feel badly that you're upset today, Mr. Astarte. Is there something you'd like to talk about?," may have shown Mr. Astarte that Olive was concerned about him, and he may have been willing to tell her his problem. Olive could have communicated at eye level with Mr. Astarte and respected his personal space, and thus avoided potential injury from the wheelchair.

Staff need to know that alternatives for dealing with challenging care situations are available. At times the duties of the nursing assistant must be delayed in order to ensure a positive outcome with residents. Some training participants react to this statement by explaining that they have no extra time to "chat" with residents who are upset or agitated; their hectic workload does not permit such "luxuries." However, investing a minute or two to listen to the concerns of the resident can save time in the long run by avoiding confrontations and showing the resident that he or she matters enough to spend time actively listening to his or her problem. Abuse of staff by residents is an important topic for training participants, providing them with the opportunity to discuss the challenging and frustrating care situations they face daily.

Module 7: Ethical and Legal Issues of Reporting Suspected Abuse

You have just observed a co-worker hitting a resident after the resident yelled at her. You know that the nursing assistant involved has many personal problems, and has been putting in a lot of overtime. She knows that you witnessed the incident. She approaches you and begs, "Please don't report me. I shouldn't have done it, but she called me names. I really need this job."

The majority of participants in this program's pilot test said they would respond by confronting the nursing assistant and warning her against hitting a resident. Participants must be made aware of their ethical and legal responsibilities regarding reporting suspected abuse. Many past training participants have commented on the pressures against reporting their co-workers. One nursing assistant confessed that she had learned to "look the other way" when she witnessed elder abuse because "nothing ever happens to the worker and I get the cold shoulder from the rest of the staff."

This participant's honesty is indicative of the serious consequences of failing to report suspected abuse. If the co-worker in the scenario decided to ignore the abuse, the nursing assistant could continue to abuse the resident. She could also abuse other residents. The severity of the abuse could increase and cause a serious illness or the death of a resident. If it was discovered that the co-worker was aware of the abuse, legal action could be taken against him or her. (Trainers should consult their state's reporting requirements.)

Nursing facility staff should be resident advocates. Many residents cannot speak for themselves and may not be able to call on anyone to act in their behalf. Direct care staff have the greatest opportunity to protect the welfare of residents by reporting any suspicions of abuse. Reporting takes courage, and this courage needs to be supported by the facility's administration. Staff members also need to know that it is not their responsibility to substantiate or to investigate the alleged abuse. They should know how to report the incident, using the chain of command within the facility. They should also be aware of the investigatory process and the roles of ombudsmen and state inspectors. The training facilitator should consult the state's reporting laws to ensure that accurate information is provided to direct care staff.

Module 8: Intervention Strategies for Abuse Prevention

Tisha has been working at a nursing facility for 3 months. She was recently assigned to a new floor, where she is working with Shannon, a nursing assistant who has worked on the floor for a long time. Mrs. Vulpis is a resident who is somewhat confused, has difficulty speaking, and requires assistance with eating. She eats her meals in her room because the residents in the dining room distract her. Tisha has just sat down with Mrs. Vulpis to help her eat lunch when Shannon approaches her. She tells Tisha to leave Mrs. Vulpis on her own and go on with her work. Shannon explains, "This way, we'll get done sooner and have a longer break. Besides, Vulpis won't know the difference and no one will ever find out. The 3-to-11 shift has more time than we do to sit with her to make sure she eats enough." Tisha believes she should stay with Mrs. Vulpis.

Conflict between residents, between residents and staff, or between staff members directly influences the quality of life for residents. Often, abusive situations occur as a result of conflicts that get out of control. Tisha is new to the facility and wants to get along well with her co-workers, but she knows that what Shannon is suggesting is not right. Tisha's ability to manage this conflict will influence Mrs. Vulpis' care.

The Institute for Mental Health Initiatives (1991) created a framework that can help every member of the nursing facility community to manage conflict appropriately while providing humane, dignified care. The technique, called RETHINK, offers a step-by-step approach to dealing with conflict:

R **Recognize** when you are angry or stressed and learn to help yourself relax.

E **Explain** the situation from the other person's point of view (i.e., empathize).

T **Think** about how you may contribute to the problem.

H **Hear** what the other person is saying; actively listen to the feelings as well as to the words.

I **Include "I"** statements to explain how you feel, rather than starting a sentence with "You. . . ."

N **Negotiate;** try to work things out to everyone's satisfaction.

K Show **kindness** even when expressing frustration.

This framework may seem cumbersome at first, but staff quickly become accustomed to the process by practicing each letter of RETHINK using role plays and case scenarios. Some training participants have commented that on the occasions that they were close to losing their temper with a difficult resident, just remembering the word RETHINK provided them with a second or two to reconsider their approach to the challenging resident.

In addition to using the RETHINK method of conflict management, utilizing the resident care plan; observing and reporting changes in resident behavior; and appropriately using distance, touch, posture, and voice tone and volume enable staff members to provide the best possible care to residents.

Resident Care Plan The resident's care plan is one of the strongest tools available for providing high-quality care to staff, particularly when all members of the care team have the opportunity to contribute to the assessment of the resident. Nursing assistants are an invaluable source of information about resident needs, and this information is instrumental in determining the best approaches to addressing those needs. This individualized blueprint for care should be accessible to the entire care team as a guide to effective care for residents.

Observation and Reporting Direct care staff are able to detect subtle changes in resident behavior and disposition. For example, incontinence may cause aggressive behavior in residents. Caregiver observation may reveal subtle changes in resident behavior, which may indicate the need to void. Toileting residents before they become incontinent may help to circumvent episodes of aggressive behavior. Observation is also important when coping with residents who exhibit repetitive behavior. Instead of becoming frustrated or annoyed, caregivers can observe what distracts the resident from the activity and can determine what the behavior indicates. Not all observations will lead to dramatic results; however, reporting observtions may help in developing an intervention strategy that will assist staff in defusing their frustration, thus avoiding a potentially abusive or neglectful outcome.

Appropriate Use of Distance, Touch, Posture, and Voice Tone and Volume Good-quality staff interactions with residents is the key to providing good care and to maintaining healthy staff attitudes, which allow them to continue to function well in their roles. Body language, facial expressions, tone of voice, and an awareness of how actions or attitudes may exacerbate a challenging situation contribute to the success or failure of providing proper care. A nursing assistant who rushes into a resident's room, throws the covers off the bed, and stands with her hands on her hips, demanding that the resident get out of bed probably will not experience a positive outcome. During training sessions, participants critique this type of encounter, offer suggestions for a more effective approach, and then role play the revised scenario. This kind of practice sharpens the creative skills of participants and offers them a safe place to test new skills. Staff need validation that certain tactics may not succeed with a particular resident. They also need to know that what works today may not work tomorrow. Staff must be made aware that they can remove themselves from a tense situation (first ensuring that the resident is safe) and seek help from a supervisor or a co-worker.

EVALUATION OF THE MODEL PROGRAM

The abuse prevention curriculum was initially tested in 10 nursing homes with 211 randomly selected nursing assistants in the Philadelphia area. A pretest/post-test instrument modeled after the survey used by Pillemer and Moore (1989) was utilized to establish the level of abuse both committed and observed by staff in the study sample. Supervisors were surveyed to evaluate the nursing assistants' performance both before and after training. Prior to training, participants completed a questionnaire that covered the following areas: frequency of abusive behaviors by staff, aggression against staff by residents, number of conflicts with residents in the preceding month (e.g., conflicts over visitors, food, resident complaints), and caregiver attitude (e.g., "Do you agree that residents are like children and need discipline from time to time?").

Rates of self-reported abusive behaviors on the pretest were high. In the month preceding the training, 51% of staff reported that they had yelled at a resident in anger; 23% had insulted or sworn at a resident; 8% had threatened to hit a resident or had thrown something at a resident; 17% had excessively restrained a resident; 10% had pushed, grabbed, or shoved a resident; and 2% had slapped a resident.

The post-test evaluation, conducted 2 months after the training program, repeated the items on the pretest. A number of positive changes were noted in the 114 nursing assistants who completed both the pretest and post-test. The percentage of participants who agreed that residents are like children in need of discipline dropped from 56% to 37% (Wilcoxin test, $p < .001$). Each of the individual conflict items was significantly lower at the post-test. Participants also reported reductions in acts of resident aggression toward caregivers. Finally, self-reported abusive actions by staff declined after the training. The mean score on the abuse scale dropped from 2.1 to 1.6 (t test, $p < .07$) (Pillemer & Hudson, 1993).

Past participants in the abuse prevention training program have indicated that they are disturbed by abuse in their facilities, but they feel powerless to prevent it. They feel relief at receiving an opportunity to discuss these problems openly and in a nonjudgmental atmosphere. Staff enjoy the interactive nature of the program. In noting the differences between this program and other in-service training experiences, the participants have described seminars in which they felt "talked at" and in which open discussion was not encouraged. A safe, comfortable environment must be established in order for staff to be involved in role playing new intervention strategies and practicing conflict management skills.

The conditions that exist in nursing facilities provide a fertile environment for abuse and neglect. The evaluation data from the Philadelphia study and trainers' experiences in conducting the program with hundreds of direct care staff in many areas of the United States argue strongly for the inclusion of this type of abuse prevention education as part of the basic and continuing training for all long-term care staff.

REFERENCES

Abeles, R., Gift, H., & Ory, M. (1994). *Aging and quality of life*. New York: Springer Publishing.

American Association of Retired Persons. (1989). *The board and care system—A regulatory jungle*. Washington, DC: Author.

American Association of Retired Persons. (1993). *The regulation of board and care homes: Results of a survey in the 50 states and the District of Columbia*. Washington, DC: Author.

Ammentorp, W., Gossett, K., & Euchner Poe, N. (1990). *Quality assurance for long term care providers*. Newbury Park, CA: Sage Publications.

Anetzberger, G., Lachs, M., O'Brien, J., Pillemer, K., & Tomita, S. (1993, June). Elder mistreatment: A call for help. *Patient Care*, 93–130.

Brannon, D., & Smyer, M. (1994, Fall). Good work and good care in nursing homes. *Generations*, 34–38.

Cantor, M., & Chichin, E. (1989). *Stress and strain among home care workers of the frail elderly*. New York: Brookdale Research Center on Aging.

Coalition of Advocates for the Rights of the Infirm Elderly. (1991). *Ensuring an abuse-free environment: A learning program for nursing home staff*. Philadelphia: Author.

Down, I., & Schnurr, L. (1991). *Between home and nursing home: The board and care alternative*. Buffalo, NY: Prometheus Books.

Eisler, P. (1994). Criminal care: A Gannett News Service special report. USA Today, 1–8.

Feldman, P. (1994, Fall). "Dead end" work or motivating job? Prospects for frontline paraprofessional workers in LTC. *Generations*, 5–10.

Feldman, P., Sapienza, A., & Kane, N. (1990). *Who cares for them? Workers in the home care industry*. Westport, CT: Greenwood Press.

Foner, N. (1994). Nursing home aides: Saints or monsters? *Gerontologist, 34*, 245–250.

Institute for Mental Health Initiatives. (1991). *Anger management for parents: The RETHINK method*. Washington, DC: Patterson Printing.

Kaye, L. (1992). *Home health care*. Newbury Park, CA: Sage Publications.

Lewin/ICF Inc. & James Bell Associates. (1990). *Descriptions of and supplemental information on board and care homes included in the update of the National Health Provider Inventory*. Washington, DC: U.S. Department of Health and Human Services, Office of the Assistant Secretary for Planning and Evaluation.

Massachusetts Department of Health Care Quality. (1984). *Incident report* [Video]. (Fanlight Productions, 47 Halifax Street, Boston, MA 02130.)

National Association for Home Care. (1995, July 14). *Home care employment outpaces all health industries*. Report No. 621. Washington, DC: Author.

Pillemer, K., & Hudson, B. (1993). A model abuse prevention program for nursing assistants. *Gerontologist, 33*, 128–131.

Pillemer, K., & Moore, D. (1989). Abuse of patients in nursing homes: Findings from a survey of staff. *Gerontologist, 29*, 314–320.

Tellis-Nayak, V. (1993). Presentation at CARIE annual meeting, Philadelphia.

Tellis-Nayak, V., & Tellis-Nayak, M. (1989). Quality of care and the burden of two cultures: When the world of the nurse's aide enters the world of the nursing home. *Gerontologist, 29*, 307–313.

U.S. Department of Health and Human Services, Office of Inspector General. (1990). *Resident abuse in nursing homes: Understanding and preventing abuse*. Publ. No. OE1-06-88-00360. Washington, DC: U.S. Government Printing Office.

U.S. General Accounting Office. (1989). *Board and care: Insufficient assurances that residents' needs are identified and met*. Publ. No. HDR-89-50. Washington, DC: U.S. Government Printing Office.

U.S. Senate Special Committee on Aging. (1989). *Board and care: A failure in public policy*. Washington, DC: U.S. Government Printing Office.

Watson, M. (1994, February). *Silent suffering: Elder abuse in America*. Conference Summary of the Pre–White House Conference on Aging. Long Beach, CA.

APPENDIX
GLOSSARY OF ABUSE AND NEGLECT

The Philadelphia Elder Abuse Task Force, founded in 1984, specifically defined the following types of abuse based on the State of Pennsylvania's definition:

Physical abuse—Inflicting injury, unreasonable confinement, or punishment with resulting physical harm, which may also include using physical restraints for punishment or for the convenience of staff or handling an elderly person roughly enough to cause bruising. *Examples:* Slapping, kicking, shoving, rough handling, shaking.

Psychological abuse—The threat of injury, unreasonable confinement and punishment, or verbal intimidation/humiliation, which may result in mental anguish, such as anxiety or depression. *Examples:* Yelling, screaming, using demeaning language or ridicule, ignoring.

Sexual abuse—Sexual contact that results from threats, force, or the inability of the elderly person to give consent, including but not limited to assault, rape, and sexual harassment. *Examples:* Rape, harassment, fondling, inappropriate touching, exhibitionism.

Financial exploitation—An improper course of conduct, with or without informed consent of the older adult that results in monetary, personal, or other benefit, gain, or profit for the perpetrator, or monetary or personal loss for the older adult. *Examples:* Stealing, "borrowing," ignoring reports of loss or theft.

Active neglect—The willful deprivation of goods or services that are necessary to maintain physical or mental health (e.g., deliberate abandonment, deliberate denial of food or of health-related services). *Examples:* Purposely withholding food, help, fluids, cigarettes; not helping a resident whom you know needs help.

Passive neglect—The deprivation of goods or services that are necessary to maintain physical or mental health without a conscious attempt to inflict physical or emotional distress (e.g., abandonment or denial of services because of inadequate knowledge, infirmity). *Examples:* Telling a resident you will return in 5 minutes and forgetting to do so; forgetting to place the call light within the resident's reach.

13

Prognosis:
Elder Mistreatment
in Health Care Settings

Lorin A. Baumhover and S. Colleen Beall

The chapters in this book highlight a number of issues and related concerns in assessing and addressing cases of elder mistreatment within health care settings. Although the precise number of reportable abuse and neglect cases is unknown, elder mistreatment is not a rare phenomenon. It is often carried out in the privacy of personal residences by and against people who have limited contact with the outside world. Many victims of mistreatment are seen periodically or episodically by professionals in health care settings. Thus, health care providers may be the only professionals with opportunities to detect the effects of mistreatment, which are hidden from other potential observers. Given the growth of the elderly population and the high rate at which older people use health care resources, opportunities to observe elder mistreatment will increase in the next 50 years.

This book is not intended to create a class of victims where none exists, nor to suggest that most older people are the victims of mistreatment at the hands of their caregivers or others. Most older people are not victimized, but are well cared for by family members and others, frequently to the point where caregivers suffer financial and physical problems as a result of the caregiving burden. It is undesirable for individuals or society to view each person as a victim of some external force. The notion that society is responsible for inflicting physical or psychological damage on an entire class of people is not healthy for any society. These arguments notwithstanding, many older people are victimized. The 700,000–1 million older people who experience moderate to severe mistreatment every year represent a sizable group of people (National Center on Elder Abuse, 1995).

The lack of standard definitions for the various types of elder mistreatment has been well documented in the elder abuse literature. Despite the negative sequelae associated with any form of mistreatment, many health care providers narrowly focus on physical neglect and physical abuse in defining the problem. This book provides health care providers with examples of the entire spectrum of elder abuse, and suggests ways in which they may assist in identifying and treating elder abuse victims.

THE "DIRTY DOZEN" BARRIERS TO IDENTIFYING, REPORTING, AND MANAGING CASES OF ELDER MISTREATMENT

Health care providers have difficulty identifying, reporting, and managing cases of elder abuse. Twelve reasons for this difficulty are examined in the following sections.

Elder Abuse Coexists with Other Social Problems

Like other persistent social pathologies in society, elder abuse is caused by and related to a variety of individual and social problems. Adult Protective Services (APS) investigators have long been aware that in elder abuse and neglect cases, illness, poverty, codependency, alcoholism, and dysfunctional families are associated with elder mistreatment. Elder mistreatment does not exist by itself and is caused by or related to these other social ills. All professionals, including health care providers, who work with elderly people have difficulty isolating the symptoms of mistreatment from the psychosocial context in which they are observed.

Elder Abuse Coexists with Other Medical and Health Problems

Three concurrent developments—normal aging, disease, and mistreatment—often coexist. As people age, many social, sensory, and physiological changes take place. These changes include a tendency for skin to bruise more easily, increased difficulties in both hearing and vision, and changes in appetite that may result in weight loss, which may or may not be related to chronic disease or medications. These changes may affect a clinician's ability to differentiate the aftermath or the effects of abuse from normal aging changes. The differential diagnosis is made more complicated still by the symptoms associated with a variety of chronic conditions common in elderly people.

Elder Abuse Is Often Not Perceived as a Crime

Historically, family members have engaged in acts of considerable violence toward one another, ranging from female infanticide to patricide (Reinharz, 1986). Some observers have remarked that the family is the most violent social institution except for the military during war. Seen in a historical context, elder abuse is a family matter. Society's perception is that family members have a long history of cohabitation, and have developed typical patterns of responding to each other. Some perceive an intergenerational transfer of violence to be almost "normal," that a child who perceived or experienced abuse may "pay back" his or her parents later by abusing them (Straus, Gelles, & Steinmetz, 1980). Observers of even severely dysfunctional families may be reticent to intervene in the violence because it is somehow seen as off limits or inappropriate to take action when family members harm each other.

Denial of Elder Abuse Is to Be Expected

Early in the assessment process, a clinician should expect elderly victims and their abusers to deny that any abuse has occurred. The literature suggests that relatively few individuals will admit to being victimized. A strong cultural tradition exists in the United States for "circling the wagons" when a family member is confronted by an accusation, regardless of the accuracy of the charge. APS investigators frequently report that the veracity or the extent of the mistreatment has little bearing on the likelihood of disclosure. Elderly victims typically say that they do not want the abuser punished or removed from the home; they simply want the abuse to end.

Elder abuse victims frequently do not report their mistreatment because they fear public exposure, embarrassment, and humiliation (Quinn & Tomita, 1986). Sometimes victims feel shame for having raised a child who hurts them or for living with a spouse who mistreats them. Other elder abuse victims feel guilty, that they must have done something to deserve the mistreatment. Some victims do not want to break the code of family solidarity, and some victims fear retaliation by the abuser. Still other victims fear that if their abuser is jailed, no one will take care of them. They may also fear having to testify against their abuser because this would bring them even more shame and humiliation. Certainly, the fear of relocation to a nursing facility or an alternate living facility is sufficient to silence some older people. Many older people fear losing their limited independence; they feel it is even worse than death itself. Some older people fear losing the affection of their batterers.

Most elder abuse victims are women and may have been raised to be passive and to accept their circumstances without complaint (Hudson, 1986). This may be particularly true when elder abuse represents a case of spouse abuse. Also, some older abuse victims cling to misguided notions that somehow the abuse will stop by itself, or that it is only temporary or episodic.

Regardless of the reason for denial, clinicians should not suspend questioning if the suspected abuse victim initially denies abuse. Continued probing is warranted if discernible indicators of abuse exist.

Elder Abuse Victims Are Hard to Find and Hard to Reach

Elder abuse is better hidden from public scrutiny than is child abuse. Older people are typically found in situations, lifestyles, and communities that differ from those occupied by people under age 70. Elderly people often report higher rates of social and geographical isolation. Elderly people living alone make up close to one third of all older people. Approximately 9 million Americans age 65 and over live alone (U.S. House of Representatives, 1991). Older people traditionally have been disproportionately represented in rural areas. That older people spend considerable amounts of time within their homes, more so than other age groups, is not seen as being unusual. As people age they are involved in fewer social roles than they were when they were younger. Social isolation is exacerbated if an older person is bedridden or incapacitated. Such limitations may increase the social distance that older people feel between themselves and other individuals. One of the predisposing conditions to elder mistreatment is the lack of people visiting an elderly person's residence. Whether the result is self-neglect or caregiver abuse, mistreatment is significantly less likely when neighbors, family members, church groups, and others frequent an older person's home.

During the assessment process, clinicians should take a social history, which includes direct questions regarding both social and geographic isolation. For example, clinicians may ask questions such as, "Does someone come by or call you every day?," "Do you have a close relative or friend that you can call for help?," "How many people come by to see you every week?" These questions, particularly in cases of self-neglect, may help clinicians more fully interpret other potential indicators of maltreatment.

Elder Abuse Can Occur in Institutionalized Populations

When compared to younger population groups, the U.S. elderly population is disproportionately confined to long-term care facilities; approximately 5% of the over-65 population is institutionalized at any given time (U.S. House of Representatives, 1991). Older people occupy up to 50% of all acute care beds. The number of residents of nursing facilities will continue to increase, primarily because of growth in the proportion of people age 85 and over. Current projections indicate that from 1990 to 2005, the number of people living in nursing facilities will increase from 1.5 to 2.1 million, and will increase again to 2.6 million by 2020. An additional 10% of the over-65 population is seen as being sufficiently physically or mentally ill as to require institutionalization, were it not for the presence of family and other alternative caregiving situations. This level of disability suggests a population more at risk for abuse than any other age group.

Health care providers frequently assume, particularly in neglect cases, that removing an elderly person from a particular environment will end the mistreatment (Clark-Daniels, Daniels, Baumhover, & Pieroni, 1989). Relocation to an institutionalized setting (e.g., long-term care facility, assisted living facility, acute care hospital) is seen as an outcome goal. An alternative living arrangement does not necessarily preclude continued or possibly increased mistreatment of older people. Although relatively few cases of elder mistreatment are perpetrated by paid caregivers, mistreatment can and does occur in institutions. (The federal government has mandated an abuse registry for nursing assistants in every state.) Family members may continue to visit elderly relatives in order to financially exploit or psychologically intimidate them.

Health Care Professionals Are Unclear About How, Where, and When to Report Abuse

Although health care providers are knowledgeable about mandatory reporting to state departments of public health regarding sexually transmitted diseases and other information routinely gathered for the Bureau of Vital Statistics, they may lack awareness of elder abuse reporting procedures. The how and the where of reporting elder abuse are less important than the when. Both the laws regarding mandatory reporting and the agency-assigned statutory authority to investigate cases vary by state. However, the reporting repository is usually the APS unit of the state human services department, or the state human resources department. In some instances, the APS unit is located in a state unit on aging, or in the state public health department. The usual pattern in both acute care and extended care facilities is to bring in a social worker to take photographs, interview the parties involved in the alleged mistreatment, and make a referral to the appropriate agency. Every state has a standard reporting form, typically a 1- to 2-page description of the event and some basic sociodemographic information on the victim and alleged perpetrator.

Of greater concern to health care professionals, however, is when to report. There is considerable confusion about the necessity for absolute certainty that abuse or neglect has occurred before a report is made. Based on both civil immunity and mandatory reporting requirements in most states, health care providers should not expect to feel completely sure that abuse, neglect, or exploitation has occurred before they make a report. Establishing that mistreatment has occurred is not the responsibility of the health care professional.

Three people are involved in this scenario. The first person is a reporter, often a health care professional who suspects that mistreatment has occurred. The reporter documents whatever evidence is available, and reports it. The second person is an APS investigator, who, on the basis of the report, determines whether mistreatment has occurred. It is the responsibility of the APS investigator, not the health care professional, to investigate the case in order to determine if a finding of mistreatment can be made. The third person is a prosecutor, either a district attorney or another designated official from the county or state, who may bring charges and prosecute an elder abuser. This third stage is frequently not reached because the APS investigator attempts to work with family members and other social and health agencies to ensure that abuse does not recur.

Elder mistreatment frequently involves shades of gray with considerable uncertainty on the part of the reporter and, sometimes, even the victim. This is because the obvious indicators of rope abrasions, cigarette or iron burns, bruises, or lacerations are frequently not seen. More likely seen is evidence of lack of social services, inappropriate shelter, insufficient food, inability to access medical care, or income diverted from medication purchases. These indicators are more nebulous.

Health Care Providers Find it Difficult to Receive Feedback on Abuse Referrals

Two complaints are often voiced by health care professionals, particularly home health nurses: 1) "Nobody does anything when I report a case," and 2) "Nobody lets me know what happens after I refer a case." Because the lack of feedback frustrates health care providers, they may curtail future reports.

"Nobody Does Anything" APS case managers are guided by the principle of client self-determination; that is, the individual's rights to autonomy and self-determination supersede the right of the state to intervene. With a mentally competent individual, the state-initiated limits are clear concerning client relocation, modifying expenditures, or changing caregiving arrangements. Health care providers often expect more dramatic changes than what is possible to achieve through traditional APS interventions.

"Nobody Lets Me Know What Happened" A health care provider should inform the APS investigator during intake that he or she wants

regular updates about the investigation. Virtually all states allow for anyone having a clear medical connection to the case to receive updates. The APS investigator may not divulge which actions are being taken against a perpetrator, but it is realistic for the health care provider to expect updates on actions taken on behalf of the patient or client.

Many Clinicians Are Reluctant to Report Abuse Even When Confronted with Abuse

Although state annual reports (see, for example, Pennsylvania Department of Aging, 1994) consistently indicate that health care professionals are more likely than are employees in other occupational categories to report cases of abuse, neglect, and exploitation, many professionals are reluctant to report abuse, even when they find it in their office or practice setting, for the following reasons:

- Concern that they must be absolutely certain that abuse has occurred before reporting it
- Fear of being forced into a lengthy court appearance as a result of filing a report
- Belief that they can better handle actual elder abuse themselves than by reporting it to the authorities because of their relationship with the victim and his or her family
- Fear that reporting potential abuse will inflame the abuser
- Fear that members of the families of abuse victims will realize that they are the only ones who could have reported the abuse and neglect
- Fear that little or nothing will be done to help the victims if they do report
- Fear that because abuse victims will likely deny the abuse, reporting will damage their relationship with the patient or client

Although all of the reasons in this list may limit the actions taken by physicians, nurses, and other health care providers, the fact remains that it is only health care providers who may see bruises that are hidden beneath clothing. The clinical setting provides an optimal opportunity to assess both the extent and type of injuries. This opportunity places a special burden on health practitioners to respond to cases of mistreatment.

Elder Abuse Can Exist Without Obvious Signs

Psychological or emotional mistreatment is common. Verbal harassment, taunts, ridicule, threats, and intimidation do not result in bruises, welts, or lacerations (Tatara, 1993). Violations of civil rights in which older people are prevented from receiving adequate medical care or are confined to a bed or room against their will, and even some episodic sexual abuse, may leave no physical evidence. The absence of concrete evidence should not be construed as absence of negative sequelae or emotional trauma. Behavioral indicators such as cowering, fearfulness, or unusual clinging to a caregiver may be important indicators in the absence of trauma.

Elder Abuse Tends to Escalate over Time

First observation, or first assessment, by the clinician is important because a considerable body of evidence demonstrates that most elder abuse is not isolated incidents (American Medical Association, 1987). Mistreatment is likely to escalate in frequency and severity over time. The use of weapons is likely to increase over time. The long-term trajectory of abuse is such that if intervention is not initiated after abuse is first observed in a clinic or examining room, the chances are good that it will continue.

Elder Abuse Is Different from Child Abuse

The definition of risk factors is less rich for elder abuse than it is for child abuse. The risk factors that have been identified frequently overlap and are nonspecific and nonexclusionary. Many definitions describe modal characteristics of the elderly population, particularly the segment over age 75. The majority of this population are female, widowed, have reduced financial assets, and have more than one chronic ailment, and yet are not victimized. This ambiguity surrounding risk factors and even characteristics of perpetrators is reflected in many of the current assessment scales. Most of the protocols have never been "validated" because any attempt to do so would emphasize the inability of the tools to distinguish cases of mistreatment from noncases.

Considerably more state and federal resources are available for investigating and managing child abuse cases than for elder abuse cases. Federal funds are earmarked for child protective services providers, for establishing a national child abuse registry, and, in some instances, to assist prosecution. None of these resources is yet available for elder abuse cases. A 1990 report revealed that in terms of protective services, states spent an average of $3.10 on each elderly resident as compared to $45.03 for each child (U.S. House of Representatives, 1990).

Unlike elder abuse, the study of child abuse has a long history, which is reflected in a network of social workers, clinicians, and law enforcement personnel. This network has developed intervention teams, established clinical protocols, and created investigation kits and a variety of other first-response materials. Child abuse has been medicalized, has an official etiology, and has more fully developed assessment and management guidelines than does elder abuse. Child abuse has become inculcated as a standard part of the medical curriculum in pediatrics, with its own medical jargon.

Children can be removed from abusive environments, including their homes, by the state without worrying about the autonomy, self-determination, and competency issues that affect older people. The state can move more quickly and more effectively in child abuse cases because statutory authority lies with the state for the protection of children. The emphasis on civil rights in U.S. society is such that self-determination issues frequently prevent APS investigators from acting in what they believe to be the best interest of the older patient or client.

Ageism, or the systematic devaluation of older people because of their age, may cause clinicians to respond less aggressively to possible elder abuse. Ironically, by the mere fact of living a long life, people lose social value. Many people report (e.g., in focus group discussions) feeling more negatively about cases of child abuse than about cases of elder abuse. Clinicians frequently ask themselves, "Is it worth my time getting involved with a person so old?"

PRESCRIPTIONS FOR IDENTIFYING, REPORTING, AND MANAGING CASES OF ELDER MISTREATMENT

As Glendenning and Decalmer (1993) have noted, it is not clear that decisions made regarding the abuse and neglect of elderly people are based on reliable research or on the result of informed discussion. Although researchers have begun to identify indicators of abuse, the indicators are imprecise. For example, distinctions have been made between violent feelings and violent actions. However, the behaviors that are the immediate triggers to episodes of mistreatment remain unclear (Quinn & Tomita, 1986). Until some of these factors can be elucidated, both predictors and interventions are likely to remain clumsy.

Although the best treatment is prevention, knowledge of the etiology of elder mistreatment is too incomplete to develop an effective vaccine. Thus, primary prevention is not yet achievable. However, secondary and tertiary interventions to minimize the long-term disability associated with prolonged exposure to the social pathogen of elder abuse are possible. A few prescriptions for health care providers are highlighted here.

Broaden the Definition of Elder Mistreatment

Most health care education emphasizes the recognition of physical signs, diagnosis of physical illness, and treatment of physical symptoms. Thus, most definitions of elder abuse in the health care professions have tended to focus on physical neglect and abuse. This focus, regardless of the level of compassion of health care providers, will necessarily restrict their capacity to recognize the full range of elder mistreatment and to maximize the quality of life of its victims. This book provides examples from a broad range of types of elder mistreatment and suggests appropriate roles for health care providers in the detection and resolution of mistreatment.

Possess a High Index of Suspicion

The recognition that elder abuse is a social and medical problem is growing. Reports place prevalence estimates at about 3% (Pillemer & Finkelhor, 1989). Most health care providers recognize that they have encountered at least one elder abuse case. Despite these statistics, elder mistreatment may not be considered a possible diagnosis for a patient or client who presents with subtle signs of neglect, or who does not fit a high-risk profile of advanced age and high dependency needs, or whose abusive caregivers ask the "right questions" in order to give the appearance that they are concerned and well-intentioned people. A disease that is not considered in the differential diagnosis will not be treated. Because many victims of elder mistreatment are out of touch with the outside world, a clinical examination and subsequent intervention may be the only opportunity to prevent future abuse.

Screen for Abuse

The increased public attention on elder mistreatment has resulted in the broad promulgation of guidelines and protocols by the American Medical Association and other professional organizations for approaching and documenting cases of suspected elder abuse, neglect, and exploitation. Screening for abuse and neglect can and should be accomplished within the context of a standard physician–patient encounter (see Chapter 3). Given the potential for negative sequelae and escalating severity, the onus is on the physician-provider of explaining the failure to screen for a condition that can be as life threatening as a serious disease. Although health care providers may not always be able to discern the subtle effects of nonphysical mistreatment, long-term patterns of abuse are likely to become apparent in careful assessments of patients.

Screening guidelines for recognition, documentation, and intervention in "nontraditional" (i.e., nonphysical) forms of abuse are particularly inadequate. The symptoms of psychological abuse generally are behaviors expressed in interactions with other people, not the types of hard evidence that medical and nursing educations prepare health care practitioners to observe and quantify. The imprecision of risk instruments may not correctly attribute observed symptoms to abuse, but often alert practitioners that "something" is wrong. Although the positive predictive value of such vague "diagnoses" is poor, these "diagnoses" must be considered in the absence of better screening criteria.

Screening instruments have a number of shortcomings, but they do act as a reminder to screen for abuse and as a standard format for documenting risk factors for abuse. Using these instruments will remind clinicians to ask patients or clients about possible mistreatment and to consider whether patient reports adequately explain the observed symptoms. Interviewing skill and clinical judgment are important in the determination of abuse and neglect.

Recognize Institutional Contributions to the Problem

Health care providers, particularly nursing assistants or home health aides, not only fail to recognize the more subtle cases of elder mistreatment, they occasionally perpetrate and perpetuate it. (Reported acts of elder abuse by nursing assistants are in the minority.) These acts of violence are more likely among caregivers who have little or no educational preparation for working with frail elderly populations and little or no professional affiliation. Beth Hudson Keller's chapter (Chapter 12) does an excellent job of highlighting this issue. The subtle forms of mistreatment that nursing assistants and their counterparts in hospitals, home health agencies, and other settings may perpetrate or encounter in their work environment differ little from the verbal and psychological abuse perpetrated by family members caring for elderly relatives. This behavior can be understood within the context of a caregiving environment, in which nursing assistants or family members perform repetitive tasks for low wages and little recognition. However, the actions cannot be condoned or overlooked.

As further pointed out by Keller, health care providers can and must be sensitized to recognize their own abusive behaviors and the attitudes that permit and encourage the behavior to occur. Professionals who work with nursing assistants or personal care aides should be alert to the need to provide them with additional training and constructive feedback and to restrict ageist comments about patients or clients that may influence the attitudes of other care providers. Positive feedback for a job well done despite difficult patients or clients, family members, and/or working conditions is an important component in preventing institutional abuse.

Know the Patients or Clients and Their Environments

Although victims of elder mistreatment may occasionally present in the emergency room of a hospital to be cared for by medical residents, technicians, and nurses with whom they have had no prior contact, the majority of elder mistreatment victims are eventually seen by their primary care physician and his or her office staff. As Holly Ramsey-Klawsnik notes in Chapter 4, a primary care provider's knowledge of the patient's medical and social history, current diagnoses, and medications, as well as the rapport established over many years, may be invaluable in encouraging disclosure of an event viewed as shameful and humiliating or in providing information to assist the APS investigator in his or her investigation. Ramsey-Klawsnik suggests that collaboration between APS and health care professionals may provide for more comprehensive, less fragmented treatment following physical abuse than would be provided if either professional tackled the problem alone.

Primary health care providers (e.g., physicians, members of their office staff, nurses, home health professionals) also are likely to know whether family members of an elderly patient have a history of providing assistance when health care crises arise. Family members who have accompanied patients to clinic appointments, have visited in hospitals, and have asked questions about episodic health problems or medications are unlikely to provide poor care intentionally. Marked increases in dependency or additional strains on the family that may compromise the quality of patient care may be known to the primary care provider. Conversely, family members without a history of involvement in the care of patients with chronic needs for assistance may be more likely to be abusive.

Do Not Become an Accessory After the Fact

Failure to report suspected or known elder abuse is a crime in many states. Most penalties for failure to report by mandated professionals are small. Failure to report can be readily justified as a clinical judgment that no abuse was present and, thus, no report was required. Nonetheless, because of the increasing number of guidelines for treatment of victims of elder abuse written since 1985, a variety of legal and professional sanctions, such as registries for health care providers convicted of abuse, loss of jobs, loss of privileges, professional reprimands, or loss of licensure, may be imposed.

Avoiding penalties is not the primary reason to report elder abuse. As mentioned previously, the opportunities to observe mistreatment in many elderly victims are limited by the relative isolation of older people and the imprecision of the indicators. In cases in which their suspicion of elder abuse is low, health care professionals face a variety of ethical dilemmas in deciding whether to report a case. Nevertheless, professionals should consider whether inaction violates the dictum of the Hippocratic Oath to "do no harm." Professional judgment, along with a weighing of likely costs and benefits of action and inaction, should guide behavior.

Seek Consultation

Few generalist health care providers possess expertise in identifying and responding to suspected elder abuse. These practitioners should consult with a health care provider with expertise in identifying signs of elder mistreatment, particularly when examining patients for whom the etiology for symptoms is unclear. A variety of approaches to consultation is available, but the model employed is less important than the advice of an experienced person.

The multidisciplinary team approach is one consultation model. As outlined by Dr. Sue Parkins in Chapter 9, the composition of the team may vary with the presenting complaints, symptoms, or treatment regimen of the patient involved. Other hospitals may employ a team, the membership of which is relatively static. Nevertheless, the mission of the team is to obtain input from a variety of professionals in order to devise one or more appropriate diagnoses, treatment plans, or both. If the result of consultation is a potential diagnosis of abuse, a report to an APS agency must be made in states with mandated reporting, and should be considered where reporting is optional, regardless of the team's recommendations for treatment.

Understand the Role of Adult Protective Services

After a report of abuse is made, it is the responsibility of APS to follow up. Although health care providers are clearly responsible for treating any medical sequelae of abuse, they are expected to relinquish control of the patient's social treatment. The shortcomings of the legal system and the APS system in handling elder abuse cases affect how health care practitioners view their own role. Mandated reporting based on suspected abuse may cause irreparable harm to the provider–patient or professional–client relationship. Many providers remain unclear about what APS is mandated to do, and fail to comprehend when no change in a dangerous living arrangement is effected.

APS workers have a difficult job in balancing their investigative function and social service provider role. The two roles often are in conflict. By law, competent clients' rights to make unusual, expensive, or dangerous decisions must be respected. Many clients have a limited number of potential caregivers and social supports. Counties also may experience severe shortages of emergency placements (e.g., safe-houses) and alternative permanent placements (including assisted living facilities, adult foster care, board and care homes, and nursing facilities), even for clients willing to accept these alternatives. As long as APS operates under investigative mandates in the absence of resources sufficient to provide a full range of intervention services, many interventions will represent less than ideal solutions to complex problems.

Provide Health Education

Patients seek at least three services from physicians and other health care providers: information, treatment, and support. With the increased emphasis on preventive health care and the increased sophistication of patients, health care professionals are likely to be questioned by patients about risk factors for mistreatment and by caregivers about caregiver support services. Health education activities may be implemented at any point in the treatment spectrum, from primary prevention to tertiary treatment.

The sensitization training program for nursing assistants (described in Chapter 12) could be adapted to educate caregivers when elderly patients are discharged from inpatient settings. Training may be particularly appropriate in cases in which care needs have increased suddenly or dramatically, as, for example, when a formerly independent 77-year-old woman is discharged from a hospital following a stroke that leaves her with vision, speech, and mobility limitations. Experience with family caregivers suggests that many are aware of their need for increased knowledge, improved coping skills, and emotional support. Caregivers are willing to attend programs providing these components when the programs are available and accessible (Scogin et al., 1989).

The Mount Sinai Medical Center's Victim Support Group (New York, NY) provides an example of health education and support related to tertiary intervention (Wolf & Pillemer, 1994). The group was recognized in 1992 for providing a forum within which victims could ease their sense of isolation; explore their feelings of victimization; and find a supportive, surrogate family. According to group leaders, the group educated members about their options and increased their sense of control over their situation.

Be Aware of How Health Care Financing/Management Issues May Affect the Patients Under Your Care

Financing and management of health care services are undergoing a revolution. Although the exact shape of the emerging system is not clear, some features of its outline are visible. The new system will rely to a greater extent on providers that resemble health maintenance organizations. Preventive care will become more important because it is more cost effective. It is less clear that such systems will foster continuity of care by a single provider. Thus, providers' knowledge about individual patients, a factor that can be invaluable in assessing subtle, psychosocial indicators of abuse, may be compromised.

Hospital payment systems have already undergone a revolution. Beginning with diagnosis-related groups and other capitated payment systems, inpatient stays are increasingly driven by length-of-stay limitations. Criteria that encourage early discharge may limit a professional's ability to resolve abuse cases.

Home health care is becoming a more important part of the provider network. Research suggests that home health care providers have knowledge deficits concerning high-risk indicators for elder abuse and about reporting requirements (Clark-Daniels, Daniels, & Baumhover, 1990). Training programs, such as one provided to home health nurses in Alabama or an adaptation of the nursing assistant program provided by the Coalition of Advocates for the Rights of the Infirm Elderly (CARIE) (see Chapter 12), offer hope for improving the ability of in-home care providers to recognize and report various forms of elder mistreatment. Home health care providers, already an important resource in APS interventions, are likely to become even more important.

REFERENCES

American Medical Association, Council on Scientific Affairs. (1987). Elder abuse and neglect. *Journal of the American Medical Association, 257*(7), 966–971.

Clark-Daniels, C.L., Daniels, R.S., Baumhover, L.A., & Pieroni, R.E. (1989). *Voices in the wilderness: Alabama health care professionals' responses to elder abuse.* Paper presented at the 85th Annual Meeting of the American Political Science Association, Atlanta.

Clark-Daniels, C.L., Daniels, R.S., & Baumhover, L.A. (1990). The dilemma of elder abuse: Home health and public health nurses' responses. *Home Healthcare Nurse, 8*(6), 7–12.

Glendenning, F., & Decalmer, P. (1993). Looking to the future. In P. Decalmer & F. Glendenning (Eds.), *The mistreatment of elderly people* (pp. 159–168). London: Sage Publications.

Hudson, M.F. (1986). Elder mistreatment: Current research. In K.A. Pillemer & R.S. Wolf (Eds.), *Elder abuse: Conflict in the family.* Dover, MA: Auburn House.

National Center on Elder Abuse. (1995, September). *Understanding the nature and extent of elder abuse in domestic settings.* Fact sheet distributed at the 12th Annual Adult Protective Services Conference, San Antonio, TX.

Pennsylvania Department of Aging. (1994). *Older adults protective services: 1993–94 report.* Harrisburg: Author.

Pillemer, K.A., & Finkelhor, D. (1989). Causes of elder abuse: Caregiver stress versus problem relatives. *American Journal of Orthopsychiatry, 59,* 179–187.

Quinn, M.J., & Tomita, S.K. (1986). *Elder abuse and neglect: Causes, diagnosis, and intervention strategies.* New York: Springer Publishing.

Reinharz, S. (1986). Loving and hating one's elders: Twin themes in legend and literature. In K.A. Pillemer & R.S. Wolf (Eds.), *Elder abuse: Conflict in the family* (pp. 25–48). Dover, MA: Auburn House.

Scogin, F., Beall, C., Bynum, J., Stephens, G., Grote, N.P., Baumhover, L.A., & Bolland, J.M. (1989). Training for abusive caregivers: An unconventional approach to an intervention dilemma. *Journal of Elder Abuse and Neglect, 1,* 73–86.

Straus, M.A., Gelles, R.J., & Steinmetz, S. (1980). *Behind closed doors: Violence in the American family.* New York: Doubleday.

Tatara, T. (1993). *Elder abuse: Questions and answers—An information guide for professionals and concerned citizens* (3rd ed.). Washington, DC: National Center on Elder Abuse.

U.S. House of Representatives, Select Committee on Aging. (1990). *Elder abuse: A decade of shame and inaction.* Washington, DC: U.S. Government Printing Office.

U.S. House of Representatives, Select Committee on Aging. (1991). *Aging in America.* Washington, DC: U.S. Government Printing Office.

Wolf, R.S., & Pillemer, K. (1994). What's new in elder abuse programming? Four bright ideas. *Gerontologist, 34,* 126–129.

Index

Page numbers followed by "*f*" indicate figures; page numbers followed by "*t*" indicate tables.